YERS 1973-74
JOE SCOTT PRES.
FRED SHERO COAC
& GEN. MGR.
PELLETIER P.P.D.
PARENT BOB TAYLOR
BERRY BILL BARBER
IMPE DON SALECKI
ASHBEE JIM WATSON
PONT BRUCE COWICK

THE OFFICIAL ILLUSTRATED HISTORY

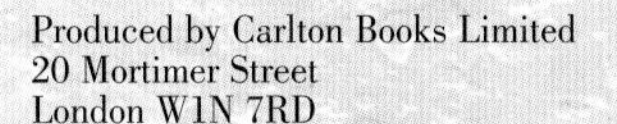

Produced by Carlton Books Limited
20 Mortimer Street
London W1N 7RD

This edition published
in 1999 by Whitecap Books Ltd,
351 Lynn Avenue
North Vancouver, B.C.
Canada, V7J 2C4

ISBN 1 55285 000 5 (hardback)
1 55285 002 1 (paperback)

Project Editor: Chris Hawkes
Project art direction: Trevor Newman
Picture research: Lorna Ainger
Production: Sarah Corteel

Printed in the United States

For all who have played hockey and for all who love hockey, past, present and future.

The authors would like to thank many family, friends and colleagues for their help in producing this book:
Ellen Pincus; Alisa Pincus; Suzanne Pincus; Andrew Malcolm; Jane Rodney; Phil Pritchard; Craig Campbell; Craig Bales; Gary Meagher; Benny Ercolani; David Keon; Chris Tredree; Greg Inglis; Susan Aglietti; Jim Gregory; David McConnachie; Ed Horne; Rick Gentile; Roseanne Giegerich; Marthe Love; Adam Schwartz; Anita Cechowski; Jennifer Perkinson; John Halligan; Susan Raposo; Mary Pat Clarke; John Hewig; Christine Simpson; Denise Gomez; KC Johnson. Connie Malcolm; Robert Reid; Lillian Pincus; Stephen Pincus and Fred Rosner.

NHL®

The Story of the Coolest Game on Earth

THE OFFICIAL ILLUSTRATED HISTORY

ARTHUR PINCUS

WITH DAVE ROSNER, LEN HOCHBERG AND CHRIS MALCOLM

WHITECAP BOOKS

BAUER
R5000
BAUER
BAUER COMPOSITE
39
BAUER
REACTOR

Contents

PEPSI
GMC
HEALTHSOUTH
SBERG
21

Foreword

WHEN DALLAS STARS CAPTAIN DERIAN HATCHER TOOK the Stanley Cup for its ride around the Marine Midland Arena ice early in the morning of June 20, 1999, he was connecting to the roots of hockey. Etched into the sides of the Cup's base (and scratched into a few spots in its bowl) are the names of the players who have won the Cup. Nothing symbolizes the history of this great game better than that magnificent trophy.

Hockey's history is filled with tales of heroes and heroics etched in memory. The performance of both the Dallas Stars and the Buffalo Sabres on that night add greatly to the legend of the game and its players. It's a legend that began for the National Hockey League more than 80 years ago and that began for the Stanley Cup more than 100 years ago. As for the sport of hockey itself, well, there are a number of views, but certainly it is more than 125 years old.

You are about to read a history of our game and I am delighted you are taking this journey. To encompass the history of hockey and the National Hockey League in one volume is quite a task.

For anyone to complete the task successfully, you must start with an historical treasure trove of photographs, and that has been done here, using the resources of the Hockey Hall of Fame and NHL Images to tell the story of the game in visual form. It is a feast for the eyes. Next you need to tap into the people who care about and love the game of hockey. For that there is no one better suited than Arthur Pincus, who is the General Editor of this book, and the staff of talented writers he assembled – David Rosner, Len Hochberg and Chris Malcolm. For six years Arthur worked at the National Hockey League as our Public Relations Vice President. Recently he ventured out on his own to use the skills he has developed over his career. It's good for all of us to know that he is staying close to the game we love and that "historian" can now be added to his resume.

I am sure you will enjoy your trip through hockey's past and by doing so, you will have your focus squarely on hockey's future.

Please enjoy.

Gary B. Bettman

Gary B. Bettman
Commissioner
New York, June 1999

Introduction

WHAT'S YOUR FAVORITE HOCKEY STORY? IS IT MARK Messier's guaranteed victory? Lester Patrick's one-game star turn in goal during a Stanley Cup Final? Or maybe it's Rocket Richard's 50 goals in 50 games? Who's your favorite star? Wayne Gretzky? Gordie Howe? Bobby Orr? Or maybe Howie Morenz? There are other stars and other stories, many others. Whichever story and whichever player it is, there is one thing certain: if you are a fan of hockey, you know that there is a wealth of stories of heroics and accomplishment, enough stories to fill a book.

If you are new to the game – and in the best tradition of hockey, welcome all – the stories will quickly appear before you and become part of your body of knowledge. For the new fan, by learning about hockey, you learn all that is best in sport. You learn about accomplishment, courage, teamwork, spirit and dedication. Across the spectrum of sports, none teaches these attributes as well as hockey. To be a fan of hockey is to learn and what a pleasant way to do that!

For the recent convert to the sport, two images of the last few months tell so much of the great place you are about to inhabit – the world of hockey.

The first image is a solitary one, rare in a sport that teaches and requires teamwork like no other. It is April 18, 1999, and the place is Madison Square Garden in New York. On the ice, a solitary figure clad in Ranger blue and with No 99 on his back skates in a spotlight. Unmistakably and forever, the Great One, Wayne Gretzky. After 20 National Hockey League seasons, 894 goals, 1,963 assists and 2,857 points; after four Stanley Cups, after a career as the greatest athlete ever in team sports, Wayne Gretzky's last appearance in an NHL arena came alone. His New York Rangers team had just ended its season and his fans clamored for him to take just one more skate. And he did. And they clamored for more. And he skated on, a solitary figure on the surface he knew so well. For the fans blessed to watch Wayne Gretzky throughout his career, the moment was bittersweet. How lucky we were to have seen him; how sad that we would see him no more. The dignity that Gretzky showed that day and every day, the awe that the fans held him in and the connection between the player, the game and the fans were never more evident.

Some two months later in the early morning hours of June 20, 1999, in the Marine Midland Arena in Buffalo, NY, a gaggle of Dallas Stars players, coaches and trainers rolled on the ice in joy and exhaustion. After almost six hours on the clock and two hours of a game, the Stars had survived the longest deciding game in Stanley Cup Finals history by defeating the Buffalo Sabres, 2-1 in goals and 4-2 in games. The scorer of the winning goal was Brett Hull; the goalie beaten was Dominik Hasek. The stories beam from each like a beacon. For Brett Hull is the son of greatness, son of Bobby Hull, and the two are the only father and son in any sport to win Most Valuable Player awards. But now, both have their names etched into the Stanley Cup itself and their connection extends back to the beginning of Bobby Hull's career in Chicago in the "Original Six Era" of the 1950s.

And on the other side is a dejected, defiant, incandescent goaltender from the Czech Republic. In the 1990s, no player showed the impact of the international star in the hockey constellation as did Dominik Hasek. Winner of the Hart Trophy as League MVP: twice. Soon to receive his fifth Vezina Trophy as outstanding goaltender. Olympic Gold Medalist. But on this morning, a Stanley Cup was not to be. Still, Hasek points to the future of this sport as few do. International stars play on the NHL's stage, melding with the stars of hockey's traditional backgrounds. No sport does it so well and the only borders in hockey are the dasherboards. And no scene told that story better than the one on the ice that morning.

The history of the National Hockey League is rich and full and the prospect of putting it between the covers of a book is one that is both daunting and thrilling. For the NHL and the sport of ice hockey have always taken pride in their history, in their roots and in their traditions. To cover that history – which extends for more than 100 years – and cover it well could overwhelm the most ardent

The first puck drop between the Penguins and the Hurricanes – hockey has grown beyond belief.

of sports historians. Yet, to do justice to that history, with all the characters, defining moments and spectacular competition gives the writers a sense of awe, excitement and anticipation. And that is the attitude we hope the reader approaches this Color Illustrated History of the National Hockey League – with anticipation. And we think there is reason to be excited and much to anticipate.

The history of the NHL only goes back to November 1917, but the history of the NHL is also the history of hockey. And so our journey begins not in a Montreal hotel ballroom in 1917 but on the frozen Long Pond of Windsor, Nova Scotia; in the city of Kingston, Ontario, and on an indoor rink in Montreal in March 1875. It goes back to England where the game of hurley was played and became, most believe, the basis for the sport of ice hockey.

It grew across the vast geography of Canada and then, as with any great idea, it was exported. It went South to the United States, across the oceans to Scandinavia, Russia and Asia.

Hockey is Canada's gift to the world.

So how do you take that history and bring it manageably to the reader? Well, first you take the reader on a visual tour of the sport and its history. Photographs are a great way to look inside the sport's evolution – from equipment to facial hair, you will be able to see how the sport and the people who played it changed. And to tell the stories in words, we broke the task up into manageable pieces. The great thing about hockey is its wealth of stories, passed on from generation to generation, not unlike the great symbol of the game, the Stanley Cup.

So to manage this seemingly unmanageable task, we have broken up the history of the NHL in decade-long chunks. Each chapter tells a unique self-contained story. For as the research reveals, each decade has a significant and singular aspect to it. The birth of the League, the move to the US, the glory days of the '30s and '40s, the Golden Years of the '50s, the landmark expansion of the late '60s, right to the end of the century with the first Stanley Cup victory by a team from the American South, the Dallas Stars – that's a long way from Nova Scotia.

In each decade, we take a narrative look at the big events. And each chapter is accompanied by the "other" stories, some big, some small, but each of them poignant and revealing. These highlighted items are aimed at putting a distinct face on the personality and the personalities of the decade. We also attempt to show the changing face of the game itself through the decades and profile the people who made it great.

To put this big book together we have enlisted three talented sports journalists, David Rosner, Len Hochberg and Chris Malcolm. Each has been a longtime fan and reporter on the game. The best part of cutting this mammoth project down to a workable size was the conversations we all had, stirring memories and images all the time. But once the conversations ended we all turned to the recorded history of the game to help tell the stories you are about to read.

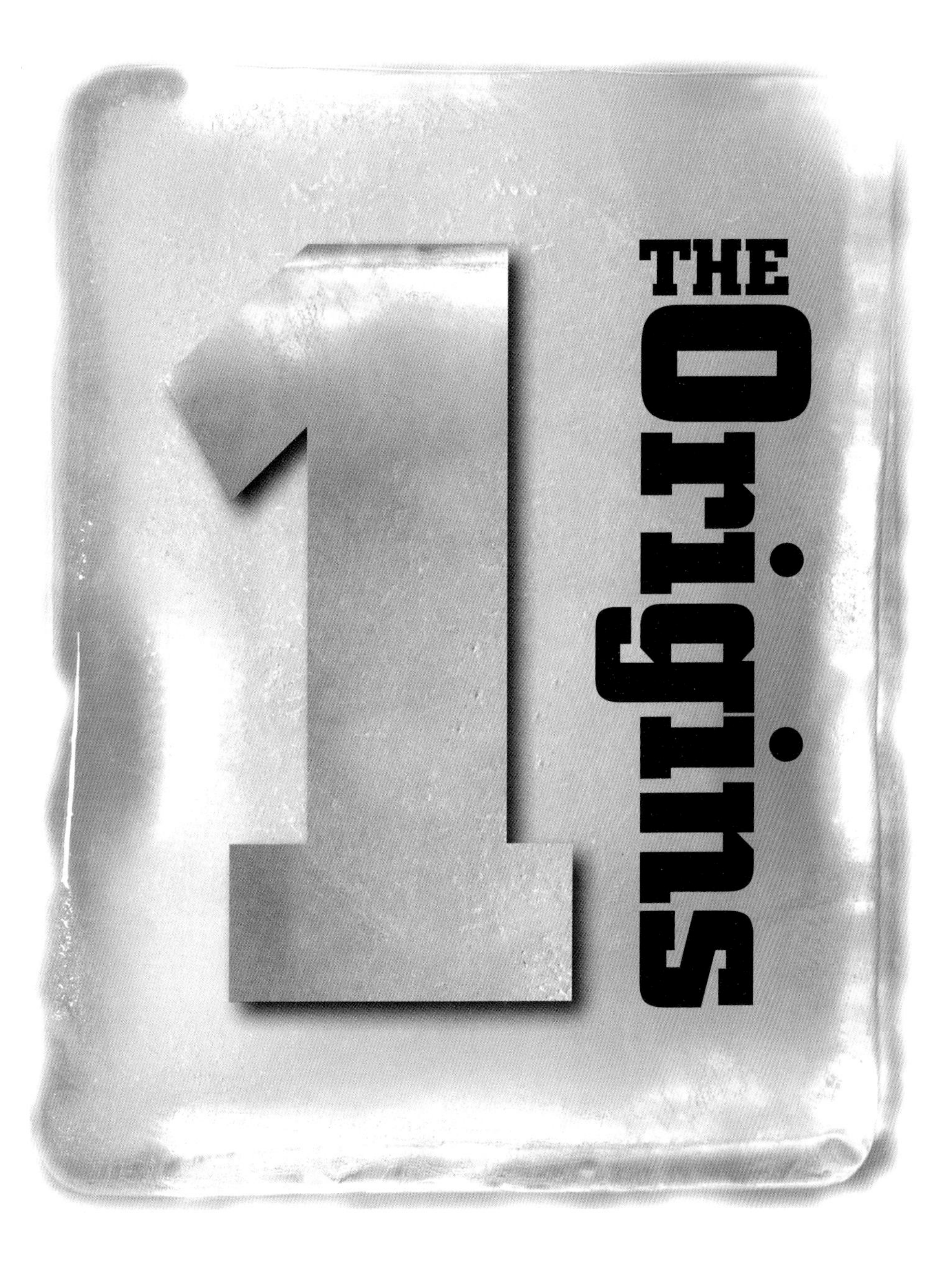

On Frozen Ponds

A group of figures glide across a frozen pond in eastern Canada as the sound of wooden sticks clicking off the rough and natural ice and the shouts of other skaters chasing a ball sneak through the trees that rim the snow-covered shores.

(Facing page): An early game at McGill University: pond hockey comes to the city.

WAS THIS THE FIRST OFFICIAL HINT OF A GAME TO BE called ice hockey? Who decided to use sticks? How were the rules determined? And what sparked this simple game to grow into one of the most popular and successful sports businesses in the world?

Some of the answers can be gleaned from newspaper accounts and oral histories while other questions will continue to be debated by those who follow the game. But it is right to say that the early form of the game sprouted in sparsely populated Nova Scotia, spread to the dominant Canadian urban center of Montreal, and thrived in places like Kingston, Ontario. And in those early years of an ever-transforming sport, each of these places – plus others – left their indelible marks on the way the game is played today.

Using curved sticks and a ball, shinty players transferred English field games to the cold surfaces around King College in Windsor, Nova Scotia, one of the first Canadian settlements. English cricket and rounders, Scottish shinty and Irish hurley were all part of the earliest form of what was known as ice hurley. From there the game spread, as soldiers were transferred among the various forts in eastern Canada; in fact, a Colonel Hockey used the game to keep his troops sharp.

And the game spread like any good news, with each group of players passing along the lessons to other groups in other locales. One of those unintentional emissaries was James Creighton, a Nova Scotian engineer who moved to Montreal and eventually played in what is considered the first official game. On March 3, 1875, two teams of nine players faced off, with Creighton's team winning two games to one. The ***Montreal Gazette*** reported the following day that the traditional ball was replaced by a flat block of wood to keep the puck from rising. The reporter also noted that the game was like lacrosse, a popular sport among native peoples, except that hockey was on ice.

In a region of North America which endures long winters, it is no surprise that the sport caught on. In Kingston, Ontario, where similar games of shinty were being played in the first half of the 1800s, a newspaper account reports that nearly 300 people gathered to watch a stick-ball game on the Kingston harbor ice. But while the historic role of host to the first game was bestowed upon Montreal, Kingston was instrumental in organizing games and teams and still hosts the longest running hockey rivalry between Queen's University and the Royal Military College of Canada.

The game – and the idea of a sport on ice – spread, and not just across Canada. There are various reports that similar forms were played in Ireland and in Russia through the 1800s. In 1899, a team of Russians faced an English team on a frozen Neva River in St Petersburg, but the Russian version of hockey stuck with a ball instead of a flat puck and the rosters included one world-class figure skater and a champion speed skater. The consensus among historians is that the first hockey game in England was played in 1895 with the first ice arena built in 1903.

Women also began to play the game, including the daughter of Lord Stanley himself. In 1889, the Governor-General's daughter, Isobel, played for a Government House team against the Rideau ladies hockey team. Three years before that, a woman called Annie McIntyre helped form a team on the lonely plains of Saskatchewan and by the early 1900s, there was an abundance of women's hockey clubs playing from Vancouver to Newfoundland. The rules were the same and women wore turtleneck sweaters, wool hats and very little padding, just like the men of that era.

JAMES **CREIGHTON**

WHEN YOU HEAR PROFESSIONAL PLAYERS SAY they play for the love of the game, it's not hard to think of Creighton skating endlessly across the lonely frozen ponds of Nova Scotia of the 1850s. Creighton grew up figure skating and eventually took up hockey for fun before he attended university and then moved to Montreal to begin a career as an engineer. There he taught friends recreational hockey and played in the first Montreal game in 1875, thus becoming one of the leading emissaries of the winter sport which swept across the country. In that game, two teams of nine played with a flat wooden puck, a change from the ball used in Nova Scotia. Long before the organized leagues sprouted up, it is believed that Creighton wrote one of the first versions of the game's rules and even played team trainer as he ordered shipments of the special hockey sticks crafted back in his native Nova Scotia. Later, Creighton joined the Rideau Rebels of Ottawa and played next to Edward and William Stanley, the sons of Lord Stanley, who initiated what would become the Stanley Cup.

THE EARLY GAME

By the very nature of the game, ice hockey has always looked the same. There have always been ice, skates, sticks, and goals. But many of the refinements of the early game took place between the birth of the sport and the beginning of the NHL in 1917.

THE EARLY FORM OF THE game was played with short curved sticks and a ball, similar to the game of hurling played on the grassy fields of the United Kingdom. The skates were crude, usually wooden blocks with a metal blade strapped to one's winter boots or shoes, and padded equipment was virtually nonexistent. By the late 1860s, leather skates with better blades were made for the quick stops and starts of hockey, and one-piece sticks were carved from hornbeam trees, also known as ironwood.

The first official documented game was played in Montreal on March 3, 1875. Nine players on each side moved a flat wooden puck up and down the ice trying to throw it between two upright poles in the ice with no nets or crossbars. Following the rules of rugby, there were no forward passes, and the absence of nets allowed players to score from either side of the goal lines. As with any successful sport, evolution changed the game but revolution was never needed.

In the inaugural Winter Carnival tournament held on the St Lawrence River in Montreal in 1883, teams shrank to seven players a side and, two years later, the entire tournament moved to an indoor arena. Pictures of these rinks show a wide open ice surface with sharp 90-degree corners. There were no raised boards, only a slight curb to keep the puck in play. Large crowds showed up for some games as evidenced by the 5,000 who attended the first Stanley Cup match between the Montreal AAAs and the Ottawa Capitals.

Uniforms of the day were usually high turtleneck sweaters and knitted wool caps with colorful designs in some cases. Most players wore little more than shin pads before the 1900s and most wore padded leather gloves after the turn of the century. Full body protection, such as elbow pads and shoulder pads, were still 30 to 40 years away. Shots were rarely lifted off the ice until 1893, forcing goaltenders to adopt larger shin pads from the game of cricket and a wider goaltending stick to block the rising pucks.

But in 1899, the closed box net goal was also adopted and the goaltender's job became a little bit easier. Still, game scores throughout the first two decades of the twentieth century were high, with teams frequently scoring double digits in a single game. Players posted gaudy statistics in comparison to today's scorers: in 1907, Ernie Russell scored 42 goals in nine games for Montreal, and in 1910 Newsy Lalonde led the National Hockey Association with 38 goals in 11 games. Good players would routinely jump from team to team across the leagues, serving whoever wanted hired "ringers".

And if you thought spectators were more gentlemanly at the turn of the century, guess again. Rivalries between cities and teams spurred some angry crowds, and a 1916 game was terminated when Quebec fans pelted the visiting Toronto team with bottles and chairs, attacking the players as they ran for their train.

As organized hockey grew though, the various leagues still played by different rules. Goaltenders dressed in thick leg pads were not allowed to drop to the ice in the some leagues, but flourished with this style in others. Even the NHA and the PCHA were distinctly different; the NHA played with six men to a side while the PCHA used seven. But as the NHA turned into the National Hockey League, the main governing body for professional hockey, the game became more homogenized.

The game moves indoors: Montreal AAA v. Montreal Victorias, Victoria rink 1891.

The Renfrew team of 1909 celebrated St. Patrick's Day with a unique greeting card; and Hobey Baker (right) the first American hockey hero.

STARS ON ICE

Newsy Lalonde was one legend in his own time. A wonderful scorer with an equally wonderful name, Lalonde was first a star lacrosse player, a sport which demanded quick reflexes and fine vision.

LALONDE SCORED 29 GOALS in his first season with Toronto in the Ontario Professional Hockey League. Then, playing for Renfrew of the new National Hockey Association (NHA), Lalonde scored nine goals on March 11, 1910, the best single-game mark throughout the NHA's eight seasons. Later, he helped to bridge the National Hockey Association and the National Hockey League (NHL) and went on to win NHL scoring titles in 1918-19 and 1920-21 as a player coach with the Montreal Canadiens.

The game was growing in the United States at the same time. In 1889, the American Amateur Hockey League was formed and became the first organized conference in the United States. Many cities south of the border had artificial ice, and teams popped up all across the eastern United States. Among their players was Hobey Baker of the St Nicholas Club of New York, a former multi-sports star at Princeton from 1910 to 1913 who could skate and handle the puck better than any other American player.

But above all the other players of the era was Joe Malone, who made his professional debut in 1908 with the Quebec Bulldogs. He was to make his biggest splash once the NHL was formed in 1917, scoring 44 goals in 20 games and seven in one game alone, still an NHL record. But during his first years in the game, he carved out a reputation as a slick and deceptive player, earning the nickname "Phantom Joe". In 1911-12, Malone led Quebec to the Stanley Cup with 21 goals, then ripped off 43 goals the following season.

Rules and Regulations

THE CHANGES IN THE GAME WERE COMING AS FAST as a two-man breakaway up the ice. In the 1880s, the Montreal Winter Carnival had staged a tournament which restricted teams to seven players per team, the first time this number was accepted as a rule. Then, in 1893, the Amateur Hockey Association of Canada, which included a handful of Canadian colleges and the Montreal Amateur Athletic Association, began to compete for the Stanley Cup, a special trophy donated by Frederick Arthur, Lord Stanley of Preston and the then Governor-General of Canada. Formal rules concerning the Stanley Cup challenge were set forth in 1903, and teams who won their respective league titles began to challenge for it annually.

There were plenty of candidates, as leagues were blossoming across both Canada and the United States. Most began as spin-offs from other leagues as a result of arguments among competitive owners or through financial failure. In 1890, the Ontario Hockey Association was formed to oversee the growing leagues, which included teams sponsored by colleges, mining and lumber companies, politicians and even banks. In 1903, after the Canadian Amateur Hockey League (CAHL) refused to allow new teams, the Federal Amateur Hockey League (FAHL) was formed and immediately included two teams from Montreal, still hockey's true hotbed. In an illustration of the contentious nature of interleague politics, the FAHL's

FREDERICK ARTHUR, **LORD STANLEY OF PRESTON**

THE STANLEY CUP CAN BE TRACED BACK TO A man who was both Prime Minister of the United Kingdom three times and an original hockey dad. After his time as a British Member of Parliament and as Secretary of State for the British Colonies, he was appointed Governor-General of Canada in 1888. An avid winter sportsman, he sponsored the Dominion Hockey Challenge Cup, which eventually became known as the Stanley Cup. The original silver bowl, bought in London for approximately $50, was first awarded in 1893 to an amateur team from any of the various leagues who challenged for it. By 1910, the trophy had become a professional team award and in 1914 the NHA built a formal playoff system around it. The first American team to win it was Seattle of the PCHA who beat Montreal of the NHA in 1917. Then in 1926, the young NHL made the Stanley Cup their championship trophy exclusively. But Lord Stanley, who became one of the first inductees of the Hockey Hall of Fame in 1945, never saw a team win the trophy, as he returned to England months before the first challenge series in 1893.

Montreal Wanderers and the CAHL's Ottawa Silver Seven played a two-game series for the right to play for the Stanley Cup. The first game reached overtime, but an argument over the officiating led to both sides abandoning the series. However, Ottawa went on to win the Stanley Cup.

The formation of the first truly professional men's team, though, is credited to a dentist by the name of J.L. Gibson, who openly hired the best Canadian amateurs and formed the Portage Lakes in 1903. The team was so good other towns began to play the best talent they could find, and so was born the International Pro Hockey League. This sparked a debate over whether professional players should be entitled to compete for the Stanley Cup, once reserved for amateurs only. Some of the best players of this era moved from team to team, always lured by a big paycheck and the distinction between amateur and professional was murky at best. But paying players well was the wave of the future, as the Ontario Professional Hockey League proved when it was formed in 1908 and proceeded to attract even more big names.

Enter the Patricks

IN 1914, THE STANLEY CUP BECAME THE EXCLUSIVE TROPHY of the NHA and the Pacific Coast Hockey Association (PCHA), two dueling leagues. A spat among Canadian Hockey Association (CHA) club owners had spawned the NHA in 1910, resulting in a seven-team NHA with three teams in Montreal: the Wanderers, Shamrocks, and Canadiens. It was regarded as the league that had the best hockey and the best players.

On the other side of North America, the PCHA was born in 1911. Founded by two shrewd brothers, Frank and Lester Patrick, the new league chose to use seven players per team and lured away notables like Newsy Lalonde and Bert Lindsay to make a splash. Frank and Lester had both played in the NHA themselves but moved west to stake their own claim.

Financed by the sale of their interests in the Patrick Lumber Company, the brothers became two of the game's greatest innovators as they founded American teams and instituted rule changes to free up the game. For example, the PCHA was first to record assists on goals, allow goaltenders to lie down to make a save, and let arenas paint blue lines on the ice to divide up the zones more clearly, a move that led to the modern-day offside rule. The Patricks also put numbers on players' jerseys for easier identification from the stands and invented a version of the penalty shot.

Ice hockey, the Patricks seemed to stress, needed to be different. And it needed to be modern. While raiding NHA teams for talent, they built new arenas with artificial ice: the Victoria rink was a 4,000-seat arena which cost

Joe Hall (left) an ill-fated star of the early days; (right) the Ottawa Silver Seven of 1905, Stanley Cup champions.

$110,000 and Vancouver's $300,000 home seated 10,500.

In 1914, the two leagues decided to face each other annually for the Stanley Cup and the traveling distance forced the series to alternate from the east coast to the west each year. Toronto beat Victoria in 1914, confirming the popular belief that the NHA was the superior league. But with Fred "Cyclone" Taylor, whom Frank Patrick had brought in in 1912 to help fill seats, and Frank Nighbor, the Vancouver Millionaires became the first western team to win it when it tore up Ottawa in two games. The following season, the Montreal Canadiens won the franchise's first Stanley Cup led by goaltender Georges Vezina, after whom the Vezina Trophy is now named.

Before that 1915-16 season, the Stanley Cup was opened up to teams beyond Canada and quite unintentionally the final year of pre-NHL professional hockey involved the internationalization of ice hockey's top trophy. The Seattle Metropolitans, champions of the PCHA, played hosts to the defending champion Montreal Canadiens of the NHA in 1917. Again, playing under the seven-man rule of the western league, Montreal won the first game 8-4 before Seattle won the next three games: 6-1, 4-1, and 9-1. Bernie Morris scored six goals in the final game of a series that made the Stanley Cup truly an international prize.

Following that season, five of the six team owners grew tired of the antics of the Toronto Blueshirts owner Eddie Livingstone. George Kennedy, owner of the Montreal Canadiens, had been feuding with Livingstone on and off for years over anything from game scheduling to the allocation of players and finally the other teams decided they had had enough. The Canadiens were joined by new NHL members: the Ottawa Senators, the Montreal Wanderers, the Quebec Bulldogs and the Toronto Arenas, although Quebec did not field a team the following season. With two teams in Montreal, the city again became the center of hockey attention, 42 years after the first game was played.

FRED "CYCLONE" **TAYLOR**

ANYONE WITH THE NICKNAME "CYCLONE" HAD better be fast, and Taylor was among the quickest on skates. He was the finest star of his time, helping the NHA draw fans in 1909 and then making waves when he jumped to the rival PCHA. After playing in several leagues as a young man, Taylor signed with the Ottawa Senators in 1908 and helped them win a Stanley Cup before signing the richest deal ever for an athlete of that era to play for the Renfrew Millionaires of the new NHA. His style and skills were somewhat ahead of his time – he played the equivalent of a defense position but rushed forward on the offensive attack. He joined the Vancouver Millionaires of the PCHA in 1912, was the league's all-time leader in assists, and ranked fifth overall in goals scored. In 1915, when Vancouver became the first PCHA team to win the Stanley Cup, Taylor scored seven goals in three games. He was inducted into the Hockey Hall of Fame in 1947.

A Thorn in the Side

The current New York Yankees' owner, George Steinbrenner, has drawn the ire of many people throughout his years in baseball, from the fans all the way to the commissioner and even his fellow team owners. Some have wanted him expelled from the sport; he has been suspended a few times. But try to imagine the officials disbanding the American League solely to rid themselves of The Boss. Something like this happened in ice hockey in 1917.

The Seattle Metropolitans of 1917 (opposite): the first US-based Cup winner.

FRANK **CALDER**

HE GUIDED THE NHL INTO A fully fledged sports entity, as league president from the first season in 1917-18 until he died of a heart attack in February 1943. He became a Hall of Famer four years later. Calder's tenure as president is second in duration only to Clarence Campbell's. He bought a trophy to go the top rookie each season (which was first awarded in 1936-37), and it is for him that the Calder Memorial Trophy is named.

STEINBRENNER CERTAINLY HAS STIRRED EMOTIONS, BUT all that seems tame in relation to the feelings engendered by Eddie Livingstone. He owned the Toronto Shamrocks and then the Toronto Blueshirts in the NHA, and his fellow club owners wanted him out. So much so that to do it they dissolved the NHA.

And, as a result, the National Hockey League was born.

It would hardly be correct to proclaim Livingstone as the founder of the NHL, but ...

Livingstone's trouble began in 1915-16, when, as owner of the Shamrocks, he bought the Blueshirts. Other owners were against him having both Toronto teams and, while Livingstone eventually folded the Shamrocks team and transferred the players to the Blueshirts, the bickering continued over numerous matters.

It came to a head in February 1917, when the six-team NHA lost the 228th Battalion Club to World War I. Livingstone recommended a revamped schedule with five clubs, but the other owners had another idea: they disbanded the Blueshirts and the players were divided among the four remaining clubs.

Livingstone was promised that the players would be returned to him at the end of the season, but that was merely a diversionary tactic. After the 1916-17 season, the eight-year-old NHA was reorganized as the National Hockey League. There were two Montreal teams and one each in Quebec City and Ottawa, plus a new Toronto franchise, which was granted to owners of the Mutual Street Arena, not Livingstone, and became known as the Arenas.

"He was always arguing about everything," said Ottawa Senators' owner Tommy Gorman of Livingstone. "Without him, we can get down to the business of making money."

Frank Calder, the secretary-treasurer of the NHA, was named NHL president, overseeing a 22-game schedule from December 19 to March 22. The plan was to divide the season in two, with the winner of each half of the schedule to meet for the NHL title. The winner then would play the PCHA champion for the Stanley Cup.

Small Beginnings

THE FINANCIALLY STRAPPED QUEBEC BULLDOGS CHOSE not to play that first season and its players, including Joe Malone, were divided among the four other clubs.

The Montreal Wanderers had the first pick in the dispersal of the Bulldogs, but amazingly, considering it was just a few weeks earlier in an NHA match that he scored eight goals against the Wanderers en route to a 41-goal season over 19 games, they decided to pass on Malone.

Thus, the Montreal Canadiens drafted Malone and the "tradition" of many of the sport's great players ending up with the Canadiens was born.

On the opening night of the season, Malone scored five goals – a wondrous total these days, but nothing extraordinary for him back then – as the Canadiens topped the

CORB & CY **DENNENY**

THEY WERE THE NHL'S first great brother combination, entering the league in its first season, and each is among only seven players in history to score at least six goals in a game. Both did it in 1920-21, Corb for Toronto and Cy for Ottawa. Cy finished second in points five times and won the scoring title once, in 1923-24. Corb won two Stanley Cups and Cy won five. Cy was elected to the Hall of Fame in 1959.

Senators 7-4.

"Phantom Joe" who had claimed his second NHA scoring title in 1916-17, went on to become the inaugural NHL scoring champion. He scored 44 goals in 20 games, a per-game pace that has never been matched. And it took more than a quarter of a century simply for his total to be equaled, when the Canadiens' Maurice Richard got 50 goals in the 1944-45 season, albeit in 50 games.

Malone "might have been the most prolific scorer of all time if they had played more games in those days," said Frank Selke, a long-time executive with the Toronto Maple Leafs and Canadiens.

The initial NHL season was the first time the Canadiens wore the now standard "CH" as their sweater crest. The franchise made its debut in 1910 wearing a "C". When the club was sold to the owner of le Club Athletique Canadien, the crest was changed to "CA". When the NHL was formed, the team's name officially became ***club de hockey Canadien.***

The two Montreal franchises shared Westmount Arena. The Wanderers opened there with a 10-9 victory over the Toronto Arenas that was notable for two reasons: the game drew but 700 fans, and it was the only Wanderers win – ever. They lost their next five games and then on January 2, 1918, the arena burned to the ground, equipment and all, for both clubs. The Canadiens moved to Jubilee Arena, a 3,250-seat structure, but the cash-short Wanderers dropped out of the NHL.

The NHL was less than two months old and it was down to three teams. It was just before the league began that a headline in the ***Toronto Globe*** proclaimed: "Pro Hockey on Last Legs."

Money was scarce in the NHA and PCHA and so was the player pool, depleted by World War I. Still, the NHL pushed on, and midway through that first season a significant rule change was enacted.

DAVE **RITCHIE**

THE MONTREAL WANDERERS DEFENSEMAN IS CREDITED with scoring the first goal in NHL history, one minute into the first game on the opening night on December 19, 1917. He went on to score another goal that night in a 10-9 win over Toronto. Ritchie's career peaked rather early, though, as he scored only 13 more goals in the remainder of his six-year career, which ended with his fifth club, the Canadiens, in 1925-26. Oddly, during that time Ritchie took three seasons off, from 1921-22 to 1923-24, in order to become a referee.

CULLY **WILSON**

WHEN THE TERM "GOON" WAS first coined, Wilson may have been nearby. He was with the Seattle Metropolitans in 1918-19 when he was banned from the PCHA for a stick attack on Mickey Mackay of the Vancouver Millionaires. He then signed with the Toronto St Patricks for 1919-20 and led the NHL in penalty minutes with 86. But Wilson also scored 20 goals and 26 points that season to finish seventh in scoring. Playing for the Calgary Tigers of the Western Canada Hockey League in 1923-24, Wilson set a then pro hockey record with a hat trick in 61 seconds.

Changes to the Game

GOALTENDERS HAD NEVER BEEN ALLOWED TO LEAVE THEIR feet purposely to make a save (the NHA imposed a $2 fine on a goaltender who went to the ice to make a save). But Calder changed that rule, saying, "As far as I'm concerned, they can stand on their head if they choose to." Unwittingly, Calder had initiated a phrase that has become part of the sport's vernacular, uttered countless times through the years after a goaltender plays a great game.

The goaltending, however, wasn't outstanding, as the Canadiens' Georges Vezina led the league with a 3.93 goals-against average; he had an NHL-best one shutout.

Vezina and the Canadiens won the first half of the season with a 10-4 score, with the Arenas going 8-6 and the Senators 5-9 (the Wanderers were 1-5). Toronto won the second half with a 5-3 mark, one game better than Ottawa and two ahead of Montreal. The Arenas and Canadiens met for the NHL title, with Toronto taking the two-game playoff, based on total goals, 10-7.

The Arenas advanced to play for the Stanley Cup against the PCHA champions. Out west, Vancouver defeated Seattle in a similar two-game, total-goals series.

The Cup finals went to a fifth and deciding game before the Arenas beat the Millionaires to give the Cup to the first NHL champion.

The NHL's second season was supposed to be a four-team affair, but Quebec still did not have the necessary funding. So again the three teams of Montreal, Ottawa and Toronto played a split schedule, this one reduced to 18

CLINT **BENEDICT**

HE WAS THE NHL'S FIRST GREAT goaltender and among the best from any era. He won four Stanley Cups – three with Ottawa and then a fourth with the Montreal Maroons in 1926. Benedict was mostly responsible for the 1918-19 rule change which allowed goaltenders to leave their skates to make a save, after he kept "accidentally" falling to the ice. He was the first NHL goaltender to wear a mask – after he suffered injuries from shots by Howie Morenz in 1929-30. Benedict was elected to the Hall of Fame in 1965.

NEWSY LALONDE

NEXT TO JOE MALONE, HE WAS the league's most prolific scorer in its formative years. Lalonde began playing with the Canadiens in 1909-10 and spent much of his career with Montreal, although he retired as an NHL player in 1926-27 as a New York American, for whom he also coached. He was player-coach of Montreal in the first five NHL seasons, twice leading the league in scoring and connecting for six goals in a game in 1919-20. Lalonde also coached during the 1930s, for Ottawa and again Montreal. He was among the NHL's great early tough guys, and he was inducted into the Hall of Fame in 1950. Lalonde was also voted Canada's greatest lacrosse player of the first half of the century in 1950.

games. Calder was given a five-year contract extension.

The game that we see today continued to develop back then, with several critical rule changes. The NHL implemented two blue lines 80 ft from the end boards, something that the PCHA had already done. Secondly, forward passing was allowed for the first time, but only in the neutral zone. Kicking the puck also was allowed between the blue lines.

As for penalties, minor ones still lasted three minutes and majors remained at five. But the rule changed so that teams now had to skate shorthanded during the infractions, as opposed to allowing substitutions as in the past. If a player was issued a match penalty, his team had to play a man down the rest of the game. Previously, goaltenders had to serve their own penalties, but that, too, was changed.

There was one other statistical development for 1919-20: assists were now being tabulated.

On the ice, the regular season had little of consequence. Newsy Lalonde, the Canadiens' player-coach, led the league with 23 goals and 33 points. Malone, his teammate, played in only eight Montreal home games that season (scoring seven goals), because he found a job that he said "promised a secure future, something hockey in those days couldn't".

Toronto, the defending champions, were supposed to be strong again but finished third in each half of the season. Instead, Montreal won the first half and Ottawa the second, and the Arenas wound up withdrawing from the league, citing financial trouble.

So, the only two teams remaining vied for the NHL title, with the Canadiens winning the playoff in five games to contend for the Stanley Cup. Montreal faced the PCHA's Seattle Metropolitans in a final series as noteworthy as any in hockey history.

Playing in Seattle, the home team won two of the first three games. The fourth game was a 100-minute scoreless tie. The fifth game went to the Canadiens, which set the stage for a decisive Game 6, a game that was never played.

Both teams had been hit with the Spanish influenza epidemic which spanned North America, but the Canadiens were hit worse than the Metropolitans, none more than defenseman Joe Hall. Even the Montreal team owner George Kennedy was stricken. The Canadiens could not continue, but the Metropolitans declined to accept the Cup by default and no Cup winner was awarded for the 1918-19 season. Cup officials deemed that Toronto – a franchise that no longer existed – would retain the Cup. It was the only season since the inception of Cup play in 1893 that no champion was determined.

The Canadiens boarded a train to return home, minus Hall, who remained hospitalized. He developed pneumonia and, at the age of 38, died. Hall was nicknamed "Bad Joe", and he was one of the baddest guys in hockey.

"The game of hockey suffered a huge loss with his passing," PCHA president Frank Patrick said of Hall, who previously had played with the Bulldogs as early as 1905. "Off the ice he was one of the jolliest, best-hearted, most popular men who ever played the game."

"He wasn't mean, despite what people said about him,"said Malone, his friend and teammate. "He certainly liked to deal out a heavy check and he was always ready to take it as well as dish it out. That in itself was remarkable when you consider that Joe weighed in at only 150 lbs. As far as I'm concerned, he should have been known as 'Plain Joe' Hall and not 'Bad Joe' Hall. That was always a bum rap."

The Survival Instinct

HALL'S DEATH MARKED A TRAGIC END TO A TWO-SEASON span of turbulence and precariousness for the fledgling league. At this point, not much indicated that the NHL would survive, much less prosper. But that's exactly the course the league began to travel under Calder's direction in 1919-20. (But not before another solemn turn: Montreal's Kennedy never recovered from the flu, and in the autumn he succumbed to complications from the disease.)

The schedule increased by 33 percent, to 24 games, still under a split format. And the number of clubs doubled – not all that hard considering only two finished the previous season. The Toronto franchise was back after reorganizing, this time named the St. Patricks. And Quebec, on the shelf for two years, also returned – and the Bulldogs got back their dispersed players, including Joe Malone, who decided he would play again full time.

Malone returned to his perch atop the league's scoring list, totaling 39 goals and 48 points to just take the edge over the 1918-19 winner, Lalonde, his former Canadiens teammate who had 36 goals and 42 points. Along the way, Malone turned in one of the NHL's great performances. On January 31, he scored a record, which still stands, of seven goals in a 10-6 victory over the unlucky St Patricks. That came exactly three weeks after Lalonde had connected for six, also against Toronto, in a 14-7 trouncing. Then, in the season's finale, Malone scored six goals in a 10-4 victory over the Senators.

Thirteen of Malone's 39 goals came in two games. Unfortunately for the Bulldogs, that constituted half of their total score for the season. They finished 2-10 and in last place in each half of the season, and on March 3 con-

JOE MALONE'S SEVEN-GOAL GAME

**There was hardly anyone there.
It was the middle of winter, the game was played outdoors, and it was 25 degrees below.**

IT WAS QUITE A SETTING for Joe Malone to do something that has never been done again – not by Gretzky, not by Howe, not by Richard, not by Lemieux, not by anyone except the NHL's very first superstar.

It was January 31, 1920, and Malone scored seven goals for the Quebec Bulldogs against the Toronto St Patricks. In NHL annals, seven men have managed to score six goals – including Malone, barely five weeks after his record performance – but seven goals in one game have remained unattainable since.

Malone, called "Phantom Joe" because he would seemingly appear out of nowhere to score, was everywhere that day.

"It was amazing the way Joe used to get himself open to score," said Frank Selke, a coach and executive for nearly six decades. "In that respect his style was similar to Gordie Howe's."

In an era of brash, rough play, Malone was known for – besides his scoring – clean, sportsmanlike play. He also was humble.

"I used to play practically the whole game," Malone recalled years later. "We'd have two or three utilitymen on the bench, but they'd only play if someone got hurt. So I think I had more chances to score."

Malone began playing with the Bulldogs at the age of 18, in the 1908-09 season. Twice he led the NHA in scoring. When the Quebec franchise became financially nonviable as the NHL started in 1917-18, the players were dispersed. Malone went to the Canadiens.

ceded a record 16 goals to the Canadiens (16-3). Meanwhile, for the first time, one club won both halves. Ottawa was 9-3 and then 10-2, negating the need for a playoff. The Senators were the NHL champions, and the PCHA's Metropolitans traveled east to contend for the Stanley Cup.

Ottawa handled Seattle – at least on the ice. The biggest problem was with the ice. The natural ice in Ottawa was so soft because of warm weather that after the Senators took a 2-1 lead in games, the series had to shift to the Toronto Arena, where an artificial ice surface was in use. Seattle took Game 4 before the Senators prevailed in the deciding match 6-1 to keep the Cup with the NHL.

During the season, a Senators-St. Patricks game in Toronto featured a record 8,500 fans. The final series in Ottawa opened before a sellout 7,500. World War I was over, allowing more people to pay attention to hockey and the NHL to begin to flourish.

Ottawa's title began a run of three Cups in four seasons. The Senators dominated with defense and goaltending. Their goaltender Clint Benedict set a league record with five shutouts in the 24-game season (the only five shutouts in the NHL that season) and finished with a 2.66 goals-against average. And that included the 10 goals Malone and the Bulldogs hung on him in the season finale.

Despite the exploits of Malone and Lalonde, the NHL was entering a defensive phase. Ottawa's trick was to get the lead and then go into a defensive shell, keeping both defensemen and a forward in its zone at all times. Critics cried "boring" and said it would kill hockey. But as it happens to this day in all sports, while other NHL clubs were criticizing the tactics, they also were mimicking the Senators' successful style.

The NHL continued to grow, despite the defensive style of play which permeated the game. After Ottawa won its third Cup in 1924, Calder changed the rules, making it illegal for more than two defenders to be in the zone if the puck was not. "I think the fans want to see more scoring," Calder said.

And the NHL was off and running.

He scored at a record pace during that inaugural season: 44 goals in 20 games. Tucked into his little corner of the world, Malone was among the era's great athletes in a sports world booming with promise following the end of World War I.

With the Bulldogs up and running in 1919-20, Malone returned to Quebec City and won his second NHL scoring title and fourth overall, this time with 39 goals in 24 games.

Three of them apparently came in a two-minute span that late January day. (If hat tricks had been invented by then, nobody would've thrown a hat because it was too cold. Besides, there was barely anybody there to throw one.) A would-be eighth goal was reportedly disallowed.

Rookie Ivan Mitchell was the distressed Toronto goaltender. Exactly three weeks earlier, the Canadiens' Newsy Lalonde had dropped in six in a game against Ivan the Terrible (who had a 4.44 goals-against average in a 22-game NHL career that spanned three seasons).

Malone had set the bar very high on the very first night of NHL play back in 1917-18, scoring five goals (and no, Mitchell was not in the building that night!).

Malone then finished the 1919-20 season by scorching the league's top goaltender, Ottawa's Clint Benedict, for six goals in a 10-4 win over the Senators.

So far, only five more players in NHL history have scored six: brothers Corb and Cy Denneny in 1920-21, Syd Howe in 1944, Red Berenson in 1968 and Darryl Sittler in 1976.

Malone played through the 1923-24 season, retiring with what at the time was an NHL career-best 143 goals in 125 games. He was elected to the Hall of Fame in 1950.

Malone was 5 ft 11 in and just 150 lbs and, as Selke said, "Joe was no Howie Morenz as far as speed was concerned." No, all Malone did was score.

"Today's game is faster, and the players are better than we were," Malone said years after retiring.

Maybe so, but none of them has done what Malone did.

Coming to America

When the NHL governors decided their young four-team league was ready to grow – and, particularly, to expand into the United States – they began recruiting investors in America's major northeastern markets.

The star-power of Howie Morenz (opposite) helped create two New York teams.

That's why they invited Boston magnate Charles Adams to the 1924 Stanley Cup final for a first-hand look at the pro game: by the time scoring flash Howie Morenz had led the high-flying Montreal Canadiens to the championship, Adams was sold.

His only question: would selling his fellow Americans on "that Canadian game" be so easy?

On October 11, 1924, at Montreal's Windsor Hotel, his Boston Bruins were formally granted the first American franchise in Canada's national game. Barely seven weeks later, on December 1, the Bruins beat their fellow expansion team, the Montreal Maroons, 2-1, at Boston Arena in the first NHL game ever played in the United States. So what if they proceeded to lose their next 11 games and finish dead last? For even before manager-coach Art Ross could whip them into a Cup contender by their third season, the Bruins made such a first impression in their amateur hockey hub that they became box office champions seeking a larger home.

If such overnight success gave the NHL a desperately needed toehold in the Land of Opportunity, its dream of achieving major league acceptance there hinged on winning over New York. That invasion began the following season, 1925-26, when the NHL welcomed the New York Americans as well as the Pittsburgh Pirates. The New York franchise proved the undeveloped league could not only make it in North America's biggest market but even fill its biggest arena. Big Bill Dwyer, a notorious bootlegger eager to add a hockey franchise to his string of Prohibition speakeasies, bought the defunct Hamilton Tigers for $75,000 and rented the new Madison Square Garden from its reluctant landlord. Boxing promoter Tex Rickard was in the process of building his new Garden when his second-in-command, Colonel John S. Hammond, persuaded him to sample a Canadiens game in Montreal. But it was not until the New York Americans formally opened the Garden that Rickard became a convert: the sellout crowd of 17,442 convinced him that not only was hockey here to stay but that his adopted town was big enough for two teams – and that his Garden should have a franchise of its own. Thus did "Tex's Rangers" debut the following season, an instant Broadway smash not only at the box office but also on the ice.

ART **ROSS**

Nowadays he may be remembered for donating the Art Ross Trophy to honor each season's NHL scoring champion, but his contributions to the game are best commemorated in every minute of play – on the puck that bears his design. Since 1940, when he beveled the edges to make the vulcanized rubber disk truer, faster, and safer, it has borne his signature as the "Official Art Ross" NHL puck. A Cup winner as an aggressive defenseman (1907 and 1908) and as an abrasive coach-manager (1929, 1939, and 1941 for the Boston Bruins), his legacies are his innovations: strategies such as "kitty bar the door" hockey, and inventions such as the B-shaped goal frame and puck-trapping net. Between all that, he found the time to conduct an infamous feud with Toronto manager Conn Smythe – they refused to talk to each other for 12 years, even at official NHL meetings.

Credit "the Silver Fox", Lester Patrick. After founding the PCHA, he and his brother Frank had innovated the forward pass and other rules which transformed hockey into a game of breathless speed with the spectator appeal for uninitiated Americans. The Silver Fox's reputation as king of hockey's royal family preceded him to New York in 1926, when Hammond hired him to manage and coach the expansion Rangers. Hammond wanted him so badly that he actually fired Conn Smythe, the manager who built the team from scratch, on the eve of the season. Patrick's legend may have been written in the 1928 finals – when at 44 he replaced his injured goalie to lead the Rangers to an overtime victory and inspire them to become the first US-based NHL team to win the Stanley Cup – but his legacy is the American game itself. For all he achieved in a career spanning half a century, it is only fitting that the Lester Patrick Trophy annually honors contributions to hockey in the United States – a monument to the pioneer generally credited with ingraining the pro game into the northeastern US.

All of that dates to the turning point of 1926. For not only did the first-place Rangers' grand entrance cement New York as hockey's American capital, but their fellow expansion teams gave the NHL a foothold in the midwest. The Chicago Black Hawks and Detroit Cougars (who would evolve into today's Detroit Red Wings) also made successful, if not as splashy, debuts in 1926-27.

That brought the NHL to 10 teams – six of them based in the United States. The league split into two five-team divisions: the American Division comprised five US-based teams, but since there were only four Canada-based franchises, the Canadian Division had to include one of the US teams. Ironically, that team was the New York Americans, right down their star-spangled red, white, and blue uniforms.

Thus did the NHL expansion transform Canada's national pastime into an international pastime. By the end of that three-year growth spurt – from four teams all in Canada to 10 teams spreading through America's major markets and amateur hockey hotbeds – the NHL owned the ice world. What's more, it had sole possession of the coveted trophy emblematic of hockey supremacy, the Stanley Cup. All it needed now was to settle down and mature into a major league.

The Detroit Cougars of 1928 take to the outdoor rink for a practice session.

LEGEND OF THE SILVER FOX

With his premature gray making him look even older than his 44 years, Lester Patrick was already a legend – "the Silver Fox" himself – when he wrote one of the all-time legends into Stanley Cup lore.

HE WAS COACHING THE New York Rangers in the second game of the 1928 Cup finals when his goaltender, Lorne Chabot, was knocked out by a drive to the eye. In that era when teams carried only one netminder, Patrick asked Montreal Maroons coach Eddie Gerard if the Rangers could substitute either of two goalies watching from the Forum stands. Legend has it that when Gerard refused him in a note – "If you need a goalkeeper, why the hell doesn't Lester play?" – Patrick huffed, "I will, by God, I will! The hell with Gerard! I'll go in and play goal myself!"

In Patrick's own less-melodramatic version, it was his star center, Frank Boucher, who suggested, half jokingly, "How about you playing goal?" Patrick demurred – "I'm too old" – but when Boucher and captain Bill Cook pressed him in the dressing room, he bowed his silver head in thought. "OK," he decided, "I'll do it!" Ripping off his tie, he called to the Ranger trainer, "Strip off Lorne's skates and uniform – I'm in goal!"

Lester Patrick: "I'll do it," he said and a legend was born.

Patrick was actually trembling as he donned Chabot's bloodstained pads. After all, the Ranger coach-manager hadn't played in two years, and then it was as a defenseman. But after play resumed early in the second period of a scoreless game, with the heavily favored Maroons smelling blood, the Rangers checked tighter than ever to protect their boss. "Let 'em shoot," Patrick would yell as he fielded shots by scrambling crablike on his hands and knees.

He faced 19 shots, several of them in sudden death, and amazingly stopped all but one in inspiring the Rangers to a 2-1 victory. His 43-minute stint enabled them to win on Boucher's goal seven minutes and five seconds into overtime and tie the series at one game apiece.

Joe Miller was recruited for the remainder of the series, again ending Patrick's playing career. For the Rangers, the real celebration followed not the fifth-game Cup clincher but the second game, when the jubilant players hoisted the teary-eyed Silver Fox onto their shoulders and skated him on a victory lap to an ovation from the Forum faithful.

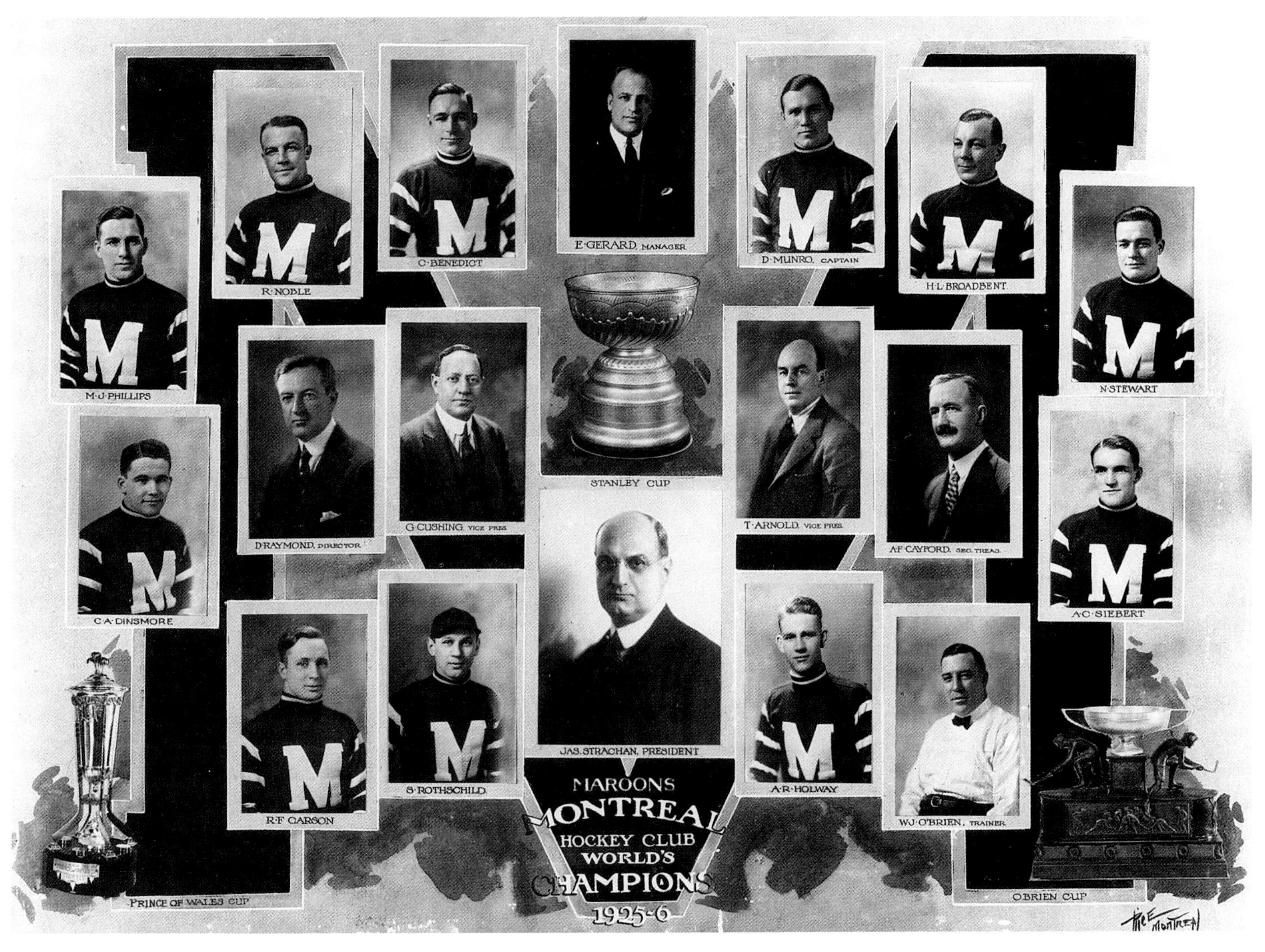

The Montreal Maroons of 1926: Champions with all the hardware to prove it.

A Store of Talent

THE NHL'S DOMINION OVER THE PRO GAME SOLIDIFIED into a monopoly with the 1926 folding of the Western Canada Hockey League (WCHL). The WCHL had rivaled the NHL for talent – and for the Stanley Cup – since the 1924 demise of the PCHA, whose success in Portland and Seattle had convinced the all-Canadian NHL that professional hockey could succeed south of the border. But the NHL's westward expansion into Chicago and Detroit finished off the WCHL, which, in turn, infused the expanding NHL with the wholesale purchase of all the defunct league's players – led by nearly two dozen future Hall of Famers. Among them were managerial geniuses who would dominate the NHL for decades (Lester Patrick, Art Ross, Jack Adams, Dick Irvin) and players who would star immediately (Eddie Shore, George Hainsworth, Frank Boucher, Bill Cook), thus consolidating all the best talent in one league.

When the NHL awarded all the WCHL players in a random draw, it was the Bruins who won the grand prize – Eddie Shore. Preceded by the Bunyanesque reputation he had built as the "Edmonton Express", Shore's aggressive style defined the gritty personality of his new team and, indeed, his new league: rough and tough. Hockey's best defenseman (and often its best player) immediately turned the Bruins into a hit on the ice, promptly leading them to the 1927 Cup finals, and at the box office, prompting them to build the Boston Garden just in time to reward their growing fan base with a Stanley Cup in 1929. His free-swinging knockdown style made him the biggest drawing card wherever the Bruins played.

While Eddie Shore drew fans into arenas and out of their seats with his reckless abandon, Howie Morenz did it with his breathtaking speed and spectacular scoring. If Shore's blood-and-guts game drew the hockey equivalent of fans who watch auto racing for the collisions, Morenz attracted those mesmerized by pure speed and skill. When Tex Rickard finally agreed to build an ice plant in Madison Square Garden after seeing a game in Montreal, it was on one condition: "Only if you guarantee this guy Morenz for the opener." Sport's ultimate promoter, Rickard knew an American box office draw when he saw one, even if he'd never seen a game before.

Morenz emerged as hockey's golden boy in the era known in America as the "Golden Age of Sport". In his book ***The Golden People***, the American writer Paul Gallico defined them as transcendent larger-than-life heroes, "outstanding not only for their accomplishments but for the mirror they held up to their times." There was Babe Ruth in baseball, Red Grange in football, Jack Dempsey in boxing, Bobby Jones in golf, Bill Tilden in tennis, and, the lone foreigner, Howie Morenz in hockey – or, as American sportswriters took to calling him, "the Babe Ruth of Hockey".

In Canada, Morenz was so much more, the center of Montreal's own renaissance. His aptly nicknamed "Flying Frenchmen" were responsible for promoting hockey not only to unexplored America but to English Canada. Even as New York emerged as the NHL's newest spawning ground, Montreal asserted itself as hockey's hub. Never was that truer than 1924 when the Montreal Forum opened as the first big-league arena designed expressly for hockey. Then again, it was also designed expressly for the Maroons – to facilitate their entry into the NHL as the representative of English Montreal. With the Canadiens locked into a contract to play in Mount Royal Arena, they could only watch in envy as the $1.5-million Forum was built for their brand-new rivals. Ironically, when warm weather turned Mount Royal into slush, they got to play the first game in the Forum, christening the ice palace on November 29 with a 7-1 victory over the Toronto St. Pats before more than 8,000 fans. The feud between Montreal's archrivals grew even more bitter after 1926 when the French-backed Canadiens moved permanently into the home of the English-supported Maroons.

Bigger and Better

WHILE MONTREAL BUILT A SHRINE, THE US MARKETS constructed bigger arenas: Madison Square Garden opening in 1925, the Detroit Olympia in 1927, Boston Garden (originally called "Boston Madison Square Garden") in 1928, Chicago Stadium in 1929. But more than arenas, they were building a foundation – a growing American fan base to fill them.

No less a literary giant than Damon Runyon became a fan: "Fortunately," he wrote, "hockey is not a game I do not fail to misunderstand." Somewhere in that sentence he pledges allegiance to this new sport. Paul Gallico may not exactly have been a fan, considering hockey a "minor sport", but that didn't keep him from regularly dropping by the Garden to pick up fodder for his ***Daily News*** column. "That many customers must be right," he conceded in his 1937 memoir ***Farewell to Sport***. "I have always suspected that the real appeal of hockey, and the reason for its immediate success when introduced from Canada in 1925 are that it is a fast, body-contact game played by men with clubs in their hands and knives lashed to their feet, since the skates are razor-sharp, and before the evening is over it is almost a certainty that someone will be hurt and will fleck the ice with a generous contribution of gore before he is led away to be hemstitched together again."

The appeal of the new game to so many new fans was the new stars. Soon legends like Newsy Lalonde and Joe Malone, scorers who had arrived in the fledgling league as established stars and nurtured it through infancy, would pass the torch to a new breed of NHL-produced stars.

But not before Malone dominated the 1919-20 scoring race, grabbing 39 goals in 24 games for the Quebec Bulldogs, one of the league's founding members but icing a team for the first time. On January 31, 1920, Malone scored seven goals in a 10-6 victory over Toronto – an NHL record that still stands. The Ottawa Senators ran away with the NHL title, then defeated the PCHA champion Seattle Metropolitans to capture the Stanley Cup. The next season, the Senators defeated the PCHA champion Vancouver Millionaires in a deciding fifth game to successfully defend the Cup.

A NIGHT AT THE GARDEN

On opening night at Madison Square Garden, Tex Rickard hardly expected to have a Broadway hit on his hands.

Rickard liked what he saw.

A BOXING PROMOTER AT heart, he had built the Garden to stage prize fights, remaining cool to the idea of filling its dark nights with ice hockey. Even when his trusty second-in-command, Colonel John Hammond, tried selling him on hockey, Rickard dismissed it as a "Canadian game" with no roots in the United States and no future in New York City.

Until December 15, 1925.

That night made Rickard a believer. He had reluctantly agreed to give hockey a try only after a trip to Montreal the previous season to check out the Canadiens, accompanied by the quintessential New Yorker Damon Runyon. And now, on that December night, Rickard watched the New York Americans open his Garden with a flourish right out of a Damon Runyon story, starting with the owner himself. A notorious bootlegger, Big Bill Dwyer used some of his Prohibition profits to buy an NHL franchise and rent Madison Square Garden. So what if he'd never seen a hockey game before opening night? Neither had any of the guys and dolls in the sellout crowd of 17,442 drawn to Eighth Avenue and 50th Street by the novelty of the ice game.

The Garden's formal opening brought the crème de la crème of New York society to the rinkside, the ladies wearing gowns, the gentlemen in top hats and derbies. While the Governor-General's Foot Guards from Canada paraded the Montreal Canadiens around the ice, the West Point Cadet Band introduced the home team. As if the Americans needed any more to announce their arrival than their own red, white, and blue sweaters patriotically spangled with large stars and stripes. "Geez," said Montreal star Aurel Joliat, "they looked like they'd come right out of a circus. We didn't know whether to play hockey against them or ask them to dance."

Seeing hockey arrive in such style that not even the Americans' 3-1 loss could dampen enthusiasm, Rickard was sold. So popular were the Americans that the Garden impresario immediately decided New York could support two hockey teams and that his arena (which was merely renting to the "Amerks") should have its own wholly owned club. Just 11 months later, "Tex's Rangers" were playing their own smoke-filled room and offering the same brand of entertainment, from the "fancy skating" exhibitions between periods to the fast-paced, hard-hitting game itself. But the house team couldn't have been more different than its tenant: an instant winner with a Broadway cachet versus a perennial loser with a colorful air of Prohibition illegitimacy.

On November 16, 1926, the New York Rangers debuted with a 1-0 Garden win over the Cup champion Montreal Maroons in what the *New York Times* called "a fast and savagely played game". It was so rough that Frank Boucher, such a gentleman that he would be given permanent possession of the Lady Byng Trophy after winning it seven times, got into the only fight of his career. Not that the blood offended the weeknight crowd of 13,000, not even the men in tuxes and women in furs. Hockey in the Roaring Twenties was a rough-and-tumble sport capturing the times as well as the fans. In an effort to appeal to New York's large Italian and Jewish populations, a Garden press agent actually renamed two players, changing Oliver Reinikka to Ollie Rocco and Lorne Chabot to Lorne Chabotsky.

Notwithstanding the smoky haze wafting from the balcony, the Garden in the 1920s became the fashionable sporting equivalent of Broadway. It was no coincidence that Ranger games began at 8:45 p.m., the opening faceoff coinciding with curtain time at the nearby Broadway theaters. Nor was it a coincidence that the classy team known as the "Broadway Blueshirts" drew a large celebrity crowd. Babe Ruth would show up at rinkside in his flashy beige camel-hair coat and matching cashmere cap, while Lou Gehrig would quietly visit the Ranger dressing room. Nothing, however, could match the Rangers' show business following. There were enough movie stars among the rinkside regulars to cast countless Broadway shows: Humphrey Bogart, Fredric March, Paul Muni, George Raft, Edward G. Robinson ... A tough crowd for a tough sport.

WHEN OTTAWA WAS HOCKEY'S CAPITAL

At the turn of the century, the Ottawa Silver Seven made history as hockey's first dynasty by winning the Stanley Cup three years in a row.

Ottawa Senators of 1927: the last triumph of an early dynasty.

IN THE ROARING TWENTIES, the renamed Ottawa Senators made history as the NHL's first dynasty by winning the Cup four times. By 1934, they *were* history.

Just like that, Canada's capital city – the birthplace of the Stanley Cup itself – was without a major league team in its national pastime. What made the Ottawa franchise's disappearance so much more shocking was that it boasted the richest tradition in all of hockey. With nine Stanley Cup titles, Ottawa folded as by far the most successful champions the game had seen and they would not be caught until long after their posthumous selection as the greatest team for the first half of the twentieth century. Even now, only two franchises have managed to surpass Ottawa's nine Cups – the Montreal Canadiens with 24 and the Toronto Maple Leafs with 13.

The capital's franchise gained fame as the Ottawa Silver Seven in 1903 back when the game was played with seven on a side and its roughest practitioners fulfilled Lord Stanley's dream of bringing home the silver bowl he donated a decade earlier. By the time they had won their third straight Stanley Cup behind "One Eyed" Frank McGee's record 14-goal game, the Silver Seven ranked as the first national heroes of Canada's sport.

A charter member of the NHL in 1917, having changed their nickname to the Senators in time to win the Cup in 1909, they brought the most enduring fame to Ottawa as the league's first powerhouse. The Senators dominated with five first-place finishes in the league's first seven years. More significant, they upheld the NHL's honor by defeating the PCHA and WCHL champions to capture the Stanley Cup in 1920, 1921, and 1923. By 1924, their sit-on-the-lead system had forced the NHL to legislate an anti-defense rule prohibiting more than two defending skaters from hanging back in the defensive zone when the puck was outside it.

Despite all that on-ice success, Ottawa could not overcome its handicap as the NHL's smallest market competing against an expanding number of major American cities. After winning the first all-NHL final to capture their last Stanley Cup in 1927, the Senators were in such financial straits that they petitioned the NHL to grant them a larger share of box office receipts on the road, given their all-star drawing power. Refused that, they began breaking up the championship team by selling off their stars. One by one, they sold all their future Hall of Famers: Hooley Smith, Cy Dennehy, Punch Broadbent, Frank Nighbor, and, worst of all in a record 1930 deal, colorful superstar King Clancy.

Before the 1931-32 season, the Senators took a leave of absence from the NHL. They returned under new management for 1933-34, but with the team gutted, the owners broke, and the fans dispirited, they finished dead last and moved to St. Louis (where the once-proud franchise endured one more last-place season as the Eagles before folding for good). The final Canadian home game would have to last Ottawans 58 years, until the NHL's 1992 return to the capital with an expansion franchise whose nickname would evoke a glorious tradition – the Ottawa Senators.

The Senators defended their regular-season title in 1921-22 led by scoring champion Punch Broadbent, whose NHL record of scoring goals in 16 straight games still stands. But they were upset in the playoffs by the Toronto St. Pats, who beat Vancouver to win the Stanley Cup. The Senators returned to the top in 1922-23, ousting Vancouver and then sweeping the WCHL champion Edmonton Eskimos for the Cup.

The Senators cruised to another first-place finish in 1923-24 behind Frank Nighbor, who became the first recipient of the Hart Trophy as the league's most valuable player (MVP). The Canadiens, led by rookie sensation Morenz, surprised Ottawa with a two-game sweep for the NHL title. Paced by Morenz's seven goals in six playoff games, they swept Western representatives Vancouver and Calgary to win their first Stanley Cup in the NHL.

Lester Patrick (right) with 1928 champion Rangers. The Cook brothers, Bill (lower left) and Bun (upper right) were two of his stars.

Expansion

THE NHL EXPANDED TO SIX TEAMS IN 1924-25, welcoming the Boston Bruins as its first US franchise as well as the Montreal Maroons. The Hamilton Tigers, four seasons after becoming the first franchise to relocate (from Quebec), finished a surprising second behind Toronto. But their players, upset that the schedule had been lengthened from 24 to 30 games without a salary increase, refused to take part in the playoffs unless they received an additional $200 each, and were suspended by NHL President Frank Calder. Montreal beat Toronto for the NHL title but lost the Stanley Cup final to the WCHL Victoria Cougars, the last non-NHL team to win the Cup.

The NHL expanded into two more US cities in 1925-26, welcoming the New York Americans and the Pittsburgh Penguins. With the Hamilton Tigers folding, the Americans took their place and bought their players. The second-year Maroons surprised the first-place Senators for the NHL title behind a bright young star named Nels Stewart, who won the scoring title and the Hart Trophy. The Maroons went on to beat Victoria for the first of 14 Stanley Cup championships won on the Forum ice (including 12 by the Canadiens).

The growth to the "south" was not without its problems and it foreshadowed difficulties the sport is feeling more than 70 years later. The ***Boston Herald*** of January 31, 1926, predicted a rough road ahead. "Trouble is brewing in the ranks of the National Hockey League," the ***Herald*** reported, "and before another season starts next winter, there may be a hockey players' union." There was no union, but the larger buildings, the wealthier owners and

the allure of the glamor cities like New York, Boston and Chicago became strong attractions to Canada-based players. Smaller cities like Ottawa, Hamilton and Victoria could not compete. The NHL added three more expansion teams in 1926-27, welcoming the New York Rangers, Detroit Cougars, and Chicago Black Hawks. With the demise of the WCHL, Detroit bought Victoria's roster and Chicago bought Portland's. The Rangers finished first in the American Division but were upset by the Bruins, who were led by Eddie Shore. That made the Bruins the first US team to reach the Stanley Cup finals, but Ottawa beat them for its fourth Cup of the decade – and the first since the NHL took sole possession of Lord Stanley's grail as its own championship trophy.

Morenz had a breakthrough season as the game's biggest superstar in 1927-28, winning the scoring title and the Hart Trophy. But when his Canadiens were upset by the Maroons, the junior Montreal team was a heavy favorite to beat the Rangers in the Cup final. That was before Coach Patrick replaced injured Lorne Chabot in goal to lead the Rangers to a 2-1 overtime victory in the second game, inspiring them to a five-game upset for the first Stanley Cup ever won by a US-based NHL team. Patrick would inspire the Rangers to three Cups by 1940, the first American franchise to achieve such a hat trick.

In the first all-American Stanley Cup final, Boston swept the Rangers for its first Cup. But the real story of the 1928-29 season was defense: Ace Bailey of the Toronto Maple Leafs led the league in scoring with just 32 points in 44 games, and the 10 teams averaged under 1.5 goals per game. George Hainsworth of the Canadiens led the goaltending dominance with a still-standing record of 22 shutouts, leading seven goalies in double figures.

As a result, the NHL began the next season with a new rule allowing forward passing in the offensive zone – just two years after it was permitted in the neutral and defensive zones. When the change proved too effective, with forwards parking themselves at the goalmouth and scoring more than doubling, on December 21, 1929, the league added the offside rule, prohibiting any player from preceding the puck across the blue line. An ideal balance of offense had been struck. And what emerged was a game with an appealing blend of speed, scoring, and hard hitting to capture a new American audience.

LIONEL **CONACHER**

HE MAY NOT HAVE BEEN THE BEEN THE BEST HOCKEY player in his own family, but that couldn't stop him from being named Canada's male athlete of the first half of the century in 1950. Of course, it helped that he was also named Canada's greatest football player of the half century. For all his sporting skills, 'the Big Train' made a name for himself as a lumbering defenseman – the first of the three Conacher brothers to star in the NHL en route to the Hockey Hall of Fame. Never mind that younger brother Charlie was by far the best of the Conachers, breaking in on the Maple Leafs' famed Kid Line, becoming the NHL's best right wing, winning two scoring titles, leading the league in goals five times and winning the Cup in 1932. Lionel could boast one more Cup, winning with the Black Hawks in 1934 and Maroons in 1935. Kid brother Roy also won two Cups for the Bruins in 1939 and 1941 along with a scoring title.

GEORGES **VEZINA**

THE CHICOUTIMI CUCUMBER – SO NICKNAMED FOR his Quebec hometown and his renowned coolness under fire – had never missed a game in 15 years as pro hockey's No. 1 goaltender, anchoring the Canadiens to their first two Stanley Cups. He played 367 consecutive games in the Montreal goal until, on November 28, 1925, he collapsed to the ice, bleeding from the mouth and suffering chest pains and dizziness. He was diagnosed with tuberculosis, never to play again. Later that season, gaunt and wheezing through ravaged lungs, he returned for a final visit to the Montreal dressing room. Tears rolling down his face, he stared at his old pads and skates, then left with the sweater in which he had won the Cup two years earlier, waving farewell to his teammates. Days later, on March 26, 1926, he died at the age of 37. A legend in his time, he became immortalized when the Canadiens established the Vezina Trophy, perpetuating his legend as the highest annual honor an NHL goalie can win.

GEORGE **HAINSWORTH**

HOW FITTING THAT THE FIRST WINNER OF THE Vezina Trophy was the very man who replaced Georges Vezina in the Montreal net, a 31-year-old rookie trying to win over fans still mourning their beloved goaltender. Hainsworth's coming-of-age came in the 1928-29 season, when he piled up an astonishing 22 shutouts in a 44-game schedule, earning the Vezina Trophy for the third straight year. In establishing a shutout record that has stood unchallenged even as the schedule has almost doubled, he allowed only 43 goals for a goals-against average of 0.92. Hainsworth led the Canadiens to successive Stanley Cups in 1930 and '31. Standing just 5ft 5in, he covered every inch of the net and totaled 94 shutouts, an NHL record that would be surpassed only by Terry Sawchuk's 103. He was traded to Toronto, played three full seasons before heading back to Montreal, retiring at the age of 41.

NO SMOKING
NO SMOKING

Hockey Night in Toronto

Over just five and a half months in the depths of the Great Depression, Conn Smythe built a miracle. Only they didn't call it a miracle back in 1931, when he broke ground on an ice palace for his Toronto Maple Leafs – they called it "Smythe's Folly".

The Maple Leafs, the Blackhawks and the 48th Highlanders open the Gardens in 1931.

IN SUCH HARD TIMES, THEY SAID, HE'D NEVER BE ABLE TO GET it built, much less fill its seats. On the day when even the indomitable owner was about to surrender his dream to a shortfall in start-up financing, his assistant Frank Selke literally ran to the union hall with a desperate scheme. He persuaded 1,300 breadline-bound union workers to accept 20 percent of their wages in stock. Smythe immediately leveraged that into increased bank investment, then managed to complete construction on time (165 days) and on budget ($1.5 million).

Maple Leaf Gardens sprang to life as more than just a building, albeit the largest arena in Canada. For this was an ice palace fit for a queen (right down to the large portrait of Queen Elizabeth, which would one day grace the south end), conferring instant respectability on a sport with a somewhat unsavory image, transporting it from smoke-filled halls onto a glamorous stage befitting a national pastime. On November 12, 1931, a capacity crowd of 13,233 spectators paid between 95¢ and $2.75 to see the Maple Leafs christen the Gardens. Many came attired in tuxedos and gowns, emphasizing Smythe's strict dress code designed to fashion a beer-free atmosphere where "women could spend the price of a season subscription on a dress without fear of having it ruined". Not even a Black Hawks' victory could spoil a grand opening that struck all the right chords, right from the 48th Highlanders band's rendition of "Happy Days Are Here Again".

Maple Leaf Gardens: a stage, a studio and one day a shrine.

But if Maple Leaf Gardens became a shrine, that was because it served equally as a stage and as a studio.

For all the thousands of fans who came to worship the Leafs in the church at Church and Carlton streets, millions more would "see" each game through the graphic descriptions of broadcasting pioneer Foster Hewitt. Attending games at the Gardens was a fashionable event in itself; listening to them around the living-room radio was a cultural phenomenon. For Canadians from all walks of life and all corners of a vast land, Saturday night became Hockey Night in Canada. Hewitt's broadcasts made national institutions of the Toronto Maple Leafs and Maple Leaf Gardens and put hockey on the map, making Maple Leaf Gardens its capital.

If Canadians couldn't make the pilgrimage to Toronto, ***Hockey Night in Canada*** brought the country's best-known building to them. While the vast majority would never set foot in the Gardens, all were transported there through the magic of Hewitt's transmissions and their own imaginations. Spectators in the multicolored seats may have been treated to unobstructed sightlines in the first arena built without pillars, but no view was clearer than that created by the voice emanating from the rafters.

With construction under way, Smythe had asked Hewitt to determine where he wanted the broadcast booth. Hewitt spent an afternoon walking up and down a downtown building, stopping on each floor to observe the pedestrians on the sidewalk as if they were skaters, until he found the ideal bird's-eye view from the fifth floor. That window was 56 ft above the street, which is how his broadcast booth came to be exactly 56 ft above the ice. Learning the hard way that he could get there only via a catwalk without any guardrail or handrail, he made the mistake of looking down and "went the rest of the way on my hands and knees". His advertising director took one look at the booth, a rickety wooden tube 15 ft long and 27 in wide slung from the rafters, and remarked, "Why, it looks just like the gondola of an airship."

When Hewitt began telling listeners he was broadcasting from "the gondola", it became part of the lexicon. Of the 90,000 letters he received each year, "most ended with the request: 'Any chance I can get up there in the gondola for a peek?' It was one of the best-known places in Canada, and those broadcasts went all over the world." It wasn't long before his signature call became the best-known phrase in Canada: "He shoots, he scores!"

HE SHOOTS, HE SCORES!

"Hello, Canada – and hockey fans in the United States and Newfoundland . . ."

THE MAN WHO UTTERED that most famous of openings needed no introduction. Millions of listeners always knew exactly who was speaking. They recognized his style: trenchant, theatrical, evangelical. And they recognized his transcendent call: "He shoots, he scores!" But most of all they recognized his name more than any other in Canada: Foster Hewitt.

Only Foster Hewitt could become more famous than the superstars he described. Indeed, he would become the most famous person in all of Canada. Even in wartime recognition polls of the 1940s, the Prime Minister was a mere second.

Every Saturday, an entire country gathered around its radios to hear Hewitt broadcast *Hockey Night in Canada*. With hockey already one of Canada's great unifying symbols, his early broadcasts would be credited with helping unify a vast, sparsely populated land.

For 57 years behind the microphone, as he defined the sport and refined the broadcasting of it into his own distinctive art form, Foster Hewitt was the game's chief salesman and ambassador.

All because he got roped into a radio assignment he didn't want.

"Foster Hewitt could make me them."

In 1923, he was a 20-year-old cub reporter at the *Toronto Star*, where his father, W.A. Hewitt, served as sports editor in addition to his standing as an amateur hockey power broker. On March 23, the *Star*'s radio station was planning history's second hockey transmission. Just before 6 o'clock, Foster Hewitt, who moonlighted as an announcer on CFCA's newscasts, was heading home after an 11-hour workday when the radio editor yelled, "Foster! I've got a job for you tonight."

After protesting that he had no interest in commentating on this amateur hockey game, Hewitt dragged himself to the Mutual Street Arena, where he found a 3ft x 4ft glass box containing one of those old-style telephones with the dangling earpiece. Though barely 5ft 7in, he had to crawl in and hunch on a small stool with sawn-off legs while speaking into the phone's fixed mouthpiece. With the booth completely enclosed to keep out crowd noise, he sweated so much that the glass kept fogging up, forcing him constantly to wipe it off so he could see what he was describing. Sometime that night, he coined his signature phrase: "He shoots, he scores!" But after the game went into overtime, with Kitchener and Parkdale playing "on and on for the longest thirty minutes in my young life", he swore it would be "my first – and only – hockey broadcast".

It turned out to be his first of more than 3,500 hockey broadcasts. At the *Star* the next day, letters began pouring in, and before he knew it, Hewitt had found his true calling. By 1931, when he christened Maple Leaf Gardens from his "gondola" in the rafters in his fifth season covering Toronto games, he had planted his voice in the public consciousness. On New Year's Day 1933, his broadcasts started going out over a national network of 20 stations coast-to-coast, establishing Saturday as Hockey Night in Canada. Sometime thereafter, the nation's most-listened-to show came to be called *Hockey Night in Canada*. By end of the 1930s, each game was reaching two million listeners, some 90,000 of whom sent him fan mail annually. At their peak, his broadcasts would reach six million listeners, a third of Canada's population at the time.

Punch Imlach, a Toronto institution himself, said Hewitt "did more for hockey than any man alive". To be sure, Hewitt was elected to the Hockey Hall of Fame as a "builder" in 1965, fully 16 years before he retired and seven years before his most famous single call: "Henderson has scored for Canada." Hewitt's call on September 28, 1972, thousands of miles from Toronto, in the Luzhniki Arena in Moscow, signified that Canada had the goal that wrested the seminal Summit Series from the Russians. Nearly three decades later, all Canadians remember exactly where they were when they heard those words.

But his true legacy can be measured by the dreams he nurtured and the imaginations he captured. How many kids couldn't wait to get out on the pond on Sunday morning and replay Saturday night's "He shoots, he scores"? How many future stars grew up being inspired by Hewitt's graphic descriptions of everyone from Morenz and Richard to Howe and Hull? "Foster Hewitt," star-turned-author Ken Dryden wrote, "could make me them."

Bobby Hull, another future star, remembers how the streets of his Ontario hometown were always empty on Saturday nights because the entire population was at home listening to Foster Hewitt.

"When I met him years later," Hull said, "it was like meeting God."

The 1932 Leafs brought the Stanley Cup to their new home.

The Toronto Maple Leafs

NO ONE PERSONIFIED THAT CATCHPHRASE MORE THAN Smythe, who had arrived in 1927 with a long-shot goal of reviving a declining hockey town. Hired the previous year by Colonel John Hammond, president of the expansion New York Rangers, to build a team from scratch, Smythe had assembled a roster that would win the Stanley Cup within two years. But before they even played their first game, Hammond fired Smythe as manager and shortchanged him $2,500 on his fee. When Tex Rickard, Ranger founder and Madison Square Garden president, learned of the injustice, he made good on Smythe's full $10,000 fee and begged him to stay. "I wouldn't work for Madison Square Garden," Smythe retorted, "for any price."

Smythe returned home to Toronto, vowing to win the Stanley Cup in revenge. He bet his $10,000 Ranger fee on a University of Toronto football game, then placed the whole bundle on a Toronto St. Patricks hockey game. That gave him enough to put together a syndicate to purchase the St. Pats in 1927 for a bargain $165,000.

The St. Pats were such bottom-dwellers that his first order of business was a complete makeover. A World War I hero, having won the Military Cross and then survived 14 months in a German POW camp after his reconnaissance plane was shot down, Smythe patriotically renamed them

KING **CLANCY**

THE FLAMBOYANT STAR KNOWN AS "135lb OF muscle and conversation" cannot be captured in stats. Only in stories. His stories. The best of them revolve around how the little Leaf defenseman would cut the great Eddie Shore down to size with his badgering words. Once, after goading the belligerent Bruin into dropping his gloves, Clancy dropped his own for the purpose of grabbing Shore's hand and pumping a handshake. "Why, hello, Eddie," Clancy deadpanned. "How are you tonight?" Another time, after they'd collided at center ice, Clancy sprang to his feet first and, with Shore still on his hands and knees, socked him. As soon as Shore regained his feet, he snapped, "All right, Clancy. Let's see you try that again." To which Clancy replied, "OK, Eddie. Get back down on your hands and knees." Often, Shore would convulse in laughter and Clancy would skate away unscathed. He would live not to fight another day, following his 15-year playing career with an 11-year stint as a referee, serving as the NHL's head of officials.

the Toronto Maple Leafs and stitched the Canadian insignia of the maple leaf across their blue and white sweaters. Then he proved himself the ultimate architect, rebuilding a last-place team into a crowd-pleasing winner that would enable him to build a grand new arena.

His first choice as a franchise player was feisty little King Clancy. When the Leafs board of directors would authorize only $25,000, half the Ottawa Senators' asking price for their star in 1930, Smythe played another of his long shots. He entered Rare Jewel, a two-year-old filly he'd just purchased for $250, in a stakes race at Woodbine, and even though his own trainer insisted she had no chance, Smythe bet on her big at 107-to-1. As Rare Jewel was led to the winner's circle for the first time, having netted Smythe $15,570, he turned to friends and said, "Now I can buy King Clancy."

For $35,000 plus two players worth $15,000, then the biggest deal in NHL history, Smythe had a rare jewel around which to build his ice stable. A First Team All-Star defenseman during his first four years in Toronto, Clancy would spark the Maple Leafs to greatness. Often mentioned among the most colorful players in the NHL along with the legendary Howie Morenz and Eddie Shore, King Clancy popularized hockey in Toronto – and beyond – thanks to the broadcasts Smythe had persuaded Toronto's board of directors to start airing in 1927. More than anything, Clancy's spirited play and Hewitt's theatrical play-by-play were responsible for convincing Smythe that the cozy 8,000-seat Mutual Street Arena could no longer accommodate the Leafs. Of all the visions and gambles of a visionary gambler, Maple Leaf Gardens was by far the biggest, the one which would turn his modest investment into a bonanza.

DICK **IRVIN**

IN 1930, WITH HIS RETIREMENT AS a star center hastened by a skull fracture, the Black Hawks' first captain became their coach – starting a career that would make him the NHL's most successful coach when he retired in 1956. He won a record 693 regular-season games and reached the Stanley Cup final an astounding 16 times, albeit losing 12 of those finals. Hired by Conn Smythe five games into the 1930-31 season, Irvin redirected the Maple Leafs to their first Cup and into the finals for six of the next eight years before resigning. Brought to Montreal in 1940 to rebuild a dying Canadiens franchise, he restored it to greatness with Cups in 1944, 1946, and 1953 before being replaced by Toe Blake on the eve of the greatest of all dynasties. Irvin returned to Chicago for a final season, bringing him full circle before he died of cancer in 1957. Six months later, Rocket Richard dedicated his 500th goal to his longtime coach.

New Rules

BEFORE THE GARDENS COULD BRING IN A MYSTIQUE ALL its own, the NHL underwent a makeover of its own: twice in 1929, the league rewrote its rule book to boost scoring and modernize a game strangled by defense.

The 1929-30 season began with a landmark rule change allowing forward passing in the offensive zone. Forward passes, until then limited to the neutral and defensive zones, could now be made throughout the playing surface. The problem was that the new rule enabled forwards to hang in front of the opposition goal and await forward passes. So in December 1929, the NHL legislated that no player would be allowed to precede the puck across the blue line – the modern offside rule.

The Boston Bruins promptly exploited the new passing rule with an offensive barrage. Center Cooney Weiland exploded, making a record-challenging 43 goals and a record-shattering 73 points. His Bruins posted a 38-5-1 record for an .875 winning percentage, still the best in NHL history, taking the regular-season title by a record 26 points. However, the Montreal Canadiens stunned them with a two-game sweep to win the Cup, prompting the NHL to extend the final from a best-of-three to a best-of-five series. The Canadiens, led by scoring champion Howie Morenz, repeated that feat in 1931 by defeating Boston in five games for the Cup.

With the Depression taking its toll in 1931-32, the Philadelphia Quakers folded one season after moving from Pittsburgh, and the Ottawa Senators, a charter member of the NHL and hockey's first dynasty, withdrew from play. Such Depression gloom was countered by a revival in Toronto, where optimism flowered in the Gardens. The home team christened Maple Leaf Gardens with a franchise-record 23 wins, behind the Kid Line of Joe Primeau between scoring champion Busher Jackson and Charlie Conacher. Smythe had virtually guaranteed that a new arena would restore the Cup to Toronto for the first time since the St. Pats won it in 1922, but even the ever-optimistic owner didn't expect it to happen this soon. Facing the Rangers in a storybook showdown, the Maple Leafs swept the finals in three games to capture their first Stanley Cup – and give Smythe his revenge against the very team that had fired him.

Toronto returned to the finals in 1933 by surviving the longest game yet in NHL history, ousting Boston in their rubber match when Ken Doraty scored four minutes and 46 seconds into the sixth overtime for a 1-0 victory. Gardens fans had hooted down suggestions to flip a coin or complete the game without goalies before Doraty, a 124-lb call-up said to lack the endurance to make it in the NHL, became an unlikely hero. The fifth game of the semifinals ended at 1.55 a.m. in Toronto, and that same night the Leafs lost 5-1 to the Rangers in the finals at Madison Square Garden. The Rangers went on to wrest the Cup from the Leafs in four games.

A GREAT PASS FORWARD

In 1929, after a season in which scoring hit an all-time low of under three goals per game and a single goaltender posted 22 shutouts in 44 starts, the NHL made a desperate move to take the game back from the defense: the league ruled that forward passing would be allowed in the offensive zone for the first time as well as the neutral and defensive zones.

IF THE INTENT WAS TO ignite offensive play by opening up the entire ice surface, the results were immediate and dramatic. During the first third of the 1929-30 season, scoring more than doubled, from 2.8 goals per game to 6.9. By then, the rule makers realized the pendulum had swung too far forward because, although passing was not permitted across either blue line, they had made no provision to stop players from parking themselves in front of the opposing goal and awaiting passes from teammates entering the zone. So on December 21, 1929, the NHL introduced the modern offside rule, prohibiting any attacking player from crossing the blue line into the offensive zone ahead of the puck. Overnight, the balance of offense and defense was restored. Even with offside regulating that equilibrium, the forward pass emerged as the greatest legacy of the era's rules changes.

Forward passing did more than merely open up the offense with speed and scoring; it revolutionized the game by promoting more creativity. No longer was the game dependent on the puck carrier for its tempo and initiative. Now the pace of the game, once tethered to the puckhandler's skating and stick-handling abilities, quickened to that of the pass itself. With the advent of the forward pass, other players could create the play even without the puck simply by darting to open spaces. What's more, defensemen now became part of the offense, quarterbacking a five-man unit inside the offensive zone.

No less an innovator than Lester Patrick, whose pioneering brother Frank had introduced forward passing years earlier, lobbied for the new rule legalizing it in the offensive zone. "I believe in keeping the game wide open," the Ranger manager argued. "Our followers are entitled to action, not for a few brief moments but for three full 20-minute periods of a game. The open style of play calls for better stick-handling and speedier play. What better system could the coaches and managers adopt to preserve and further popularize the fastest game in the world?"

The Kid Line of Charlie Conacher, Joe Primeau and Busher Jackson personified team play.

In just one season, the impact of the new passing rule was written all over the stat sheets as well as the ice. Shutouts plunged: from 120 to 26. And scoring soared: from the 32 points Ace Bailey needed to win the 1928-29 scoring title to Cooney Weiland's record 73 points in a similar 44-game schedule.

The rule changed hockey from a game of individual rushes to team passing combinations. Where once individual scorers dominated, now permanent forward lines were formed and quickly exceeded the sum of their parts. Of all the threesomes bolstered by the rule, the Kid Line of the Toronto Maple Leafs emerged in 1931-32 to personify the new emphasis on team play. With Joe Primeau between Busher Jackson and Charlie Conacher, the Kid Line led the Leafs to their first Stanley Cup and routinely dominated the scoring race with a frenzied style unmatched even by the legendary trios to follow.

With the forward pass promoting the type of speed and teamwork we now take for granted, this brand-new world of offense built a loyal Depression-defying fan base among uninitiated Americans. Thus was the game established, both on the ice and in the stands.

Some Dark Days

THE 1933-34 SEASON WOULD BE MARRED BY ONE OF THE darkest incidents in NHL history. At a game in Boston, reigning MVP Eddie Shore hit Leafs star Ace Bailey from behind so viciously it ended his career with a life-threatening skull fracture.

While Bailey hovered between life and death for 10 days, the Bruin defenseman was suspended for 16 games, one-third of the 48-game schedule. The Ace Bailey benefit game in February turned out to be the forerunner of the All-Star Game. Charlie Gardiner, who started in the Ace Bailey game and went on to win his second Vezina Trophy, led the low-scoring Chicago Black Hawks to their first Stanley Cup, dispatching the Red Wings in four games with an overtime shutout. Just two months later, he collapsed and died of a brain hemorrhage at the age of 29.

For the 1934-35 season, the Senators, who had returned to Ottawa after a one-year hiatus, left Canada's capital to become the St. Louis Eagles for what would be their last season. Toronto's George Hainsworth faced the first penalty shot in NHL history, stopping Canadien Armand Mondou. In a season when the floundering Canadiens traded aging star Morenz to Chicago, Montreal belonged to the Maroons, who upset the Leafs for the Stanley Cup.

CHARLIE **GARDNER**

EMERGING AS HOCKEY'S TOP GOALTENDER IN the 1930s, he was respected by teammates (who unanimously elected him Chicago captain) and opponents (Howie Morenz called him "the hardest man I ever had to beat"). By 1933-34, when Gardiner won his second Vezina Trophy, playing while suffering severe headaches all season, many were calling him the greatest goalie of alltime. With worsening pain causing him to black-out before games and forcing him to slump over the crossbar to rest when play was at the other end in the playoffs, he carried the low-scoring Black Hawks to successive wins over Detroit to open the best-of-five finals. After fading badly in the third game, he insisted he could muster his strength for the fourth. Racked with constant pain through a scoreless tie, he made 40 saves to clinch Chicago's first Stanley Cup with a double-overtime shutout. Just two months after being pushed through Chicago's "Loop" section in a wheelbarrow in the victory parade, he collapsed and died of a brain hemorrhage. He was only 29.

After Shore's check of Bailey (photo left) the Leafs and the Bruins had a scuffle. Right, Bailey (in coat) at the Ace Bailey Benefit game.

THE ACE OF HEARTS

Tears streaming down his face, Ace Bailey welcomed the NHL All-Stars as they skated over to him at center ice, greeting each with a warm handshake. All the while, the fans were welcoming Bailey back with a shower of affection befitting the date on the 1934 calendar: Valentine's Day.

IN AN IRONIC HOLIDAY twist, though, they had come to Maple Leaf Gardens armed for vengeance. Just two months earlier, Eddie Shore, hockey's best and baddest player, had blindsided the Leafs star with a vicious kidney check. The attack was all the more unforgivable because the Bruin defenseman, picking himself up from a check by Toronto's King Clancy, was retaliating by charging the first Leaf he saw. Bailey happened to be leaning with his stick on his knees trying to catch his breath when Shore ploughed a shoulder into his back, catapulting him into a backward somersault. Bailey's head hit the ice with a sickening crack heard throughout Boston Garden. He lay across the blue line, his head twisted as if his neck were broken, his legs twitching uncontrollably. He was carried off the ice unconscious, his skull severely fractured.

Two renowned neurosurgeons operated through the night to save his life, but the prognosis was so grave that the morning papers printed his death notice. After more delicate brain surgery to remove a blood clot, the doctors told reporters and the Leafs' owner Conn Smythe that they couldn't save Bailey – and gave him only two hours to live. Smythe instructed his assistant, Frank Selke, to make arrangements for the return of Bailey's body to Toronto.

Amid calls for a lifetime ban (Shore got a 16-game suspension) and a murder trial, Bailey's anguished father turned up in a Boston bar, brandishing a loaded gun and threatening to kill Shore. When Selke got wind of this, he phoned a policemen he knew in Boston. The cop found Bailey's avenging father, disarmed him, and put him on the next train to Toronto.

As the deathwatch continued outside Bailey's hospital room, nurses could be heard trying to revive him by slapping him and begging him to get back on the ice. The deathwatch lasted 10 days before doctors determined Bailey would pull through. He would never play again, his Hall of Fame career ending after just seven and a half seasons and one NHL scoring title.

On February 14, a capacity crowd of 14,074 flocked to the Ace Bailey All-Star Benefit – the forerunner to the annual All-Star Game – to give their hero a $20,000 Valentine and the Bruin villain a piece of their mind. Bailey came out on the ice wearing dark glasses, walking very gingerly. The fans cheered loudly as each of the other stars shook Bailey's hand, received an All-Star sweater, and returned to the blue line. After all the stars except one had been introduced, the fans fell silent as their eyes fell on Shore standing alone by the boards at the end of the line. When the PA announcer called Shore's name, and all eyes followed him as he skated slowly toward Bailey, it was so quiet you could hear a puck drop.

At last, they faced each other and, after an interminable moment, Shore extended his right hand. With the crowd holding its breath for another interminable moment, Bailey reached out and grasped it, firmly. As if inspired by the ear-splitting roar of the fans and the banging of the All-Stars' sticks on the ice in tribute to the gesture of forgiveness and sportsmanship, Bailey and Shore embraced each other.

Elmer Ferguson, dean of all hockey writers, referred to it in the *Montreal Star* as simply "the most completely dramatic event I ever saw in hockey".

The Red Wings' long road to the Cup in 1936 started with what remains the longest game in NHL history. Rookie Mud Bruneteau finally ended it 16 minutes and 30 seconds into the sixth overtime, scoring the game's only goal. At 21, the youngest man in the longest game, Bruneteau gave the worn Wings fresh legs, never mind that he had scored only two goals all season. He slipped past a weary Montreal Maroon defense and deked goalie Lorne Chabot out of position to send the tired fans home at 2.25 a.m., six hours after the opening faceoff. Detroit goalie Norm Smith made 92 saves through the eight-plus scoreless periods, carried his shutout streak through the second game, posted a 0.20 goals-against average in the series sweep, and then backstopped the Wings past the Leafs in the four-game final.

Montreal welcomed Morenz back to the Canadiens in 1936-37, but he broke his leg in a January home game. He never left the hospital, dying five weeks later of a coronary embolism. His death stunned the hockey world, and his funeral filled the Montreal Forum. The Canadiens recovered to win their division, but were ousted from the playoffs by Detroit. The Red Wings went on to beat the Rangers to become the first American franchise to win back-to-back Stanley Cups.

The 1937-38 season began with an all-star benefit in honor of Morenz, which raised $20,000 for his family. Nels Stewart, who had overtaken Morenz as the NHL's all-time leading scorer the previous year, scored his 300th goal, and Shore won his fourth and final Hart Trophy, but the

NELS **STEWART**

OLD POISON – SO NICKNAMED FOR THE DEADLY accuracy of his shot – graces a short line whose direct linear descendants are Howie Morenz, Rocket Richard, Gordie Howe, and Wayne Gretzky. In that pantheon of all-time scorers, Stewart's 324 career goals stood as the NHL record from January 30, 1937, when he scored his 270th to pass Morenz, until November 8, 1952, when Richard scored his 325th. Stewart's 15-year reign is a testament to how he dominated his defensive-oriented era. In his rookie year of 1925-26, he won the scoring title with 34 goals in 36 games and the Hart Trophy, then led the Montreal Maroons to the Stanley Cup. Centering the "S Line" (with Babe Siebert and Hooley Smith), he won the scoring title with 39 goals in 44 games and the Hart Trophy as 1929-30 MVP. The next season, he scored two goals in four seconds, a record that still stands.

PAUL BUNYAN ON SKATES

Ever the rugged western Canadian pioneer, Eddie Shore epitomized the macho iceman of the early NHL and embodied the rough-and-tumble game of the late 1920s and 1930s.

FOR MANY OF HIS 14 seasons as hockey's most-feared defenseman, he was at once its greatest and meanest player, its most famous and infamous character.

His Bunyanesque legend can't be measured in goals or penalty minutes – or even the four Hart Trophies he won between 1933 and 1938, still the most MVP citations ever received by a defenseman. Rather, his legend should be measured in blood and guts, his and his victims'. How tough was Shore? Once, when doctors advised him he would lose the ear dangling tenuously from his head after a fight, he insisted they sew it back on with no anesthetic while he himself held a mirror to make sure it was stitched to his liking. In all, he had 978 stitches, 19 broken noses, five shattered jaws, and assorted fractures – the battle scars of a style of play both reckless and ruthless.

Eddie Shore, a legend from out of the west.

In an era when defensemen seldom crossed the blue line, Shore was renowned for his end-to-end rushes, knocking down defenders and lifting fans right out of their seats. His free-swinging style made him hockey's biggest drawing card wherever his Bruins played. He was loved in Boston, where his arrival in 1926 instantly ignited interest in a fledgling franchise, and hated everywhere else. So great was his drawing power that when he threatened to hold out one season, NHL President Frank Calder intervened as an arbitrator to get him to sign minutes before the opening game. The literary giant Ring Lardner called Shore "the only man in hockey generally known to the people who dislike hockey".

For a time, his flair for showmanship manifested itself in his grand entrances: he'd skate out on the ice to a band's accompaniment of "Hail to the Chief", with Bruin manager Art Ross trailing him as a valet to remove his matador's cloak. But his real genius for showmanship was simply the way he played the game, with a prodigious talent that could be undermined only by his own temper.

The outburst that forever branded him the NHL's most notorious villain came on December 12, 1933, when he viciously upended Leaf star Ace Bailey with a blindside hit that fractured Bailey's skull on the ice and nearly killed him. Two brain operations saved Bailey's life, but not his career. After Shore's 16-game suspension, the haunting memory of what's known as "the Ace Bailey Incident" prompted Shore to become the first player regularly to wear a helmet.

Shore made up for his late start, taking up the game in his late teens only in response to his older brother's challenge, with an unsurpassed drive. Once in 1929, he missed the Bruins' train and hired a limousine for the 350-mile drive from Boston to Montreal, taking the wheel because the chauffeur was driving too slowly through a blinding blizzard. After letting the chauffeur drive the last leg, only to wake up to find the limo in a ditch, Shore hired a team of horses to tow it out. He arrived just in time to play all 60 minutes of a 1-0 victory over the Maroons, scoring the winning goal.

Upon his 1940 retirement, having bought the Springfield Indians of the American Hockey League, he became sport's most bizarre owner and disliked manager. He would make his players tap dance in hotel lobbies, sell programs, and paint seats. He was even more notorious for his frugality, holding practices in darkened arenas and once trading a defenseman for a net. Players in the NHL actually put in their contracts that they couldn't be sent down to the minor league team Shore ran with the same iron hand with which he had played.

Morenz funeral at the Montreal Forum: "He died of a broken heart."

THE BABE RUTH OF HOCKEY

The larger-than-life legend of Howie Morenz hardly ended with his tragic death at the age of 34.

LONG AFTER HIS BODY LAY in state in the Montreal Forum on the very center-ice circle where he dazzled fans, long after a capacity crowd sat eerily silent through the most widely attended funeral in Canadian history, he left a legend that would only keep growing.

In the Roaring Twenties – the Golden Age of Sport – Howie Morenz had emerged as the golden boy: hockey's charismatic answer to baseball's Babe Ruth, football's Red Grange, boxing's Jack Dempsey, golf's Bobby Jones, tennis' Bill Tilden.

In Canada, Morenz was "the Stratford Streak", his reckless abandon capturing the imagination as well as the selection as the best hockey player of the first half of the twentieth century. In the United States, he was "the Babe Ruth of hockey", his rink-long rushes the equivalent of the home run for neophyte fans captivated by this newfangled sport settling into major American markets.

Dashing on and off the ice, right down to his spats, he led the Montreal Canadiens to three Stanley Cups and won three Hart Trophies as MVP. As his spectacular speed burned out, though, even the NHL's all-time leading scorer became expendable, exiled in 1934 to Chicago and later New York. When the Canadiens brought him home in 1936 to buoy a sinking franchise, the fans flocked back to cheer their revitalized icon.

The Habs were in first place on January 28, 1937, when he streaked into the Chicago zone in a flash of his old dynamic self. Suddenly, an Earl Seibert hip check threw him off balance and he hurtled into the boards, where his left skate got caught. Morenz's left leg snapped with a crack that could be heard throughout the Forum, breaking badly above the ankle.

Although the four broken bones were knitting well in the hospital, Morenz's psyche never recovered. He was weak and deeply depressed. Convinced the injury spelled the end of his career, he drank heavily and reportedly suffered a nervous breakdown requiring a straitjacket. He told longtime linemate Aurel Joliat he would never skate again, then gestured towards the heavens and said he would watch the Canadiens play from the next world. On March 8, just days before he was to be released from the hospital, Morenz ate a light meal, closed his eyes, and never regained consciousness.

The cause of death was a coronary embolism, the doctors explaining that his heart had exploded. But friends believed Howie couldn't conceive of a life without hockey. Howie, they said, willed himself to death rather than face the thought of never again playing for his beloved Canadiens. "Howie," Joliat said, "died of a broken heart."

In the hours preceding the funeral service on Thursday, March 11, some 50,000 people filed past the flower-banked coffin at center ice. Thousands wiped tears from their eyes as they paid their respects. Friends consoled his wife and three children, the oldest of whom (10-year-old Howie Jr.) was the Canadiens' skating mascot. His teammates stood by the casket as a guard of honor. Floral tributes ringed the Forum, many arranged to commemorate his No. 7. The doors to the Forum were closed early in the afternoon and the service was conducted before more than 10,000 hushed mourners (including three teams, the Montreal Maroons and Toronto Maple Leafs joining the Canadiens).

Six teammates served as pallbearers, carrying the coffin to the hearse at the front of the Forum, where another 15,000 bareheaded mourners waited silently. Thousands more lined the route of the funeral cortege to Mount Royal Cemetery, where Howie Morenz was laid to rest on the snowy slopes overlooking his beloved Forum.

season belonged to a bunch of upstarts. The Black Hawks, with an unprecedented eight American players, became the first team with a losing record (14-25-9) to win the Stanley Cup (see overleaf).

The Maroons suspended operations before the 1938-39 season, leaving the NHL with seven franchises and a single division for the first time in 12 years. Frank Brimsek replaced Vezina Trophy winner Tiny Thompson in the Boston net and led the Bruins to a runaway first-place finish, earning the Vezina and his nickname of "Mr Zero" with six shutouts in his first eight games. Mel Hill earned his own nickname of "Sudden Death" by scoring three overtime goals in one playoff series to lead the Bruins past the Rangers with his seventh-game heroics, a record that has never been challenged. He scored twice more in the five-game final, both in regulation, to help the Bruins win the Cup over the Maple Leafs.

The next season would mark the sixth time in eight years that the Leafs had gone to the final without winning the Cup. Even in defeat, their perennial finals appearances had established Toronto as the capital of hockey. Maple Leaf Gardens may have been the last of the "Original Six" arenas built, but it was actually ahead of its time as a state-of-the-art facility. It was the first arena to have a four-sided time clock (1932), and the first to use herculite glass (1947), the first to install escalators (1955), the first to have separate penalty boxes (1962). When the Leafs moved to the Air Canada Centre in 1999, they left behind not just a National Hockey League treasure but a national treasure.

Mel Hill's nickname, "Sudden Death," was well-earned.

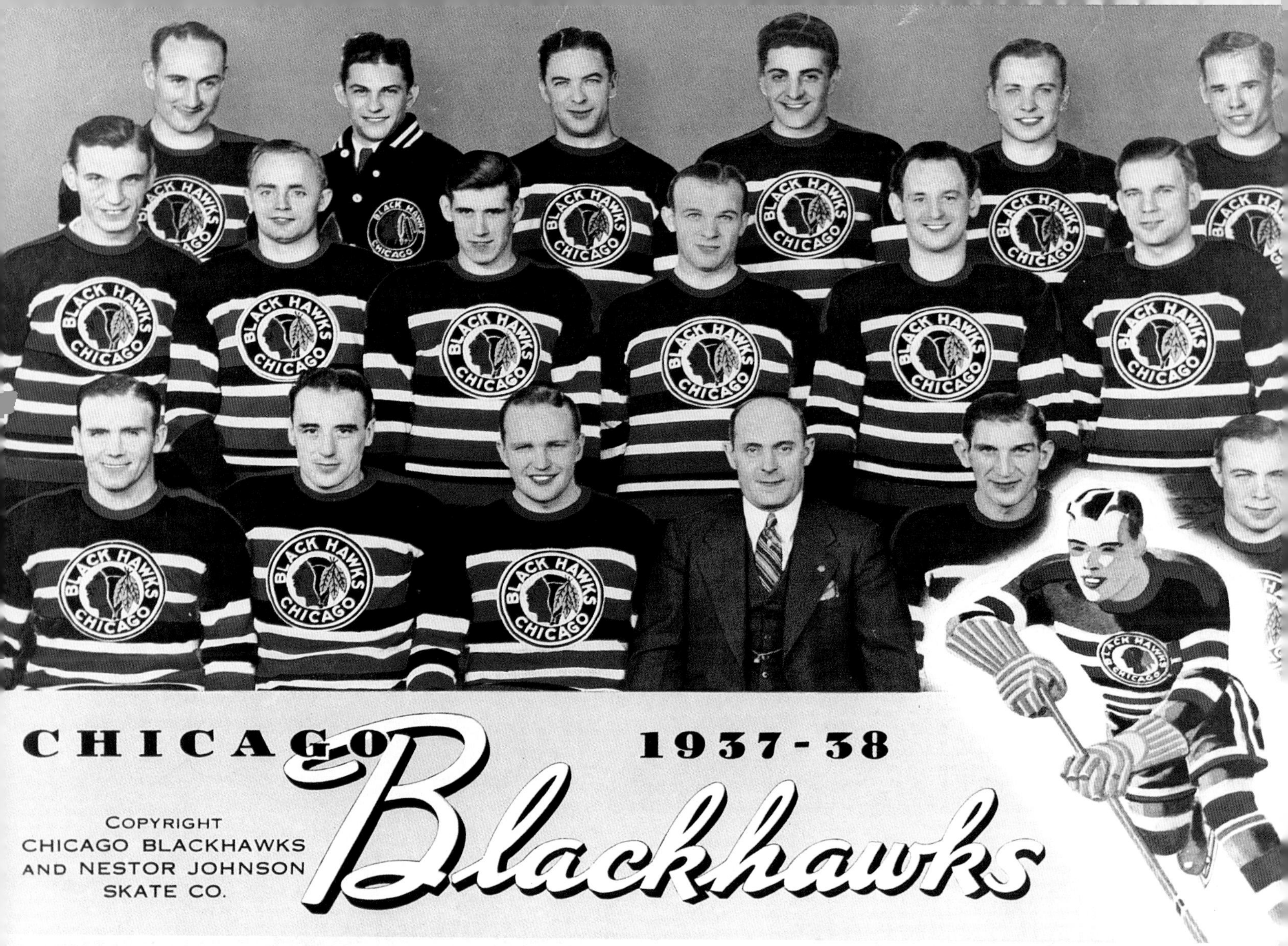

CHICAGO 1937-38 *Blackhawks*

A preseason team shot of the 1937-38 Blackhawks; Coach Bill Stewart (bottom row, center) led Major McLauglin's "All-American" team to an improbable Cup.

THE ALL–AMERICAN TEAM

Major Frederic McLaughlin was a staunch American patriot, naming the Chicago franchise he founded in 1926 after the famed Black Hawk regiment he had commanded in World War I.

SO WHEN HIS BLACK Hawks fell on hard times after winning the 1934 Stanley Cup, the eccentric owner had an idea for restoring old glory as well as Old Glory. Resenting Canada's NHL monopoly while Americans had yet to make any impact, the nationalistic major commanded manager Bill Tobin: "Ice me a team of all American players".

At a time when Taffy Abel was often the only American in the entire league, the Hawks opened the season with an all-American roster. After losing five of their first six games, they signed some Canadians to complement their eight best Americans. The half-American team was eventually built around two Minnesotans who each won the Calder Trophy as rookie of the year, goaltender Mike Karakas (1936) and center Cully Dahlstrom (1938).

McLaughlin topped off his

American Dream by hiring a Massachusetts native with no coaching experience to be the NHL's first American coach. Bill Stewart was a former NHL referee and at that time a baseball umpire as well, who had just worked in the 1937 World Series.

This team had Cinderella written all over it. The Americanization was mocked by rival managers who could point to the standings as proof: the 1937-38 Black Hawks finished a distant third in the American Division and barely made the playoffs with a 14-25-9 record. Facing 100-to-1 odds against becoming the first losing team ever to win the Stanley Cup, they upset the Montreal Canadiens and New York Americans to advance to the finals against the Maple Leafs as 10-to-1 underdogs.

With Karakas sidelined by a broken toe and Conn Smythe refusing to let an NHL goalie fill in, Stewart fought the Toronto manager outside the dressing room before recruiting minor-leaguer Alfie Moore in a Toronto pub; Moore shut down the Leafs in the opener, thumbed his nose at their bench, then was ruled ineligible. Karakas came back with a steel-toed boot to lead the Hawks to history's greatest Cup upset with victories in the third and fourth games, then was carried off by his jubilant teammates.

They remain the least successful team (.411) ever to win the Stanley Cup. Significantly, they did it with more Americans on their roster than any team in history. Stewart became the first American-born coach to win the Cup, but was fired the next season. His grandson Paul Stewart is a former NHL player and a longtime NHL referee.

That 1938-39 season, Frank Brimsek made an NHL debut which would have been spectacular even if he wasn't American. He wasted no time earning his nickname of "Mr Zero", recording six shutouts in his first eight games while twice running off streaks of three in a row. He went on to win the Vezina Trophy and the Calder, then led Boston to the Cup. The Minnesota native would jokingly tell his Canadian colleagues, "You're just a bunch of lousy foreigners." He led the Bruins to another Cup in 1941, but he was never the same after serving two years in the US Coast Guard during World War II.

His career served as a metaphor for US hockey. Where a number of Americans could be found in the NHL before the war, they completely disappeared afterwards. In the early 1960s, with the arrival of Tommy Williams in Boston, there was only one American regular in an all-Canadian league. Not until the job opportunities created by the Great Expansion of 1967 did Americans start making inroads into the NHL – from two percent in 1967-68 to 18 percent in 1994-95.

Mike Karakas wore a steel-toed boot as he led the Blackhawks to the 1938 Cup.

The Rocket

All fire on ice, Maurice Richard was born to propel the NHL into the Modern Era. He had the perfect nickname: "the Rocket." He had the perfect game: fast and furious. And, like any great goal scorer, he had perfect timing.

No star burned as brightly – or as fiercely – as Rocket Richard.

THE INTRODUCTION OF THE CENTER RED LINE – DESIGNED to speed up the grinding wartime game with an injection of passing and scoring – was about to usher the league into its modern era, and who better to launch this faster-breaking new style than the explosive Rocket?

A mercurial force of nature who could burn holes through goaltenders with his speed, his shot, and even his stare, Rocket Richard no doubt would have proved himself history's most fabled goal scorer in any era. But what explains his transcendent legend, as a cultural icon like no other, is that he did it at this particular flash point in history. A time when the sport of hockey, like the province of Quebec, needed a hero.

With the introduction in 1943 of the red line facilitating hockey's evolution from a possession game to a transition game, the Rocket fired the first shots in the revolution – blasting 50 goals in 50 games in 1944-45. If that goal-per-game pace still remains magical, even after it was finally surpassed (by Wayne Gretzky) 36 years later, back in 1944-45 it was positively epochal. In one quantum leap, the Rocket did for goal scoring what the Babe had done for home-run hitting. By the time his assault on the NHL record book ended after 18 seasons, his 17 entries ranged from his 544 career goals to playoff marks even more Ruthian.

With his flair for the dramatic, only Richard's competitive intensity would somehow burn even hotter on the playoff stage. While leading the Montreal Canadiens to eight Stanley Cups, far more than any other player had won at that stage, he cemented his reputation as history's greatest clutch performer. His record of six overtime goals stood unchallenged for four decades; four other records, including his five goals in one playoff game, have merely been tied; still others, notably his 18 game-winning goals, were broken only by present-day stars over many more games.

But it wasn't just that Richard scored goals at a record pace – it was how he scored them. He played like a proud warrior possessed, with a fierce passion that could be undermined only by his own ferocious temper. When provoked as the most marked of men, his mean temperament could self-destruct into the kind of vicious outbursts which in 1955 drew the suspension that triggered one of hockey's darkest moments, the infamous "Richard Riot". But when channeled, that same inner rage fueled a driving determination which made him unstoppable from the blue line in, no matter how many defensive "shadows" were draped on his back. From the instant he exploded on those straight-ahead charges from right wing until he'd instinctively unleash some shot from his arsenal, there was nothing so electrifying in all of sport. He was the most exciting and charismatic player of his time, if not (as old-timers maintain) of alltime.

Frank Selke, Montreal's genius of a general manager, called him simply "the greatest opportunist the game has ever known". But what goaltenders feared wasn't his shot so much as his stare: those famous coal-black eyes, piercing and menacing. "When the Rocket came flying toward you with the puck on his stick," said Hall of Fame goalie Glenn Hall, "his eyes were all lit up, flashing and gleaming like a pinball machine. It was terrifying." It's no wonder generations of headline writers have repeatedly captured Richard's fiery essence with the same descriptive phrase: "The Rocket's Red Glare."

If goalies saw him looming larger than 5 ft 10 in and 170 lb, a nation deemed him larger than life. For he was more than merely the heart and soul of the Montreal Canadiens. He was a Quebec deity, a totem for the hopes and fears of an entire French-Canadian people. Nowhere was this truer than in a city dominated politically and economically at that time by an English elite, where he was a lightning rod both for the thunderous cheers inside the Forum and for the rampaging "Richard Riot" outside it through the streets of Montreal.

When he joined Les Canadiens, having grown up so poor in Montreal that the first NHL game he saw was the first one he played, he spoke two words of English, "yes" and "no". But on the ice he spoke a universal language that bridged Canada's bilingual divide. When Conn Smythe, the irrepressible Toronto owner who first saw Richard play, he tried to buy him for his all-English Maple Leafs. But Montreal laughed at his $25,000 offer, just as Selke would reject a later $135,000 Smythe overture, saying that "no amount of money can buy the Rocket".

That explains Richard's singular stature as a priceless icon, hockey's first crossover star. But what explains the way his mystique has only continued to grow over the four decades since his retirement? Simply put, it's a phenomenon. Only that could explain how Richard garnered almost as much applause at the Boston Garden's closing ceremony as the hometown hero Bobby Orr. Or how Richard evoked a longer ovation than all the other Montreal legends at the hallowed Forum's closing ceremony, an outpouring of emotion so prolonged it brought tears to his eyes. He is Canada's

(Continued on page 65)

THE BIG FIVE–0

Over half a century later, it remains hockey's magic number: 50. Even in this space age of 100-mph slapshots, scoring 50 goals in a season is still the benchmark, still such an achievement that no sniper reached it during the 82 games of the 1998-99 schedule.

HOW IRONIC THAT A MERE 47 goals were enough to win the inaugural Maurice "Rocket" Richard Trophy, the award now honoring each season's NHL goal-scoring champion.

Just imagine how mind-boggling the feat must have seemed back in 1944-45 when Richard himself did the unfathomable: scoring 50 goals in 50 games.

In racing through the Montreal Canadiens' 50-game schedule at a goal-per-game clip, the Rocket did more than simply shatter the single-season scoring record of Joe Malone, whose 44 goals in the NHL's 22-game inaugural campaign had stood unchallenged since 1917-18. Given the changes in the style and sophistication of play, Richard's goal-a-game pace was even more awe-inspiring than Malone's two-a-game clip. Over time, it would only become more and more revered. Richard's 50-goal breakthrough endured as the NHL record for 21 years, until Bobby Hull notched 54 in a 70-game schedule in 1965-66. Even more remarkably, Richard's goal-a-game pace remained unsurpassed for 36 years, until Wayne Gretzky scored 50 goals in the first 39 games of the 1981-82 season – the feat he deems the greatest of his 61 NHL scoring records.

For all Richard's own NHL scoring records – he retired with 17 of them, from 544 regular-season goals to 82 playoff goals – none could approach his magical 50 in 50. Consider that no player had reached even the 40-goal plateau since Boston Bruin center Cooney Weiland scored 43 in 1929-30. As if answering his critics who noted that Richard's astonishing feat came against watered-down wartime rosters, the Rocket responded by scoring many big goals in big games. On 10 occasions, he scored two or more goals in a game. During one nine-game stretch, he had 15 goals, five of them on the night he also had three assists for an NHL-record eight points.

And with the dramatic flair that characterized his career, he scored the 50th goal (by whacking in a pass from linemate Elmer Lach in a 4-2 win at Boston) with just 2 minutes 15 seconds to go in the third period of the 50th and final game.

Although modern-day superstars would meet Richard's 50-in-50 standard – Gretzky (50-in-39), Mario Lemieux (50-in-46), Brett Hull (50-in-49), and Mike Bossy (50-in-50) – the magical 50 has somehow always belonged solely to the Rocket.

Another Richard goal-scoring record that served notice of what was to come was his five goals in one playoff game. Before the second game of the 1944 semifinals, he warned Maple Leaf goalie Paul Bibeault, "You were too hot for us in Game 1, Paul. But I'll give you a lot to think about in Game 2, my friend." Richard then delivered on his boast by burning the close-checking Leafs with five goals. Final score: Richard 5, Toronto 1. That equaled a playoff record he now shares with four others. When the traditional stars of the game were introduced afterwards, the Montreal Forum crowd greeted the announcement of Richard as Star No. 3 with befuddled protest, as Star No. 2 with amused recognition, and as Star No. 1 with a thunderous ovation. It's the only time a player has been awarded all three stars.

A sip from Richard's favorite Cup.

THE RED LINE

Leave it to Frank Boucher, the NHL's premier playmaker of the 1920s and 1930s, to speed up and open up the game by promoting passing with the 1943 introduction of the red line.

"MY THOUGHT WAS that hockey had become a seesaw affair," explained Boucher, who had retired as the New York Rangers' star center to become their coach in 1938-39. "Defending teams were jammed in their own end for minutes because they couldn't pass their way out against the new five-man attack."

Invited to recommend changes to the game, Boucher led a counterattack against the rules which perpetuated the grinding defense-oriented style of play. He argued that with players precluded from passing the puck forward across their own blue line, it was becoming increasingly difficult to carry it out of their defensive zone themselves with five opposing forecheckers to weave through.

"Why not allow teams to pass their way out of trouble, say up to mid-ice?" Boucher suggested. "It would open the dam for the defending team and restore end-to-end play."

With the resulting introduction of the red line as the center-ice divider at the start of the 1943-44 season, players no longer had to carry the puck over their own blue line and into the neutral zone before another forward pass could be made. They could now pass the puck right up to the center red line, greatly enhancing their mobility to clear the defensive zone without being bottled up. No longer at the mercy of strong forechecking teams that could hem them into their own zone, they could now launch a counterattack through speed and passing from as deep as behind their own goal. The only catch was that the breakout pass could not cross the red line (as a two-line pass resulted in an offside call) and the puck could not be passed across the center-ice stripe unless the original passer had already crossed his own blue line.

Allowing forward passes out of the defensive zone would accelerate the transition from defense to offense, fostering hockey's evolution from a puck-handling game to a passing game. And it would propel the NHL into the modern era. Whether it actually revolutionized the game is a matter of conjecture. For change would be more evolutionary than revolutionary: the pace speeded up, but the game remained still more of a possession game than it was a transition game.

The impact on the league was dramatic. After all, the NHL Board of Governors had adopted the new rule in the hopes that an injection of speed and scoring, through increased passing and decreased offsides violations, would attract fans to a game hurt by wartime shortages of players and money. And it offset the dump-and-chase style employed by wartime replacement players who lacked the skill to elude forecheckers and penetrate packed defenses. Thus it shifted the balance back

Leafs' Syl Apps getting a goal. The introduction of the red line took some tinkering before it helped open up scoring and the game.

to the players with creative finesse. By freeing the shackles from fleet forwards, it opened the gate for the likes of Chicago's dynamic Pony Line, with the Bentley brothers (Max and Doug) and Bill Mosienko averaging just over 5 ft 8 in and 150 lb to make an impact.

Following the introduction of the foot-thick red line, the number of goals immediately rose by more than 10 percent, from 1,083 in 1942-43 to 1,225 in 1943-44, while the number of offsides violations declined. That season, four of the six teams scored between 214 and 234 goals, this in a league where no club had ever reached even the 200-goal plateau.

Is it any coincidence that by 1945-46, a new rule required that a red light, synchronized with the official time clock, be placed behind every net to indicate goals?

MASTER HOCKEY

After an epic NHL career which spanned a record 26 seasons and bridged a remarkable five decades, it is hard to imagine that Gordie Howe was ever a rookie.

YOU ALMOST FORGET THAT he wasn't christened "Mr Hockey" at birth, that his arrival in the NHL wasn't anticipated like Beliveau's and Gretzky's would be, that he didn't quickly assert himself as the game's top player and ambassador as "Rocket" Richard did. To the contrary, the most durable player in sports history arrived as a raw rookie struggling to prove his staying power.

Raised during the Great Depression in the western Canadian wheat fields of Floral, Saskatchewan, he did not even begin skating until he was six. And then it was only because his mother, taking pity on a poor woman trying to buy milk for her children, scraped together two dollars to buy the peddler's threadbare sack of odds and ends – which happened to include an old pair of skates.

Although he didn't begin playing organized hockey until the age of eight, he grew quickly into a prodigy and, by his mid-teens, a 6-ft prospect. He was only 15 when he attended his first tryout camp in 1943, but before New York Rangers manager Lester Patrick could be impressed, Howe became homesick and left. That was fortuitous for the Detroit Red Wings, who invited him to the next season's tryout camp where manager-coach Jack Adams spotted him and labeled him "the best prospect I've seen in 20 years". Within a year, the Wings had signed him to a pro contract and placed him with their Omaha affiliate in the United States Hockey League.

In 1946, 34 years before he retired from the NHL while playing alongside his two grown sons, 18-year-old Gordie Howe made an entrance that was somewhat less grand. In his first NHL game, wearing No. 17 rather than the No. 9 he would make famous, he scored once and fought twice. Then he went on to sit for 15 games. As Adams explained, "Young man, I know you can fight. Now, can you show me you can play hockey?"

No challenge was ever answered with more authority. For nobody ever played hockey quite like Howe. If he wasn't the best at any single skill, no player was better at doing it all. He could skate, stick-handle, shoot, score, you name it – the consummate blend of savvy skill and brute strength in a sport that prizes it more than any. He finished his rookie season with a modest seven goals, but by the end of the decade he had emerged as the NHL's most complete player. He would break Maurice Richard's career record of 544 goals on the way to 801, in the process setting all the records that Wayne Gretzky would eventually catch. More enduring are the longevity records no one has even challenged: 26 seasons, 1,767 games, 21 postseason All-Star selections. They stand as testament to his versatility at adapting his style across eras before finally retiring for good at the age of 52.

For all his celebrated longevity as an indestructible man of steel, Howe's career – and, indeed, his life – were threatened in just his third NHL season. In the 1950 playoff opener with their archrival Toronto Maple Leafs, Howe mistimed a check against Ted Kennedy and crashed head-first into the sideboards, suffering a severe head injury. A 90-minute operation to relieve pressure on his brain saved his life. He was not out of danger for a few days and, during his two-week hospitalization, it was feared he might never play hockey again.

But he made a speedy recovery and returned with a devastating aggressiveness that made him more fearsome than ever, a mean streak to complement his sublime skill. The next season he won the first of his six scoring titles. In the next four seasons, he won four of them, two of his six Hart Trophies as league MVP, and three of his four Stanley Cup rings. The only legacy from the injury was a facial tic that earned him a new nickname from his teammates: "Blinky."

Before Gordie Howe's career took off, it almost ended during the 1950 playoffs.

RTHLAND PRO

THE COMEBACK KIDS

Championships in major league sports have long been decided by a best-of-seven series. Heading into the 1999 playoffs, the best-of-seven format had already determined champions in 90 World Series, 52 National Basketball Association finals, and 60 Stanley Cup finals. In all those series combined, only one team ever came back from losing the first three games to sweep the next four and win the championship: the 1941-42 Toronto Maple Leafs.

THOSE MAPLE LEAFS HAD entered the 1942 Stanley Cup finals as heavy favorites after ousting the first-place New York Rangers. But they ran into trouble when Detroit coach Jack Adams surprised them with an innovative tactic in which his Red Wings shot the puck into the offensive zone and flooded in after it with forechecking abandon. What is now known as the 'dump-and-chase' strategy enabled the Wings to produce 3-2, 4-2, and 5-2 upsets and spurred Leaf goalie Turk Broda to pronounce them "unbeatable".

Facing a sweep in Detroit, Leafs coach Hap Day countered with a daring move of his own, putting leading scorer Gordie Drillon and top defenseman Bucko McDonald on the bench and replacing them with Don Metz and Ernie Dickens, two young players who had scored two goals apiece that

season. After a 4-3 reprieve in Game 4 in which Adams was suspended for the series after racing onto the ice to attack referee Mel Harwood, Metz became the unlikeliest of heroes: the ex-benchwarmer had a three-goal hat trick and two assists in Game 5 to spark a 9-3 victory, then scored the winning goal in Game 6 as Broda posted a 3-0 shutout to set up the historic Cup comeback.

With Maple Leaf Gardens rocking with 16,218 fans, then the largest crowd ever to see a hockey game in Canada, the home team had to summon one last comeback as the Wings took a one-goal lead into the third period of Game 7. Between periods, Conn Smythe, the Leafs' founding father, paid a visit to the dressing room to deliver one last pep talk before heading overseas to military duty. When he directed his usual barbed rhetoric at All-Star winger Sweeney Schriner's line, the two-time NHL scoring champ simply grinned up at Smythe and said, "What ya worrying about, boss? We'll get you a couple of goals." True to his word, Schriner sandwiched two goals around Pete Langelle's game-winner to lead the charged-up Leafs to a 3-1 victory, capping the greatest comeback in Stanley Cup history.

Only afterwards did they reveal what inspired the comeback. In the dressing room before the fourth game, Day read a letter from a distraught young girl in Toronto who wrote that she would be ashamed to go to school the next day if the Leafs were swept. "Don't worry about this one, Skipper," Schriner called out. "We'll win it for the little girl." After capping the comeback, centers Syl Apps and Bob Davidson actually visited the girl to thank her for her help.

Pete Langelle's goal made the Maple Leafs unlikely and unforgettable comeback complete.

THE CURSE

In January 1941, nine months after the New York Rangers celebrated their Stanley Cup championship in style, the Madison Square Garden Corporation paid off the $3-million mortgage on the arena and all the officers of the corporation wanted to celebrate.

SO THEY HELD A GLEEFUL ceremony in which the Ranger president, General John Reed Kilpatrick, put the mortgage certificate in the sacred bowl of the Stanley Cup and lit a match to it. In those ashes was born the Curse.

Or maybe it was born in 1942 when Red Dutton put a hex on the Rangers for driving his New York-turned-Brooklyn Americans out of the league. No longer able to pay the six-figure Garden rent, the Amerks were forced to leave – but not before Dutton, as legend has it, vowed that the Rangers would never win another Stanley Cup as long as he was still alive.

Whatever the genesis of the Curse, it would survive the death of Dutton, the owner-turned-NHL president, in 1987 and the opening of a new Garden in 1968. It was not broken until 1994, when the Rangers lifted the Curse and the Cup for the first time in 54 years. Yet as bad as things got during those 54 years, they were never so low as in the war years.

It was 54 years before the Rangers won the Cup again.

Just three seasons after winning the Cup, they began a string of four straight last-place finishes, setting all kinds of records for ineptitude. In 1942-43, a year after finishing first, they went 25 straight games without a victory, including 21 losses. The following season, with their roster decimated by wartime call-ups and enlistment, manager Lester Patrick actually asked permission to suspend operations, only to be saved when the Montreal Canadiens lent them two players.

Those 1943-44 Rangers went on to suffer the worst season in franchise history. Things got so bad that Frank Boucher, who had retired as the Rangers' star center just in time to coach them to the 1940 Cup, attempted a comeback at the age of 42. He came back for 15 games at center, totaling 14 points and outplaying his players, before returning to the bench. His hapless team, unsuccessful in its first 15 starts, finished last by a galling 26 points, with a 6-39-5 record.

They conceded a whopping 310 goals, the NHL record until 1970-71, when the California Golden Seals surrendered 320 in a schedule which was 28 games longer. Ken 'Tubby' McAuley endured all 50 games in goal, posting a 6.20 goals-against average, still the NHL record for poor 'keeping. The worst of it came on January 23, 1944, when the Red Wings pummeled him for 15 goals on 58 shots. That 15-0 rout remains the NHL record.

answer to Joe DiMaggio, a hero who carries himself with dignity and embodies values that transcend sport and age.

It happened again at the 1999 NHL All-Star Weekend, when the league's new Maurice "Rocket" Richard Trophy was unveiled. Upon his arrival at the Tampa airport, the 77-year-old guest of honor found himself mobbed by fans, most too young ever to have seen him play. "I'm old enough," Montreal team president Ronald Corey said in introducing Richard at the trophy unveiling, "and I'm so happy to be 60 years old, because I saw him play."

Richard's real hockey legacy is not the trophy for each season's goal-scoring champion. Rather, it is his enduring impact on the style of play we now take for granted. And all the while, he lit the way for a whole new breed of super-scorers.

The first and foremost of them was just a teenager when Richard made his mark, a prodigy named Gordie Howe. By the end of the decade, Howe would join Richard in a rivalry destined to take the modern game to new heights. Yet even after Howe inevitably surpassed him, first as the game's top player and then as the best of all time, Richard never ceased being the most colorful player the game had ever seen.

For right from the start, Richard was as tailor-made for the modern era as it was for him. Just as the NHL adopted the red line to speed up play by allowing forward passes up to center ice from the defensive zone, along came this young lion whose blazing speed had instantly earned him his Rocket nickname. The only catch was that he was returning after a rookie season in which he had badly broken an ankle on one of his rink-long rushes, limiting him to 5 goals in 16 games and shattering his confidence to the point where he nearly quit at the age of 21 to become a machinist. Instead, fired up by management's knocks that he was too "brittle-boned" to play in the NHL, Richard came back with a vengeance in 1943-44: he forged a reputation for lighting the red light, with 32 goals in 46 games, and especially for clutch scoring, with 12 goals in 9 playoff games.

It was no coincidence that he achieved all that while anchoring the most prolific forward line in NHL history. The advent of the red line, promoting passing and cutting down offsides violations, brought lines to the fore throughout the 1940s. The Kraut Line in Boston, the Pony Line in Chicago, the Production Line in Detroit – all dominated the scoring races. But none could surpass the Punch Line, which was formed in 1943-44 when Montreal coach Dick Irvin added Richard to a unit that featured playmaker Elmer Lach at center and scorer Toe Blake at left wing. Blake, Richard, and Lach jelled so fast that they went 1-2-3 in that season's scoring race. Paced by the freewheeling Punch Line, the Canadiens became feared and revered again as "The Flying Frenchmen" – the perfect team nickname for the modern era.

The Pony Line (left) of Bill Mosienko, Max and Doug Bentley and the Punch Line of Maurice Richard, Elmer Lach and Toe Blake, were helped by the red line.

"ORIGINAL SIX" RIVALS

In the fall of 1949, Toronto v. Detroit wasn't just a game, but a grudge match. In the seven years since the NHL had shrunk to the "Original Six" franchises – familiarity breeding contempt, bitter rivalries, and blood feuds – the Maple Leafs and Red Wings developed into the best (and worst) of foes.

AS DETROIT CAPTAIN SID Abel put it, "They pay us to play the other teams – we'd play the Leafs for nothing."

By the end of the decade, the rivalry had reached a boiling point, not to mention a turning point. The Maple Leafs had just beaten Detroit in the finals for a galling second straight season, becoming the first NHL team ever to win the Stanley Cup three years in a row. And the Red Wings had just won the first of what would become seven straight regular-season titles, an NHL record that has never been challenged. With the schedule lengthened in just three years from 50 games to 60 games and then 70 games for 1949-50, the two teams would meet 14 times in the regular season alone: the NHL's first modern dynasty versus the heir inevitable.

For Teeder Kennedy, half a Cup is better than none.

Not that you needed such a natural rivalry to produce heated competition. That was automatic with the Original Six. In those firebrand postwar days of the six-team NHL, hockey could be as violent as it was sublime. Upon assuming the league presidency in 1946, Clarence Campbell had called it "a game of speed and fierce bodily contact – if those go out, hockey will vanish". But by 1949, an inherently rough game was faster than ever and the bodily contact fiercer than ever.

Part of it was a continuation of hockey's rugged and rowdy tradition as captured by Toronto owner Conn Smythe's colorful motto: "If you can't lick 'em in the alley, you can't lick 'em on the ice." And part of it was the natural result of putting the 100 best players in such close quarters, fighting for coveted roster spots and then battling familiar foes for the coveted Cup. But in the late 1940s, high-sticking and hooking became a common part of the game. Stick-swinging incidents and bench-clearing brawls became routine.

The change stemmed from the faster style of play facilitated by the introduction of the red line. Speed changed the game, the new dynamic requiring new skills. With the game moving at a speed overwhelming all but the most skilled players, overmatched defenders could no longer rely on old-fashioned bodychecking. Whether intentional or not, their frustrated attempts at bodychecking faster-moving targets evolved into new ways to neutralize players of finesse – slamming them into the boards, elbowing them off the puck, impeding them with the stick. It became a vicious cycle of frustration: stars as big as Rocket Richard and Gordie Howe, tired of being hooked and high-sticked and wrestled off the puck, were left with no choice but to retaliate in kind.

By definition, hockey, with its speed and congested playing area, has always been a rough game. If the game got more vicious after the war, if the stick and the boards were brought into systematic use, then that was the price for a faster, better game. The level of play had never been higher. By the late 1940s, the level of competition, making a comeback from its wartime depths, had reached a peak. The same rivalries which fueled confrontations also pushed rivals to competitive heights. All that fit right in with the NHL's whole new postwar look.

Conn Smythe and Dick Irvin always had a lot to talk about.

Even the rink itself had a new look: a fresh coat of white paint. For in the 1949-50 season the NHL began painting the entire ice surface white, making the puck more visible to fans in the stands as well as to those watching on the new medium of television. Prior to 1949-50, all ice surfaces appeared as a drab gray, their color coming from the concrete floors of the arenas.

The new white ice made the sport friendlier for fans, from the record 2.5 million spectators who attended games the previous season to the countless viewers who were soon watching on TV. Within a few years, hockey became a televised sport, with made-for-TV stars like Richard and Howe, and made-for-TV rivalries like Detroit v. Toronto.

GONE TO WAR

Early in the 1939-40 season, just after war broke out in Europe, the "Kraut Line" – the Boston Bruin forward unit so named because of the Germanic extractions of Milt Schmidt, Woody Dumart, and Bobby Bauer – was rechristened the "Kitchener Kids", a nod to anti-German fervor and the Ontario hometown of the trio who would go 1-2-3 in that season's scoring race.

DURING THE 1941-42 SEAson, in the wake of the attack on Pearl Harbor and the US entry into World War II, all three "Kraut Line" stars enlisted together and exchanged their Bruin uniforms for those of the Royal Canadian Air Force.

From the moment they finished their last game before three years of military service, with all the Bruins and Canadiens teaming to carry them off the ice as the Boston Garden organist played "Auld Lang Syne", the threesome personified the war's debilitating impact on the league and the patriotic spirit of so many involved in hockey. Before the 1942-43 season, NHL President Frank Calder announced that the league would continue to operate for the duration at the wish of both the Canadian and US governments "in the interest of public morale". But it wasn't easy as service rolls swelled with scores of players, including such First Team All-Stars as Syl Apps, Max Bentley, Frank Brimsek, Turk Broda, and Lynn Patrick.

A harsh critic of the "home defense" draft that kept many conscripted players in Canada – most with less hazardous duties at training bases where they could join armed forces teams playing morale-boosting exhibitions – was Conn Smythe, the Toronto Maple Leafs managing director. A World War I veteran pushing 50, Smythe pressed to get himself on the firing line as commander of a battalion, shipped out as a major in the Royal Canadian Artillery with his own anti-aircraft battery, and was seriously wounded in a Luftwaffe raid in July 1944. He returned home that September to find only a hint of the former NHL.

Nearly 50, Conn Smythe pressed to get himself back on the firing line.

By 1942-43, enlistments and military call-ups had put more than 80 NHL players in the armed services, gutting lineups throughout the six-team league. A new rule cut each team's roster limit by one player to 13 skaters and a goaltender, but not all franchises were affected equally.

Of the 14 players in the New York Rangers lineup when Pearl Harbor was attacked on December 7, 1941, 10 wound up in military uniform. It is no coincidence that the Rangers, Stanley Cup winners in 1940 and regular-season champions in 1941-42, were so decimated that they missed the playoffs 18 years out of the next 24 and failed to win another Cup for 54 years. Nor is it a coincidence that the Bruins, Stanley Cup champions in 1939 and 1941, went 29 years until a savior named Bobby Orr led them from the cellar to the Cup.

It was as if the war had suddenly turned the league upside down. While the Bruins and Rangers were transformed from the league's top two powers into doormats, the Montreal Canadiens underwent a resurgence from last place to long-lost glory. Detractors branded them a "wartime team", claiming they benefitted from an inordinate number of deferrals; but Montreal manager Tommy Gorman had cleverly built a mature and powerful lineup whose dominance would outlast the war, sowing the seeds of what would become the greatest dynasty in NHL history.

The NHL looked to fill the holes with medical deferrals as well as overage veterans and underage prospects. None was more underage than winger

Armand "Bep" Guidolin, who was 16 years old in November 1942 when the Bruins made him the youngest player ever to play in the NHL. He went on to play for seven years in the NHL.

Although the level of play clearly deteriorated during the war – as Major Smythe had put it in a 1944 letter from overseas, "You have to admit that one NHLer is worth two wartime NHLers" – franchises continued to draw well. After all, the game looked the same, even if fans were repeatedly reminded to please return pucks from the stands because of the wartime rubber shortage. And it sounded the same: Foster Hewitt's edited *Hockey Night in Canada* broadcasts had the same comforting effect on Canadian troops serving in Europe as radio baseball did on American servicemen.

When players began returning from service and replenishing rosters, they found a changed league. Regular-season overtime, discontinued in November 1942 because of wartime curfew restrictions on train scheduling, would not return for 41 years. But the irreversible change was in the game itself: the red line had altered the pace and flavor of the game, and many returning servicemen, having lost the best years of their careers, found their declining speed and skill no match for the faster style of play.

The hockey family continued to mourn their own. After Red Garrett became the first NHL player killed in action, at the age of 20 during a November 1944 escort run off the coast of Newfoundland, the American Hockey League honored the former Rangers defenseman by naming its rookie-of-the-year award after him.

Howie Meeker, a Maple Leafs prospect, was so badly wounded by a grenade that he was told he would never be able to play hockey again. After a lengthy rehabilitation of his injured legs, he returned to Canada and played senior hockey in Stratford in 1945-46 before joining the Leafs as a 21-year-old winger in 1946-47. He scored 27 goals – including a still-unbroken rookie record of five in one game – and outshone a rookie named Gordie Howe in winning the Calder Trophy as rookie of the year.

World War II called for unique training methods (and uniforms) for all to be ready.

A SHOOTING STAR IN GOAL

Even by the unorthodox standards of NHL goaltenders, Bill Durnan was different.

HE WAS A LATE STARTER, breaking into the NHL as a 28-year-old rookie. And he was an early retiree, quitting the Montreal Canadiens abruptly after just seven seasons. In between, he broke the mold as well as the records.

Durnan was the first ambidextrous goalie, employing a combination catching mitt and stick glove on each hand, switching the stick from hand to hand as needed, then stoning NHL shooters with a trick learned in a schoolboy church league.

He went on to become the first goalie to win the Vezina Trophy for four straight years, his first four in the league no less. And, two decades before Jacques Plante would earn his record seventh Vezina, Durnan became the first to win the trophy a total of six times.

He did all this in just seven years. As a rookie in 1943-44, he won the Vezina after allowing just 109 goals in 50 games and backstopping the Canadiens to their first Stanley Cup in 13 years. He became such a leader that in 1947-48 the Canadiens made him one of the few goaltenders to serve as a team captain. He is the last goalie ever to wear the "C", his frequent journeys to argue with referees having spurred an NHL rule change prohibiting netminders from serving as captain.

It is a measure of Durnan's greatness that he dominated his position at a time when he had to duel with the game's greatest money goalie, Turk Broda of Toronto. Broda backstopped the Maple Leafs to five Stanley Cups between 1942 and 1951, but won the Vezina only once, breaking Durnan's monopoly on the trophy and the First Team All-Star slot in 1948.

Durnan (left) and Broda; remarkable goalies of the 1940s.

Durnan rebounded the following season by playing a consecutive streak of 309 minutes and 21 seconds without allowing a goal, an unchallenged modern record spanning four shutouts in a row. He was halfway through a fifth straight shutout when Gaye Stewart scored in Chicago to end the streak right where it began two weeks earlier. Instead of celebrating the goal, Stewart skated over to Durnan and actually apologized for breaking the streak. "I had to chuckle," Durnan said later, "because, in a way, I was relieved to get it behind me."

After the streak, in which he stopped 95 shots, Durnan completed his year with 10 shutouts and a 2.10 goals-against average. But he knew his career was on borrowed time.

He had long sought the addition of a backup goalie to his team's roster. In those days each team carried one goalie and employed a spare goalie who might be at a game in case the regular goaltender was unable to finish. Durnan argued that the stress unique to sport's most pressure-packed position was too much for one netminder. He became his own best argument. The pressure ate away at him until he found himself unable to sleep the night before games, often getting sick to his stomach. Midway through a 1950 semifinal series against the Rangers, he was injured and asked to be replaced in the nets. He never returned.

The Original Six

WITH WORLD WAR II TURNING THE NHL UPSIDEDOWN, the Canadiens, suffering through the longest drought in their rich history, would rise the farthest as well as the fastest. Almost overnight, they displaced the league's two dominant powers, the New York Rangers and Boston Bruins, who would crash hard.

In 1940, the Rangers won their third Stanley Cup with Bryan Hextall's overtime goal in the sixth game of the finals against the Toronto Maple Leafs – a championship that would have to last them 54 years until their next one.

The following year, the Bruins, winning their fourth straight regular-season title behind a record 23-game unbeaten streak and recording their second straight scoring champion (MVP center Bill Cowley having succeeded Kraut Line center Milt Schmidt), won the Cup over the Detroit Red Wings with the first four-game sweep in playoff history – a championship that took them 29 years to repeat. So decimated were the league's top two teams by the wartime player shortage that they never regained their lost momentum.

The next season, 1941-42, put an exclamation mark on the pre-modern era. Scoring champ Hextall led the Rangers to what would be their last regular-season title for half a century, but it was their playoff conquerors who made history. The Maple Leafs, stunned by the underdog Red Wings in the first three games of the finals, roared back to pull off a feat never matched by any team in the NHL or the other major-league sports – sweeping the final four games of a championship series after losing the first three. Down three games to none, the desperate Leafs shook up their lineup by putting their leading scorer and top defenseman on the bench, then reeled off victories of 4-3, 9-3, 3-0, and 3-1 to capture their first Stanley Cup in 10 years – and cap the greatest comeback in hockey history. It was a fitting end to an historic era.

After that season, the floundering Brooklyn Americans, a year after changing their name from the New York Americans in their desperate search for a new identity while continuing to share Madison Square Garden as mere tenants of the Rangers, suspended operations for the duration of World War II. The insolvent franchise, after 17 wild if not winning seasons in stars and stripes, was never reactivated. That brought what had been a 10-team league just 12 years earlier down to six teams and ushered in a new period of unprecedented stability. This period, lasting 25 years and overlapping the modern era, nowadays has a name all its own: "the Original Six."

The six remaining teams which opened the 1942-43 season – the Montreal Canadiens, Toronto Maple Leafs, Boston Bruins, New York Rangers, Chicago Black Hawks, and Detroit Red Wings – would constitute the entire NHL until the Great Expansion of 1967-68.

Although Montreal and Toronto were the only Original Six franchises which were actually around at the NHL's inception in 1917, the six-team league would be, in every other sense, a North American original. With the game's best players fighting for some 100 NHL jobs, the Original Six featured a competitiveness unique to all of major-league professional sports. The quality of play was heightened by the intense competition both within teams and between teams, with frequent showdowns breeding bitter rivalries and bloody feuds. Nowhere were the rivalries fiercer than among the three franchises which promptly asserted themselves as first-division powerhouses: Montreal, Toronto, and Detroit.

The Red Wings became the first Original Six champions. They finished atop the 1942-43 standings without a single scorer in the top 10, let alone anywhere near scoring champion Doug Bentley of Chicago. Then they swept Boston in four straight games to capture finally the Stanley Cup they had blown with the previous year's humiliating collapse against Toronto's comeback kids.

The next season signaled a return to glory for the league's most storied franchise. The Canadiens were on the verge of collapse when long-time Toronto coach Dick Irvin arrived in Montreal in 1940-41 and began a 15-year tenure by discovering Maurice Richard playing junior hockey. Under Irvin, who in the 1940s became the most successful coach in NHL history en route to a then-record 690 regular-season victories, the Canadiens underwent a remarkable rejuvenation. They rose from last place to evoke the original Flying Frenchmen of the 1920s and early '30s, only now they were even more dangerous. They featured the Punch Line, scoring goals at a record pace, and goaltender Bill Durnan, saving them at a clip which would earn him an unprecedented six Vezina Trophies in a seven-year career.

STABILITY FROM THE TOP

After nearly three decades of growing pains, of franchise shifts and rule changes, of Depression struggles and two world wars, what the NHL needed more than anything was stability. Reconstructing after the upheaval of World War II, the remaining six NHL franchises had just the man for the job: Clarence Campbell.

CAMPBELL HAD SERVED as a lieutenant colonel in the Canadian Army in Europe before joining the Canadian War Crimes Unit. He spent most of 1945 and 1946 as one of the Allies' prosecutors during the Nuremberg war crimes trials, winning the Order of the British Empire.

So impressive was his résumé – Rhodes scholar, lawyer, onetime NHL referee – that the league governors persuaded Red Dutton, who had succeeded Frank Calder, the NHL's president from its inception in 1917 until his death of a heart attack in February 1943, to continue running the league, however reluctantly, until the designated successor returned from Europe. Upon Campbell's return, Dutton summoned him for an interview. "We were walking across Dominion Square in Montreal when Dutton told me he was going to resign and recommend me as President," Campbell recalled. "At noon that day, I had the job."

Campbell took over as the NHL's third president in 1946, just as the league was settling into postwar prosperity as a solid six-team circuit in an era of both stability and change. He managed the league at the direction of a board of powerful and colorful governors, serving no owners more influential than Jim Norris in Detroit and Conn Smythe in Toronto.

Clarence Campbell was the man the NHL had to have so they waited.

Stately and dignified, Campbell personified integrity and leadership, an image that served hockey well. In March 1948, he acted against the gambling that had tainted the league. Just before he took over as president, aging defensive star Babe Pratt, just two years after winning the 1944 Hart Trophy as MVP, had been suspended for nine games for betting on games involving teams other than his own. Realizing that the Pratt suspension was too mild, Campbell expelled New York's Billy Taylor and Boston's Don Gallinger for gambling (both players were alleged to have bet on games, though none was fixed).

Campbell never shied away from making the tough calls. After Game 2 of the 1947 Stanley Cup finals, in which Rocket Richard had opened head cuts with stick fouls against two Maple Leafs, Campbell stung the Canadiens by suspending their star for the next game. It gave a warning that Campbell would not tolerate stick fights.

One of Campbell's first orders of business was to heed the suggestion of Chicago newspaperman John Carmichael, with the support of Black Hawks manager Bill Tobin, to stage an All-Star game pitting the reigning Stanley Cup champions against the stars of the other five teams. Campbell jumped at the idea and earmarked one quarter of the game's proceeds for the Players' Emergency Fund, a forerunner to the pension plan. All-star benefit games had been played on three occasions in the 1930s, but this was to be the first official All-Star game. On October 13, 1947, with Richard scoring the unassisted tying goal and setting up Doug Bentley's winner, the All-Stars defeated the host Toronto Maple Leafs 4-3 to inaugurate the annual NHL All-Star Game.

That was merely one piece of Campbell's legacy. He guided the league through what has become known as the "Original Six" era, when the solid six franchises provided hockey with its Golden Age. And then he guided it through the Great Expansion of 1967, taking it to the next level by doubling the number of franchises to 12. By the time he retired in 1977 after 31 years at the helm, there would be 18 franchises. That is his greatest legacy.

The Punch Line

AFTER FIVE STRAIGHT YEARS WITHOUT A WINNING RECORD, the Canadiens opened the 1943-44 season with a 14-game unbeaten streak, a starting-gate record that would stand for 41 years. They went on to finish 38-5-7, setting a still-standing record for the fewest losses (including none on home ice), and dominating the standings by 25 points, an NHL record that stood for 52 years. Durnan, the ambidextrous netminder, won the Vezina Trophy as a 28-year-old rookie, overshadowing the Punch Line and the scoring race paced by Boston's Herb Cain. With Durnan continuing his brilliant goaltending and the Punch Line notching 21 playoff goals, the Canadiens beat Chicago in the finals to win their first Stanley Cup in 13 years.

They dominated the next season similarly, topping the 1944-45 standings by 13 points with a 38-8-4 record and packing five players among the six First Team All-Stars. The Punch Line went 1-2-3 in the scoring race, joining the Kraut Line as the only forward trios to pull off that feat (Milt Schmidt, Bobby Bauer, and Woody Dumart first did it in 1939-40) and averaging a matchless 4.4 points per game. Despite finishing seven points behind league MVP Lach for the scoring title, Richard dominated with his record-shattering 50 goals – 21 ahead of runners-up Blake and Teeder Kennedy of Toronto. The Rocket scored five of those goals in the same December game in which his three assists gave him a record eight points. For all their firepower, however, the Canadiens were upset in a six-game semifinal by the third-place Maple Leafs.

Toronto went on to win an exciting seven-game final in which the Red Wings, sounding a rallying cry of

TED "TEEDER" **KENNEDY**

WITH HIS FIERCE COMPETITIVE SPIRIT, he helped lead the Maple Leafs to seven Stanley Cups between 1945 and 1951. As he'd line up for faceoffs, Maple Leaf Garden would echo with the fans' battle cry of "Come on, Teeder! Come on, Teeder!" In 1948, after leading the Leafs to three Cups in four years, he replaced the retiring Syl Apps as captain. In his captain's role, he is best remembered for the photograph of him welcoming Princess Elizabeth to the Garden for a 1951 game. He finally garnered an individual honor in 1954-55 when he won the Hart Trophy, making him the last Leaf selected as league MVP.

"Revenge for 1942", almost pulled off the same three-down comeback with which the Leafs had humiliated them three years earlier. The Leafs jumped to a commanding lead behind three straight shutouts by rookie goalie Frank "Ulcers" McCool, but then dropped the next three. McCool, who came by his nickname the hard way, spent the series regularly doubling up in pain. He even skated off to the locker room in the middle of Game 7, but coach Hap Day talked him back onto the ice, where he clutched his stomach when play went the other way and led the Leafs to a 2-1 victory for the Cup.

With the defending champion Maple Leafs failing to make the playoffs, the Canadiens returned to the top in 1945-46. Richard slipped to 27 goals and fifth in the scoring race, well behind champion Max Bentley of Chicago's Pony Line. The Canadiens nevertheless won the regular-season title and swept Chicago in a four-straight semifinal to set up a finals showdown against Boston, whose manager Art Ross branded them "strictly a wartime team". The Canadiens responded by routing the Bruins in five games for their second Cup in three years and proving, in Irvin's words, that they were "not just a wartime club but really a great team in every era of hockey".

They went on to win their fourth straight regular-season title in 1946-47 behind Richard, whose 45 goals silenced critics who had attributed his defining 50-goal season to a wartime dilution of talent. Scoring 15 more goals than anyone else, he came within a point of scoring champion Max Bentley, won the Hart Trophy as league MVP, then led Montreal into the finals as the heavy favorite against the rebuilding Maple Leafs. After shutting them out 6-0 in the opener, Durnan quipped, "How did those guys get in the league?" The upstart Leafs proceeded to show him, stunning the Canadiens in six games to become the youngest club ever to win the Stanley Cup.

That foreshadowed a changing of the guard, as a broken leg the next season ended Blake's career and broke up the Punch Line. Meanwhile, the Maple Leafs, with winger Howie Meeker giving them their fourth Calder Trophy winner in five years as rookie of the year, had amassed a promising young nucleus to complement such veteran All-Stars as classy captain Syl Apps and big-game goalie Turk Broda.

They improved overnight the following November as Conn Smythe, their wheeler-dealer managing director, pulled off the biggest trade in hockey history: a blockbuster which sent five talented young regulars to Chicago in exchange for two-time reigning scoring king Max Bentley. With Bentley joining Apps and Teeder Kennedy to give Toronto three Hall of Fame centers – the "Dipsy-Doodle Dandy" playmaker led them by finishing fifth in the scoring race, just seven points behind scoring champ Lach – the Leafs won the 1947-48 regular-season title over the Red Wings. They then swept the Wings out of the finals for their second straight Stanley Cup, becoming the first franchise to win it seven times overall.

Although the Maple Leafs slipped badly during the 1948-49 season, barely making the playoffs after Apps's retirement, they remained a threat to become the first fourth-place finisher in history – indeed, the lowest-placed team ever – to win the Cup. The regular season belonged to Durnan, who set a modern record of 309 consecutive minutes without allowing a goal, spanning four straight shutouts; and to the Red Wings, who easily won the first of their record seven straight points titles. But if the poor play of the 22-25-13 Leafs was the surprise of the regular season, their second straight finals sweep of the Wings was even more stunning. That made Toronto the first NHL club to win three consecutive Stanley Cup championships – and the first to stake a claim as a modern dynasty.

The back-to-back sweeps notwithstanding, the Toronto-Detroit balance of power was shifting. The Leaf decline could be measured not only in the standings but on the scale, where the stocky 5 ft 9 in Broda had ballooned to 197 lbs. Smythe responded in December 1949 by putting his pudgy puckstopper on a very public diet. "We're not running a fat man's team," Smythe announced. "I'm taking him out of the nets and he's not going back until he shows some common sense." Enduring a week of practices in which he faced a shooting gallery of snipers with no stick, the "Crisco Kid" sweated off the mandated 7 lbs with a pound to spare. But not even the return of hockey's premier playoff goalie could preserve the Leafs dynasty.

The time clearly belonged to the Red Wings and, particularly, to their blossoming young superstar. A superstar who would dominate the NHL for the next quarter of a century in a way nobody ever had.

MAX **BENTLEY**

CREDIT BROADCASTER FOSTER HEWITT with coining his nickname: "the Dipsy-Doodle Dandy of Delisle." It referenced the playmaker's skating and stickhandling skill as well as his Saskatchewan hometown. At just 5 ft 8 in and 158 lbs, Max and his older (but not bigger) brother Doug terrorized Chicago Black Hawks foes as two of the league's most dangerous scorers. Doug won the scoring title in 1943, Max won it in 1946 and 1947. They made their biggest impact on the league's most dynamic unit: the Pony Line, with Max at center, Doug on the left and Bill Mosienko on the right. The only way they were stopped was when, as part of the November 1947 blockbuster trade, Max was swapped for five Maple Leaf regulars to go to Toronto, where he won the Cup in 1949 and 1951.

HOWIE **MEEKER**

HE WAS AN INSTANT SENSATION, SCORING A rookie-record five goals in one game and totaling 27 for the season to win the Calder Trophy as 1946--47 rookie of the year, a feat made all the more remarkable by the serious World War II injury which threatened to end his NHL career before it even started. But that was only the beginning for Meeker. He went on to play for eight years with the Maple Leafs, winning four Stanley Cups, before achieving greater fame as a TV analyst. But the most interesting time of his career came between 1951 and 1953, when he played for the Leafs in Toronto while also serving as a Member of Parliament with the Conservative Party in Ottawa.

Number 9

IF ROCKET RICHARD WAS THE IDEAL SCORING FORCE TO define the modern firebrand game, Gordie Howe was just the all-round force to personify the redefined game's unique blend of sublime skill and brute strength. With Howe's cool efficiency making him the perfect foil to Richard's hot intensity, is it any wonder that theirs grew into such a compelling rivalry? Both wore No. 9 on their sweaters with the grace to fashion it into hockey's royal number. Both played right wing as it had never been played before. And both scored goals more prolifically than anyone else ever had.

In 1949-50, Howe finished third in the scoring race, behind Production Line-mates Ted Lindsay and Sid Abel and just ahead of Richard, presaging his breakthrough as the game's number one player. Eventually he broke Richard's career scoring record, but their rivalry, like the rivals themselves, transcended hockey. For both transcended the sport in a way no one ever had, as hockey's first crossover stars popularizing an evolving game through its Golden Age: Richard the cultural icon, Howe the hockey ambassador. Howe proved himself the perfect ambassador for the rugged Original Six age and the sleek modern era, blending his skill and power in a uniquely complete package worthy of his nickname – "Mr Hockey". Mostly, he was to prove himself a player for the ages, adapting over the following decades as the game became more and more modern.

TURK **BRODA**

HE WON THE VEZINA TROPHY JUST TWICE and made First Team All-Star just twice during his 14-year career, but no goalie was ever more dominant come playoff time. He backstopped the Toronto Maple Leafs to five Stanley Cups between 1942 and 1951, the last four in a dynastic five-year run. His 1.98 goals-against average remains the NHL playoff record, a telling improvement on his regular-season average of 2.53. And his 13 playoff shutouts stood as the NHL record until Jacques Plante surpassed it in 1970. No wonder Broda, notorious for the girth that once led Toronto manager Conn Smythe to suspend him and put him on a very public diet, is hailed less for being big than for coming up big – the ultimate "money goalie".

SID **ABEL**

HE MAY NOT HAVE BEEN ANYWHERE NEAR AS BIG A STAR AS HIS TWO WINGERS, GORDIE HOWE ON THE right and Ted Lindsay on the left, but Abel enjoyed no small measure of fame in Detroit at the center of the Production Line. The first season they were dubbed the Production Line, 1948-49, he led the first-place Wings in scoring and won the Hart Trophy as league MVP. The next season, he finished second in the scoring race behind Lindsay and ahead of Howe as the Production Line went 1-2-3 and led the Wings to the Stanley Cup. Abel accepted the Cup as captain, as he did after two other Detroit championships, in 1943 and 1952.

CHUCK **RAYNER**

HIS CLAIM TO FAME CAME IN 1949-50 when he became just the second goalie ever to win the Hart Trophy as league MVP. He did so by leading a very mediocre New York Rangers team to a fourth-place finish and then to within a seventh-game overtime goal of the Stanley Cup. Frustrated by the anemic Ranger offense, he was notorious for leaving the crease to handle the puck and trying to become the first goalie to score a goal. Twice in 1946-47, he fired shots at the opposing goal. The closest he came was late in 1949-50, rushing up ice for the puck after Toronto had pulled goalie Turk Broda but just missing the empty net. Even more than his saves, his rink-long dashes drew standing ovations.

After taking over the coaching reins in Montreal, Toe Blake would stand in the home dressing room at the fabled Forum exhorting a new generation of Canadiens to restore an old tradition of glory. His pep-talk oratory was always loud, often authoritarian and sometimes profane.

Opposite page: Toe Blake used a variety of methods all for one purpose: to win.

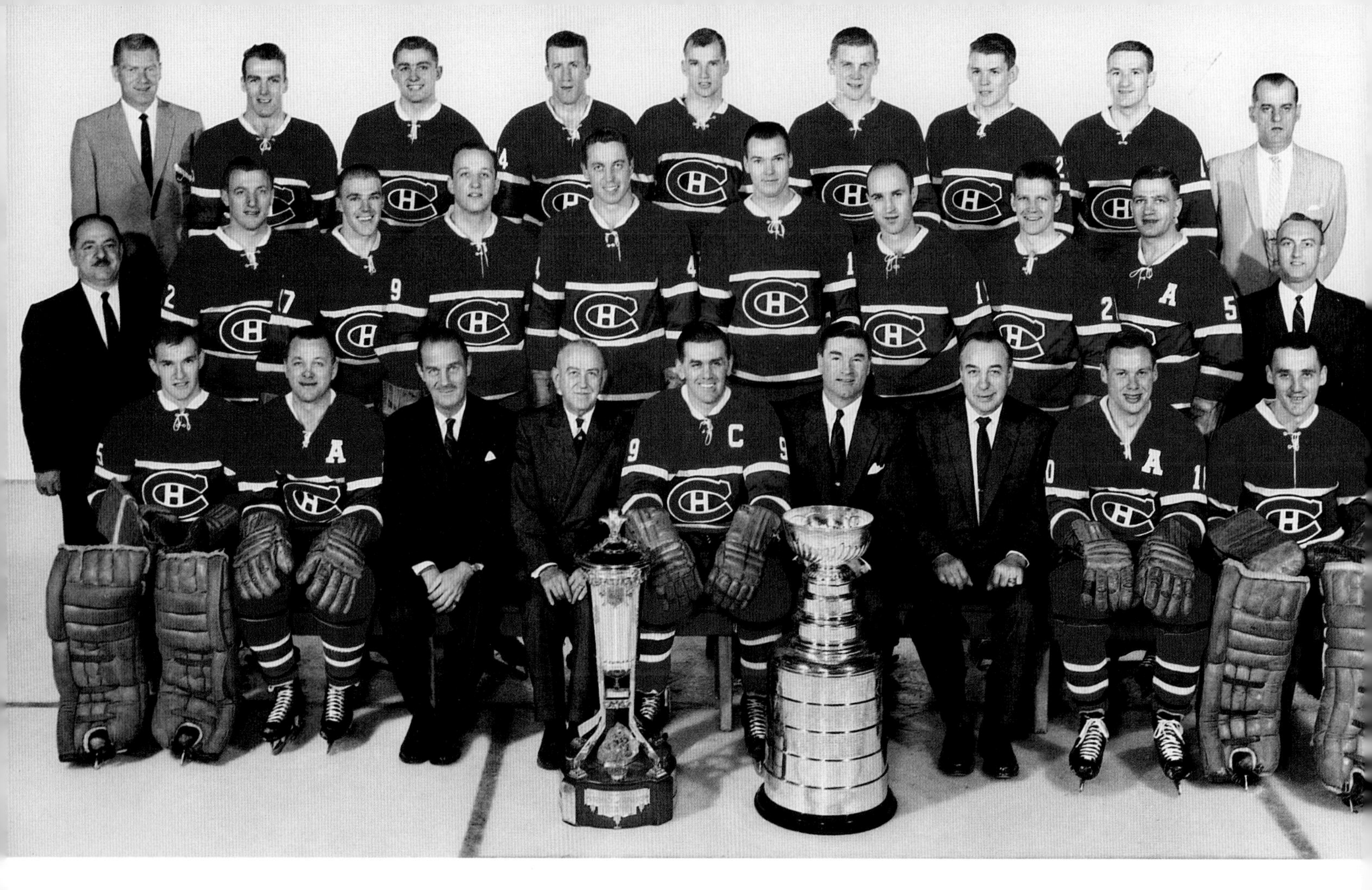

Canadiens and the Cup: A most familiar sight of the times.

But when the time came to drive home his message, he simply pointed to the writing on the wall above the large headshots of the Montreal Canadien greats. The words, immortalized in Colonel John McCrae's World War I poem "In Flanders' Fields", were inscribed there in French and English for all to be inspired:

NOS BRAS MEURTRIS VOUS TENDENT LE FLAMBEAU,
A VOUS TOUJOURS DE LE PORTER BIEN HAUT!

—

TO YOU FROM FALLING HANDS WE THROW THE TORCH,
BE YOURS TO HOLD IT HIGH!

Leave it to the Montreal Canadiens to come up with the perfect definition of dynasty – one that has carried them through 24 Stanley Cup championships, nearly twice as many as any other hockey franchise and a total unsurpassed in any professional sport. More to the point, leave it to Toe Blake's Canadiens to come up with an even more perfect definition of dynasty – one so rewritten by their juggernaut of the 1950s that every other team in hockey history must suffer by comparison.

Five consecutive Stanley Cup championships: that's what defines the dynasty the Canadiens strung together from 1955-56 to 1959-60. Yet even that daunting number cannot begin to measure the transcendent impact they had in a sport where no team had ever won more than three in a row and where to this day no other team has ever won more than four in a row. They didn't just rewrite the record book, they rewrote the rule book; they didn't just dominate the game, they changed the game.

To call them "the greatest team ever assembled" may be an understatement, but at least it's a fitting testament to the man who assembled it – Frank Selke. From the day he arrived in 1946 as Montreal's manager, Selke built a powerhouse from the foundation up, designing the farm system whose All-Star harvest came of age in the mid-1950s just in time to complement the Canadiens' aging superstar, Maurice "Rocket" Richard.

The resulting dynasty provided an astonishing ten players for the Hockey Hall of Fame, eight of them members of all five championship clubs. And that number doesn't even include their Hall of Fame coach, who somehow made them even better than the sum of their parts. "I'll always remember the first meeting the team had with Toe," recalled Jean Beliveau, who was about to succeed Richard as its best player. 'He looked around the dress-

Forever Rivals: The Leafs and the Canadiens.

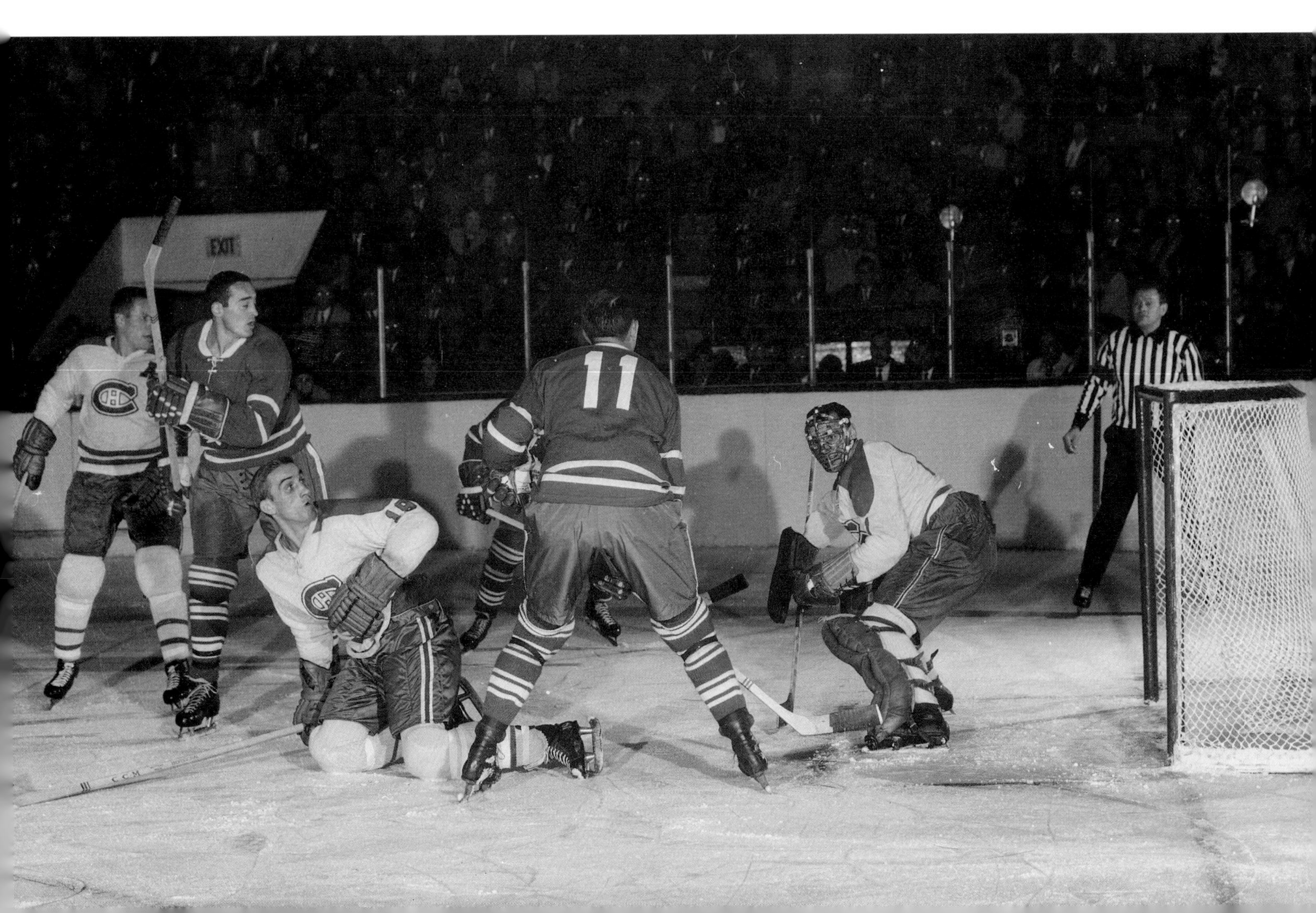

FARMER **FRANK**

Raised in the rich farming country of southwestern Ontario, Frank Selke knew a thing or two about sowing the seeds of a dynasty and reaping a harvest of prospects.

TRAINED IN THE BUILDING trades, he also knew how to help Conn Smythe build Maple Leaf Gardens and rebuild the home team into multi-Cup champions. So when Smythe forced him out of Toronto after two decades, Selke knew just what would be the best revenge. He didn't get even – he built the Montreal Canadiens into the greatest dynasty in hockey history.

A trim 5 ft 6 in with wire-rimmed glasses and a habit of rubbing his hands as he talked, Selke hardly looked like an empire builder. Incongruous as it seemed for such a colorless executive to build a most colorful franchise into the freewheeling Flying Frenchmen, he would, incredibly, leave an even more enduring legacy. Building a farm system that would perpetuate the dynasty, he cemented his place as the most successful front-office executive and the greatest general manager in NHL history.

Upon his arrival in Montreal in 1946, Selke took one look at the reigning Stanley Cup champions, noted an alarming lack of depth and youth, and unveiled plans to build a farm system which would become the organizational model for the postwar NHL. Not just a farm system, but an empire. Building up from the foundation, he poured money into the Quebec junior leagues and into the minor leagues in hockey hotbeds encompassing all geographical regions and playing styles.

The Farmer gets his man, Beliveau, as Dick Irvin flashes the "V" sign.

The feeder system embraced 10,000 players from 750 teams across Canada, controlling more talent than the other five NHL franchises combined. Of all the Canadiens' talent sources, none matched the Quebec Junior Hockey League, which Selke rebuilt as a showcase where Montreal prospects (Beliveau, Plante, Geoffrion, et al.) became household names long before they arrived in the NHL.

By 1954, the crops were in and ready to harvest, yielding a depth of talent the likes of which the NHL had never seen. That first became apparent in the 1955 playoffs after the Rocket Richard suspension had cost the Canadiens the services of their leader and "Selke's Kids" stepped up to lead the team to the seventh game of the Cup finals. Thus was the stage set for them to capture their unrivaled five straight Stanley Cup championships from 1956 to 1960.

Just as Richard was the heart and soul of that dynasty, Selke was the brains behind it. "We looked for players with more than just talent," Selke explained. "They had to be committed to the high standards of excellence in all parts of their lives that we made the trademark of the Canadiens' organization."

As their demoralized rivals waited for those dynastic Canadiens to age, Selke just kept looking to the feeder system which would produce enough prospects to keep them at the top of the NHL for decades. "They can say what they want," Selke shrugged. "When our old men stop producing, we'll bring up young men who will start producing. Canadiens will be the team to beat for the next ten years."

Beliveau: So good they bought his league.

ing room for several moments and then said, "I have great hockey players here, but the only way we're going to win the Stanley Cup is to make a unit and work together.' That was Toe's greatest strength as a coach."

And Montreal's greatest strength as a team? On offense, they were simply unstoppable, with two full All-Star lines boasting a shooting gallery that featured the elegant Beliveau, the gritty Dickie Moore, and the aptly nicknamed Bernie "Boom Boom" Geoffrion, as well as Rocket Richard and his kid brother, Henri "Pocket Rocket" Richard. On defense, they were simply unbeatable, with peerless defenseman Doug Harvey controlling the pace like a quarterback and pioneering goaltender Jacques Plante inventing new ways to keep the puck out. (Those seven all-time greats would be joined in the Hockey Hall of Fame by three teammates: winger Bert Olmstead and defensemen Butch Bouchard and Tom Johnson.) The only thing scarier than having all that talent to spread around was putting much of it on the ice at the same time, on the ultimate power play.

Their dynasty-in-the-making wasn't even a year old when the Canadiens forced what may be their most enduring legacy: a rule change to limit power-play goals. Their power play – featuring Beliveau at center, the Rocket at right wing, Moore at left wing, and Geoffrion and Harvey at the points – was so overpowering that they often scored two or three goals before the shorthanded team could kill off a two-minute penalty. So after the 1955-56 season, when Beliveau alone once scored a hat trick in 44 seconds of a power play, the rule was changed to allow the penalized player to return to the ice once a goal was scored. "They simply wanted to limit our power,"

Henri Richard, the Rocket's younger brother, had a Hall of Fame career as well.

DOUG **HARVEY**

BEFORE ORR BROKE THE MOLD, HARVEY SET THE standard for defensemen. No defenseman could singlehandedly control the tempo of a game like this consummate quarterback, speeding it up or slowing it down at will. He asserted himself as hockey's best blue-liner in the 1950s just in time to lead the Montreal Canadiens' dynasty to six Stanley Cups, five in succession. He won the Norris Trophy as top defenseman seven times in eight years and was a First Team All-Star 10 times in 11 years, capping both strings in 1962 as Rangers' player-coach. Angered when the Hall of Fame bypassed him in his first year of eligibility "because I've been known to hoist a few", he boycotted his induction the following year. But the perfect appreciation of his pace-controlling style was delivered by Montreal coach Toe Blake: "Doug plays defense in a rocking chair."

said the Rocket, "but that didn't stop us."

Nothing could. All five seasons, they led the league in goals scored and fewest goals allowed. Then they somehow became that much more dominating in the playoffs. Throughout their reign, they were never even extended to seven games once in the Cup finals. In fact, they never had to endure a seventh-game ordeal in any of their 10 playoff series, and only twice were they forced to play a sixth game. They crowned their fifth Cup in style, becoming only the second team ever to achieve perfection by sweeping all eight games of the semifinals and finals.

That capped a remarkable run in which they made the finals 10 years in a row, winning the Stanley Cup six times. To have made it eight straight, all the Canadiens would have had to do following their 1953 Cup championship was win the seven-game finals they lost to the Detroit Red Wings the next two years. They lost in 1954 on a fluke overtime goal, then in 1955 after Rocket Richard's infamous suspension from the playoffs.

Maybe that's where the dynasty started – in 1955 with the "Richard Riot". With the Rocket leading the 1954-55 scoring race and "Selke's Kids" having come of age as stars in their own right, the Canadiens were poised to unseat the Wing dynasty. But then came that game in Boston where Richard retaliated with a vicious stick-swinging outburst and punched the linesman who tried to restrain him. NHL President Clarence Campbell suspended the Montreal icon through the playoffs, precipitating the riot.

The riot cost Montreal one Cup and one coach. Dick Irvin was fired after 15 seasons in favor of a coach who could control Richard's red-hot temper. Selke's perfect choice was Blake, the former Montreal great who had played with Richard for years on the famous Punch Line and knew how to handle his fierce temperament. A taskmaster in his first NHL coaching job, Blake used to read the words inscribed in red block letters near the dressing-room ceiling, then warn his players, "Look up! If you don't catch the torch, I'll light it under you."

In Blake's first season, Beliveau broke through as the star of what many consider the best single team in NHL history, the 1955-56 Canadiens, winning the scoring title and the Hart Trophy as league MVP before equaling Richard's playoff scoring record in leading Montreal to the Stanley Cup. "I have realized my ambition, to be on a Cup-winning team," Beliveau said afterward. "I hope to be on a few more others."

WAITING ON THE BIG ONE

Once in a lifetime, there comes a teenage prodigy whose long-awaited NHL arrival is ballyhooed as the second coming.

THE LIST OF SUCH LEGENDS before their time is short: Orr, Gretzky, Lemieux, Lindros. Yet for all the intensifying media hype welcoming each one in succession, no highly touted prospect was ever anticipated quite like the first – Jean Beliveau.

The Montreal Canadiens and their fans waited years for the teen sensation who became a Quebec legend – second only to Rocket Richard – before he even played a game in the NHL. And the waiting and wooing ended when it did only because the Canadiens found a novel way to finally land him: they bought an entire hockey league.

The Canadiens knew just how good this "Kid Beliveau" was because each September at training camp the lanky center would show up their NHL veterans, only to return home to Quebec City and dominate the amateur ranks of the Quebec junior and senior leagues. Twice he came through brief NHL trials with flying colors: he teased the Canadiens in his debut at the age of 19 by being selected First Star of his first game and scoring a goal in his other game, then again two years later by scoring a hat trick and adding two more goals in a three-game stint. But both times he turned down their offers to wear the *bleu, blanc et rouge* and returned to the Quebec Aces of the Quebec Senior Hockey League. The leading scorer in that semipro league for two years running, he commanded an annual salary of $20,000 – making the same kind of money as a so-called "amateur" that Richard and Gordie Howe were as the NHL's two biggest superstars – so he could afford to be in no hurry.

Jean Beliveau proved to be worth the wait.

"It wasn't too complicated for me," said Beliveau, explaining his annual decision to remain with the Quebec Aces instead of joining the most hallowed NHL franchise. "Each time I left for Montreal and training camp, the people in Quebec would say, "Whatever they offer you, same here." So I knew that money would not be the reason that I left Quebec to play in the NHL."

The Canadiens finally purchased the Quebec Senior Hockey League and the pro rights to all its players. Then they turned it professional, making Beliveau an offer that "the highest-paid amateur in hockey" couldn't refuse. When asked at the October 3, 1953, signing ceremony how the Canadiens finally roped in their prized prospect, Montreal manager Frank Selke deadpanned, "It's really very simple. We just opened the vault and said, 'Jean, take what you think is right.'"

Beliveau signed for a $20,000 bonus and $105,000 over five years, a fantastic salary for any NHL player but unheard-of for a 22-year-old rookie. He turned out to be worth every penny. Playing with a rare blend of elegance and power at 6 ft 3 in, he elevated the game with his grace and dignity on and off the ice. His long-awaited arrival in 1953-54 sent the Canadiens to the top, the final building block in their dynasty of five straight Stanley Cup championships from 1956 to 1960.

It took him only three seasons to establish himself as the league's premier center, winning both the scoring title and Hart Trophy in 1955-56. That season, he also became the first hockey player to appear on the cover of a two-year-old magazine called *Sports Illustrated.*

While becoming the highest-scoring center the game had yet seen, he won a second Hart Trophy as league MVP in 1964. Then, in 1965, he became the first winner of the Conn Smythe Trophy as playoff MVP. He spanned two Montreal dynasties, winning 10 Stanley Cup championships, the last five in his 10-year tenure as a softspoken captain leading by example. For all the hype surrounding his arrival, the lasting image of Jean Beliveau is of him hoisting the Stanley Cup in 1971 after his farewell game, forever the regal captain and Quebec icon.

THE RICHARD RIOT

The riot began at precisely 9.11 p.m. on March 17, 1955, when a tear–gas bomb exploded in the Montreal Forum, sending 16,000 panicking hockey fans into streets already teeming with frenzied protesters . . .

OR MAYBE IT BEGAN THE day before, when NHL President Clarence Campbell suspended Canadiens star Maurice Richard, the beloved idol of all French Canada and especially Montreal, for the rest of the season through the playoffs . . .

Or maybe it began three days before that, when Richard retaliated for a high-stick in Boston by viciously slashing the Bruins' Hal Laycoe three times and punching the linesman who tried to restrain him . . .

The flash point of the riot may be hard to pinpoint, but it doesn't take a social historian to cite the underlying cause. If what's known as the "Quiet Revolution" formally began in Quebec with the Liberal Party's 1960 election, there are many who regard the "Richard Riot" as the first shot in that French-Canadian movement. The Unquiet Revolution, if you will: French-Canadians protesting an English-Canadian's suspension of their Gallic god. Campbell, of course, was a decorated hero of Canada's participation in World War II.

In the first 24 hours after banning Richard for his deliberate and persistent attacks as a repeat offender, Campbell had been deluged with death threats, most from French-Canadians accusing him of an anti-French bias. Yet not even all those threats could deter him from attending the next home game with his secretary (later his wife), as was his custom. His office was a few blocks from the Forum. As he arrived midway through the first period for that fateful St. Patrick's Day showdown for first place between the Canadiens and the Red Wings, the fans booed his every step to his usual seat. They strafed him with fruit, vegetables, eggs, pickled pigs' feet, coins, programs, overshoes, even bottles. One man extended his hand as if to shake and then slugged Campbell twice before being led away. Another man rushed in and squashed two tomatoes on Campbell's chest. When an unknown fan lobbed the tear-gas bomb into the lower-level seats near Campbell, a cloud of acrid fumes sent fans bolting toward the exits, coughing and choking, covering their faces with coats and scarves. Campbell managed to escape to the first-aid center, where it was decided to forfeit the game to the Wings (who were ahead 4-1) and clear the arena.

When the Forum patrons spilled out onto the streets, they encountered a mob of thousands more in an even uglier mood. That mob of fans, demonstrators, and hoodlums had begun massing outside the hallowed arena nine hours before game time. They brandished signs saying, "Unfair to French Canadiens." They chanted, "Kill Campbell! Kill Campbell!" By the time the Forum fans joined in, they had whipped themselves into a savage frenzy.

As the mob swelled to 10,000, outnumbering police by 40 to one, they began to riot. They threw bricks through hundreds of Forum windows, smashed the windows of passing streetcars, tore down overhead trolley cables, and threw rocks and bottles at police. The Forum was in a state of siege, and soon so would the surrounding city.

The howling mob of more than 10,000 started moving east along St. Catherine Street, cutting a swath of destruction for 15 blocks. Display windows were smashed, stores looted, cars overturned, newspaper stands torched, telephone booths toppled. Order was not restored until 3.00 a.m. By the time the damage was finally assessed, there had been 70 arrests, 12 policemen and 25 civilians injured, 50 stores looted, and $100,000 in property damage.

For Canadien fans, the additional cost could be measured in the standings. Their idol, who had watched the Forum uproar from his rinkside seat, lost his last best shot at winning the elusive scoring title, falling one point short of the only major honor that would elude him. And without him, his Canadiens would lose to the Red Wings in a seven-game Stanley Cup final. The day after the riot, Richard went on the radio with a message to calm the fans and salve a city whose civic and ethnic pride had been badly bruised: "Do no more harm. Get behind the team in the playoffs. I will take my punishment and come back next year and help the club and the younger players to win the Cup." A man of his word, he took his punishment, came back and helped the Canadiens win the Cup.

The riot begins with a fan attacking Clarence Campbell.

Dynasties Collide

BEFORE THEY COULD BUILD A DYNASTY OF THEIR OWN, however, the Canadiens first had to wrest hockey supremacy from Detroit's dynasty. So it was only fitting that they started their run at a time when dynasties collided, by winning the 1956 final in five games over the two-time defending champion Red Wings. For just as the Canadiens would monopolize the last half of the 1950s as no team in NHL history had, so the Red Wings had set the standard by dominating the first half of the decade in a way no team ever had.

The Red Wings had entered the 1950s in the midst of a record run of their own. Starting in 1948-49, they won seven straight regular-season championships, a record streak which no other NHL franchise has ever come within two titles of challenging.

After being swept out of consecutive Cup finals by the Toronto Maple Leafs in 1948 and 1949, the Red Wings finally broke through in 1949-50. The Production Line – Ted Lindsay at left wing, Sid Abel at center, and Gordie Howe at right wing – became the third forward unit ever to finish 1-2-3 in the scoring race. They led the Wings to a first-place finish by 11 points over Montreal, which was paced by Richard's league-leading 43 goals. Breaking a streak of 11 straight playoff losses to Toronto, the Wings knocked off the Leafs in a bitterly fought seven-game semifinal despite losing Howe to a life-threatening head injury. In the opener, Howe mistimed a check against Toronto's Ted Kennedy and crashed head first into the boards, requiring surgery to relieve pressure on the brain; the 90-minute operation saved his life, and within a few days he was out of danger. Without their emerging superstar, the Wings were pushed to seven games in the Cup final by the resurgent New York Rangers, the cellar dwellers whose surprising fourth-place finish earned goalie Chuck Rayner the Hart Trophy as MVP. The clock struck midnight in the seventh game of the final, however, as Pete Babando gave Detroit the championship by scoring the winning goal on a screened 25-ft shot in double overtime – the first time the Stanley Cup had ever been decided in a sudden death. In the wild celebration it unleashed, the loudest Olympia cheers greeted Howe as he walked to center ice for the Cup presentation and doffed his hat to reveal his bandaged head.

Howe bounced back from the injury stronger and tougher than ever in 1950-51, winning the scoring championship with an NHL record of 86 points. He and goalie Terry Sawchuk, the Calder Trophy winner as rookie of the year with a 1.98 goals-against average and a league-best 11 shutouts, led the Wings to their third straight first-place finish with record totals of 44 wins and 101 points. But they were upset in a six-game semifinal by the third-place Canadiens, setting up a Montreal showdown with second-place Toronto. The Leafs needed only five games to win their fourth Stanley Cup in five years, but it was the hardest of all possible five-game finals – for it marked the first time in history when every game in the final was decided in sudden-death overtime.

For one night at the end of the next season, the stage belonged to a meaningless game between two teams eliminated from the playoffs: in the span of 21 seconds, Chicago Blackhawk winger Bill Mosienko (see overleaf) scored the fastest hat trick in NHL history. The three-goal barrage, in the third period of the season finale before 3,254 Madison Square Garden diehards, left rookie Ranger goalie Lorne Anderson so shell-shocked he never played another game. Apart from those 21 seconds, the rest of the 1951-52 season belonged to the Wings, who rebounded from the previous spring's early upset to win their fourth straight regular-season title by 22 points. Again they were led by Howe, who won his first Hart Trophy as MVP as well as his second straight scoring title, and Sawchuk, who won his first Vezina Trophy with a 1.90 goals-against average and 12 shutouts. Sawchuk was even better in the playoffs, allowing just five goals and recording four shutouts through all eight games. Sweeping Toronto in the semifinals and Montreal in the finals, the Red Wings became the first team ever to win all eight games in capturing the Cup. For the Cup clincher, a couple of Red Wing fans pitched an octopus onto the Olympia ice as "a good-luck charm", its eight tentacles symbolic of eight straight wins. Thus began an octopus-throwing tradition that has long outlived the eight-game playoff format, bringing notoriety to the "Octopus Pitchers" and an average of 25 octopuses on the ice per Detroit playoff game. A mechanical octopus hangs from the ceiling today in Detroit's Joe Louis arena.

OVERTIME HEROICS

As a defenseman known for bodychecking, Bill Barilko was an unlikely hero. Then again, the 1951 Stanley Cup showdown between archrivals Toronto and Montreal was an unlikely series: the only final in history when every game was decided in sudden-death overtime.

THE MAPLE LEAFS, LEADing three games to one, forced overtime in the fifth game when they pulled their goalie and Tod Sloan scored with 32 seconds to go in the third period. Then, just 2 minutes 53 seconds into overtime, Barilko instinctively defied coach Joe Primeau's orders to stay behind the blue line to thwart a Montreal break. Off balance after charging into the zone to keep Howie Meeker's pass from sliding over the blue line, "Bashin' Bill" gave new meaning to his nickname: he flung himself airborne and drove all his 180 lbs into a blind desperation shot, gunning the puck over Montreal goalie Gerry McNeil's shoulder for the Cup-winning goal.

Overnight, after a wild Maple Leaf Garden celebration in which his jubilant mother had run onto the ice to kiss him, Bill Barilko was a national hero. A few weeks later, he was dead. He and a friend flew to northern Ontario on a fishing trip and the plane was lost. The wreckage of the crashed plane was finally found 11 years later—just weeks after the Maple Leafs captured the Stanley Cup for the first time since Barilko's heroics.

Bill Barilko's famous – and final – goal for the Maple Leafs.

HOCKEY NIGHT ON TELEVISION

Throughout the fall of 1951, Conn Smythe sat alone in his owner's lair at Maple Leaf Garden watching Toronto games on that newfangled contraption called television.

HE WAS THE LONE VIEWER of a special feed designed to determine if TV would be a suitable medium for hockey: could it capture the essence of a game most Canadians had seen only through the pictures painted by Foster Hewitt's legendary radio commentaries? Once Smythe gave the green light to the Canadian Broadcasting Corporation, everyone would now see the NHL game for themselves on what was to become the most-watched TV show in Canada and the longest running TV show in North America.

On November 1, 1952, the first *Hockey Night in Canada* television program was beamed from Maple Leaf Garden into living rooms everywhere in black and white. With Foster Hewitt announcing that Leafs-Bruins game while his son Bill took over his usual radio play-by-play description, it marked the first English-language telecast in NHL history.

Just three weeks earlier, on October 9, 1952, the first regular-season TV screening had originated from the Montreal Forum: a French-language production of the Canadiens' opener against the Blackhawks announced by Rene Lecavalier, whose dulcet radio voice had already made him a legend on *La Soirée du Hockey au Canada*. It was only fitting that on the historic night TV was introduced to hockey, so was another newcomer: Danny Gallivan covered that game on radio as the English-language voice of the Canadiens. Later that season, Gallivan would begin introducing English-language programmes from the Forum on CBC-TV. Over the next 32 years, his commentaries and catchphrases would make him a legend almost as synonymous with hockey on TV as Foster Hewitt was with hockey on radio.

Thus did the NHL make the transition into the television age.

Just one year after NHL President Clarence Campbell had branded television "the greatest menace of the entertainment world", those pioneering 1952 TV broadcasts were such an instant success that hockey was soon the highest-rated show on Canadian television. More than that, television was about to popularize the sport as never before. TV not only helped magnify the game's appeal in established hockey hotbeds, but it introduced and spread it across the puck-deprived United States.

In its infancy, TV hockey consisted of local coverage of certain home games, or even just parts of games, by each franchise through the early 1950s. It reached the network level in 1956-57 when CBS televised an experimental 10-game package, the first nationally televised game being a Rangers win over the 'Hawks from Madison Square Garden on the afternoon of January 5, 1957. Amazed at the response, especially in the South, CBS in 1957-58 inaugurated a 21-game Saturday afternoon series from Boston, Chicago, Detroit, and New York. The network then introduced a formal "NHL Game of the Week" package starting in the 1959-60 season. But by the early 1960s, the NHL was without a network contract, foreshadowing a sporadic cycle that characterized the league's TV position for much of the next three decades.

Right from the start, the NHL sought to make the game viewer-friendly. Anticipating television's emergence, the league started painting the ice white in 1949-50 to make the puck more visible. In 1951-52 the league began requiring one team to wear white and the other to wear colored jerseys to make each of them distinguishable on black and white television. For the same reason, some arenas in 1957 began replacing the solid red line with a checkered line to make it distinguishable on TV from the blue lines.

In this satellite age of multiple camera angles and replays, it's hard to believe hockey used to be televised by just two or three black and white cameras. At Maple Leaf Gardens, Smythe initially banished even those to the roof so as not to block the view of any paying fans.

At least television arrived at the right time for a sport in the midst of its Golden Age. It was full of made-for-TV rivalries and made-for-TV stars, none more photogenic than Rocket Richard and the Canadiens. *Toronto Globe and Mail* columnist Jim Coleman noted as much when he wrote in 1958, "The work of Howe, a perfectionist, often is lost on these new spectators. However, even a casual television fan can appreciate Richard, whose every appearance includes the violent promise of thunder and lightning." The promise of televised hockey, however, would be realized long after Richard's retirement.

The view from above and into the homes of millions.

BILL **MOSIENKO**

LONG KNOWN AS THE FASTEST MAN ON SKATES, IT was only natural that he should become the fastest scorer as well. On the last night of the 1951-52 season, the Blackhawk star scored the fastest hat trick in NHL history – three goals in 21 seconds! That barrage, in the third-period between two non-playoff teams in a nearly empty Madison Square Garden, broke the NHL record of 64 seconds and has been approached only by Jean Beliveau's 44-second hat trick in 1955. Mosienko got used to such fast company as right wing on Chicago's galloping Pony Line. But never did the 5-ft 8-in, 150-lb stick-handling magician create chances quite like he did on March 23, 1952. For the record, he beat rookie Ranger goalie Lorne Anderson on a close shot at 6 minutes 9 seconds, a faceoff breakaway at 6 minutes 21 seconds, then a high shot off a fake at 6 minutes 30 seconds. No *team* ever scored three goals that fast. Imagine if he hadn't hit the post 45 seconds later.

THE GOLDEN AGE OF GOALTENDERS

All three arrived on the hockey scene at the same time to dominate as no goal-tenders before or since.

ALL THREE CERTIFIED THE 1950s as goaltending's golden age. And all three redefined their position and changed the game.

So it's only fitting that all three are joined when discussing the greatest goaltenders in NHL history. First there's Glenn Hall, the Iron Man revered as "Mr Goalie". Then there's Jacques Plante, the innovative Masked Marvel. And finally, there's Terry Sawchuk, the all-time Shutout King

Their legacy reaches beyond their dominance during the Golden Age of Goaltenders, beyond their combined 14 Vezina Trophies and 11 Stanley Cups, to the way they revolutionized their position with innovations taken for granted in today's game.

THE IRON MAN

They didn't call him "Mr Goalie" for nothing. Glenn Hall earned his nickname the hard way while playing 502 consecutive games spanning seven seasons – an endurance run hailed as the most unbreakable of all NHL records.

FACING MORE THAN 16,000 vulcanized-rubber shots without a day off or a mask on, he ran the streak to 551 Red Wing and Blackhawk games, including 49 playoff games. From the start of his rookie season on October 6, 1955, until he was pulled in the first period on November 7, 1962, he played every minute of every game, a total of 33,135 minutes in a row. And he did it while playing sport's most hazardous position through all manner of injury and illness until, ironically, the streak succumbed to a pulled back muscle sustained in practice by simply leaning down to adjust a toestrap on a pad.

It's a streak made all the more remarkable for the unsurpassed level at which he played. And more remarkable still for his pregame ritual of getting sick to his stomach. So tightly wound up was Hall – he referred to each season as "a winter of torture" and each game as "60 minutes of hell" – that it's no wonder he threw up before every game and often between periods as well.

He didn't just get butterflies—he invented them. More precisely, he invented the butterfly technique. Hall's impact on changing how the position is played was second only to that of Jacques Plante. Back in the 1950s, when all goalies played a stand-up style and commonly sprawled sideways to stack their pads on low shots, Hall was considered both unique and foolish for inventing and playing the butterfly style. In the butterfly, he would drop to his knees and fan his legs out in a wide V formation, spread-eagling his pads to cover the nether region of the net post-to-post. Defying conventional wisdom by embracing a courageous style that put his bare face into harm's way, he then dared shooters to beat him high. The butterfly style, which had been born out of necessity – in his Saskatchewan youth, he lacked the arm strength to stop shots with his stick, so he took to dropping to his knees to cover the lower net with his pads – now took hold out of sheer effectiveness.

Hall may have looked like a demented acrobat, but the unconventional style made him the league's most consistent goalie for reasons other than his 551 consecutive games in goal: the Calder Trophy in 1956, three Vezina Trophies, and 11 postseason All-Star selections – seven of them First Team All-Star berths, more than Plante and Sawchuk combined. In 1957, two years after his arrival spurred the Red Wings to trade Sawchuk, Hall himself was sold to the Blackhawks 140 games into the streak. In Chicago in 1961, Hall backstopped the 'Hawks to an unexpected Stanley Cup, holding the five-time defending champion Canadiens scoreless for a 135-minute stretch in the semifinals. His success continued long after his streak stopped. At the age of 36, and finally embracing the mask he'd always disdained for fear it would compromise his vision, he led the expansion team St. Louis Blues to the 1968 finals, winning the Conn Smythe Trophy as playoff MVP despite being swept by the Canadiens.

Perhaps Scotty Bowman, his coach in St. Louis, put it best: "Goalies are a breed apart, and Hall is apart from the breed." So much did Hall dread returning to each training camp that he would hold out as a rite of fall, staying home on his 160-acre Alberta farm and claiming he had "to paint the barn". In 1971, after 18 seasons threatening to quit, Hall finally did at 40, leaving behind a consecutive-games streak that will last forever.

Butterfly man, Glenn Hall of the Blackhawks, stops another one.

THE MASKED MARVEL

Before the 1959-60 season, Canadiens goaltender Jacques Plante asked coach Toe Blake if he could wear a mask in goal. The request should not have come as a surprise from the innovator who'd already popularized the practice of roaming from the crease for loose pucks.

SINCE SUFFERING TWO fractured cheekbones off practice shots by his own teammates, Plante had worn a specially designed plastic mask in workouts. But when he asked if he could use a mask redesigned to eliminate blind spots in games, Blake flatly refused him, demanding barefaced tradition.

And then on November 1, 1959, midway through the first period of a scoreless game at Madison Square Garden, Andy Bathgate, the New York Rangers' hardest shooter, unleashed a wicked backhander. Screened, Plante never saw the puck until he felt it ripping his cheek and nose. After getting up from the blood-stained ice and making his way to the dressing room with a towel stanching the flow, he needed seven stitches to close the wound. In those days clubs carried only one goaltender. The game had been interrupted for 20 minutes when Blake asked if Plante was ready to return.

"I won't go back in," Plante told him, "unless I can wear a mask."

Blake had no choice but to let Plante change the face of hockey.

Plante returned wearing a cream-colored plastic mask and beat the Rangers 3-1. Then, over the repeated objections of Blake and Montreal manager Frank Selke, Plante kept wearing the mask, and followed the historic debut by running off a 10-game winning streak on the way to an 18-game unbeaten string.

"I had to show good results to keep the mask," Plante explained. But not even that could stop the critics from branding him a rebel, even a coward. He heard it from colleagues who scorned him for going soft, and from fans.

Jacques Plante: a mask or nothing.

"Doesn't wearing a mask prove you're *scared*?" a fan once asked.

"If you jumped out of a plane without a parachute," Plante replied, "would that prove you're *brave*?"

What Plante still had to prove, though, was the mask's effectiveness. It took a spectacular playoff performance that spring, which led the Canadiens on an eight-game sweep to the Stanley Cup with three shutouts, to force widespread acceptance of the mask as a standard piece of equipment.

He had played all season like a masked man on a mission, backstopping the Canadiens to the Cup for their record fifth straight year and winning the Vezina Trophy for his record fifth straight year. He went on to earn the Vezina seven times, the most ever, and in 1962 became only the fourth goalie ever to win the Hart Trophy as league MVP. His 431 career wins place him second only to Sawchuk's 447, and his 14 playoff shutouts remain the modern record.

His legacy lies in the inventions which made him the game's greatest innovator and one of the most influential goalies of all-time. "Jake the Snake" earned his nicknamed as the original roving goalie – playing the puck for his defensemen, stopping dump-ins behind the net, jump-starting the Montreal offense with passes up ice, diving out of the net to smother loose pucks. He explained the motivation behind the roaming by saying, "One of the junior teams I played for was so bad that I had to always chase the puck behind the cage because the defense couldn't get there fast enough."

The motivation behind the mask was more straightforward. "I already had four broken noses, two broken cheekbones, and almost 200 stitches in my head," he said. "I didn't care how the mask looked. The way things were going, I was afraid I would look just like the mask."

Clint Benedict may actually have been the first goalie to wear a mask, a primitive leather model to protect a broken nose in 1930, but it was Jacques Plante who popularized its use and perfected this new piece of standard equipment. By 1975, when he finally retired for good at 46, maskless marvels had become extinct and every goalie wore Plante's invention as his legacy.

THE SHUTOUT KING

For all his fame as hockey's No. 1 goalie, Terry Sawchuk seemed to gain as much notoriety with one haunting image in the March 4, 1966, issue of *Life* magazine: a large headshot retouched by a make-up artist highlighting in chilling detail all the facial scars and stitches he had accumulated in his perilous profession.

TERRY SAWCHUK HIMSELF stopped counting at 400 stitches in an injury-punctuated career that almost ended on his 18th birthday, before he had reached the NHL, when, during his first minor-league pro season in Omaha, he took a stick in the eye. His sight was saved only because an excellent eye surgeon happened to be passing through town.

Undaunted, Sawchuk kept putting his bare face in the line of fire. He became the first goalie to adopt a gorilla-like crouch, bending so deep that his chin almost rested on his knees, his face just two or three feet off the ice. A dynamic acrobat who relied on his catlike reflexes and explosive moves, he used the unorthodox crouch to track the puck through opponents' legs on screen shots and to snap his legs out quicker for kick saves.

The "Sawchuk Crouch" was to be copied by generations of goalies: In 1950-51, he won a record 44 games to earn the Calder Trophy as rookie of the year, and posted goals-against averages under 2.00 for an astonishing five straight seasons. During that span, he won the Vezina Trophy three times and backstopped the Detroit Red Wings to three Stanley Cups. In the first of those Cup drives in 1952, he set an unparalleled standard for goaltending excellence, leading the Wings to an eight-game playoff sweep by posting four shutouts and allowing only five goals for a goals-against average of 0.62.

By the time he was traded after the third Cup in 1955, he was already renowned as the best ever to play in that position. But the competition was closing the gap, pitting five future Hall of Famers in a six-team league – Sawchuk, Plante, Hall, Johnny Bower, and Gump Worsley. Long past his prime, Sawchuk teamed with Bower in Toronto for a most formidable platoon, sharing the Vezina in 1965 and heroically leading the aged Maple Leafs to the Cup in 1967.

Sawchuk's status as the NHL's all-time leader in victories (447) may be tenuous, but his claim to fame is one of hockey's unbreakable records: he is the NHL's all-time shutout king, with 103. And he's likely to wear that crown for a long time, with no active goalie within 56 shutouts of him.

Sawchuck: So talented, so troubled.

If Sawchuk was the greatest goalie in hockey history, he was also the most troubled. On top of all the physical injuries (herniated discs, severed hand tendons, ruptured appendix), he drank too much, slept too little, and was given to volatile mood swings. Brooding, temperamental, violent—all describe the tortured soul who was an enigma even to his family and closest teammates. Playing for the Boston Bruins in 1956-57, he came back too soon from mononucleosis, plunged into a clinical depression, and abruptly quit the game in the middle of the season. He returned the next season playing back in Detroit, but he was becoming more and more irritable and irascible towards fans, reporters, and even his own family.

"When we woke up in the morning," said Marcel Pronovost, his Wing roommate and best friend, "I would say good morning to him in both French and English. If he answered, I knew we would talk at least a little that day. But if he didn't reply, which was most days, we didn't speak the entire day."

Sawchuk had been haunted since the age of 10 when he inherited the goalie pads of his brother Mike, who died of a heart ailment at 17. Thirty years later, in 1970, Terry Sawchuk accidentally hit his stomach on a barbecue pit during a drunken yard brawl with Ranger roommate Ron Stewart. Sawchuk suffered extensive liver and gallbladder damage, and during surgery a month later, a blood clot spread and stopped his heart. He was 40.

The End of the Line

ANOTHER DETROIT TRADITION, THE PRODUCTION LINE, broke up in 1952-53 when Abel asked to be traded to Chicago to become the Blackhawks' player-coach. But that didn't stop the Red Wings from running away with the regular-season title for an unprecedented fifth straight season or keep Howe from running away with the scoring race for an unprecedented third straight year. League MVP Howe won with a record 95 points and a record-challenging 49 goals, Lindsay was second, and Abel replacement Alex Delvecchio was fifth. The Wings, however, were stunned by the Bruins in a five-game semifinal. That set the stage for the Canadiens, after a season highlighted by Rocket Richard's 325th career goal to pass Nels Stewart as the NHL's all-time leading scorer, to overwhelm the Bruins in five games for the Cup.

The Wing Dynasty returned to form in 1953-54. Detroit finished first for a record sixth straight season, Howe won the scoring title for a record fourth consecutive year, and Red Kelly became the first winner of the Norris Trophy for top defenseman. The Hart Trophy went to a member not of the best team but of the worst team in NHL history: the Blackhawks' Al Rollins, whose 3.23 goals-against average on a 12-51-7 team made him the league MVP. But the Stanley Cup returned to Wing hands the same way it got there four years earlier – in another sudden-death Game 7 final. This time, they stunned the Canadiens in a seventh-game overtime when the flawless Harvey reached up to flick away Tony Leswick's dump-in shot and it deflected off his glove, past goalie McNeil, and into his own goal. So devastated were the Habs at being beaten by a fluke goal off the league's best defenseman that they refused to take part in the postgame handshake ritual. "If I had shaken hands, I wouldn't have meant it," said Coach Irvin. "I refuse to be a hypocrite."

The next season, 1954-55, was supposed to go down as the year the Canadiens would take over from the Wing

RED **KELLY**

NO ALL-STAR WAS EVER MORE VERSATILE, MAINLY because none ever led such a double career. During his incarnation in Detroit, spanning the 1950s as the league's best rushing defenseman, he helped lead the Red Wings to four Stanley Cups in six years, won the first Norris Trophy as top defenseman in 1954, and became the last blue-liner honored with the Lady Byng Trophy for sportsmanship. Then came his reincarnation after a 1960 trade to the Toronto Maple Leafs, who took advantage of his playmaking by converting him to a center. From 1962 to 1964, he helped the Leafs to three straight Cups. While playing for that Toronto dynasty, he entered politics as a Liberal member of the House of Commons and served two terms in Ottawa. After winning his eighth Stanley Cup in 1967, the ultimate two-way player retired with more championships than any player who did not play for the Montreal Canadiens.

Dynasty, the year The Rocket would finally win his elusive scoring title. But Richard was suspended by NHL President Clarence Campbell and teammate Boom Boom Geoffrion, whose feisty style, fiery temperament, and booming shot fueled a natural rivalry with the Rocket in the three years after he won the Calder Trophy as rookie of the year, needed to make up only two points in three games to wrest the scoring title. With Montreal fans actually pleading with him to back off and cede Richard the scoring race, Geoffrion ignored their boos and won the Art Ross Trophy by one point.

Far more galling to Montreal fans, the Red Wings came from two points back to win the seventh consecutive regular-season title, a record so unassailable not even the Canadiens could challenge it. The Wings went on to beat Montreal in a seven-game final to hold on to the Stanley Cup. But it was the end of the Wing Dynasty, which was broken up when manager Jack Adams stunned the hockey world by trading almost half his squad in blockbuster deals with Chicago and Boston.

The Canadiens finally staked their claim in 1955-56. They cruised to an NHL-record 45 victories while losing just 15 of their 70 games, dethroning seven-time defending champions Detroit by a whopping 24 points. Beliveau had a breakthrough year, leading the league in scoring with 47 goals and 88 points while earning the Hart Trophy as league MVP. Harvey won his second straight Norris Trophy and Plante earned the Vezina for the first of his record seven times.

Bouchard, who had succeeded Blake as captain in 1948, was so slowed by age and injury that he retired after his 15th season and passed the "C" to Rocket Richard. Not that there was any shortage of fresh legs to step in. The best among that season's rookie crop was the 19-year-old Henri Richard, who surprisingly made the team in training camp by standing up to veterans taking runs at him. Considered too small at 5 ft 7 in and 160 lbs to stay in the league, the Pocket Rocket lacked his famous brother's scoring punch but soon made a name for himself as a playmaker. His arrival brought the final Hall of Fame piece to Montreal's dynastic puzzle. The Canadiens needed only five games to dispatch the Rangers in the semifinals, and another five to dethrone the Red Wings – and capture the dynasty's first Cup.

DANNY **GALLIVAN**

FOR SOMEONE WHO ENTERED THE MONTREAL dressing room just twice in his life, he would become as legendary as the Canadiens he helped make famous. In broadcasting nearly 2,000 Canadien games, the link bridging 16 of the dynasty's Stanley Cup champions, he became as beloved as Richard or Beliveau. Gallivan got his first break when the regular broadcaster took ill, filling in even though he'd never seen an NHL game. That audition won him the gig two years later. Arriving on the same opening night as TV made its Forum debut, Gallivan made a name for himself during that 1951-52 season as the radio and TV voice of the Habs and *Hockey Night in Canada*. It wasn't long before his colorful calls entered the lexicon, from "cannonading drive" to "Savardian spinarama". After 32 years behind the mic, he would share hockey broadcasting's pantheon with only Foster Hewitt.

A STAR-CROSSED UNION

Of all the fights Ted Lindsay fought as hockey's notorious tough guy, the greatest was one he lost. By the time he spearheaded the fight for players' rights, "Terrible Ted" had long since built his reputation as the fiercest of competitors.

The union fight cost Lindsay dearly.

THOUGH JUST 5 FT 8 IN and 160 lbs, he was feared throughout the league as both its penalty king and its best left wing – the sparkplug of Detroit's famed Production Line and the catalyst of the Red Wings' dynasty of four Stanley Cups from 1950 to 1955.

All of which made Lindsay just the man to begin organizing the first players' union at the 1956 NHL All-Star Game in Montreal. Tired of being dismissed whenever he asked about the players' share of the pension fund, he enlisted all the on-ice foes who had branded him "Scarface" to join him at a postgame meeting where he proposed they form a players' association. The All-Stars resolved to solicit support from their respective teams, and within four months they had collected the $100 membership dues from every player in the league but one.

On February 12, 1957, at a New York press conference, Lindsay announced the formation of the NHL Players' Association, extending his reputation as a relentless competitor to his new position as union president.

Not only did the team owners refuse to recognize his fledgling Players' Association, but they immediately vowed to crush it. Retribution was swift.

The Red Wings shocked the hockey world in July 1957 by trading Lindsay to the lowly Chicago Blackhawks, with manager Jack Adams claiming that his former captain had "outlived his usefulness" and was "over the hill". But with Lindsay coming off his most productive season, scoring more goals and points than he had as the 1949-50 NHL scoring champion and earning his eighth First Team All-Star selection, the trade was widely considered punishment. As was the inclusion in the deal of Glenn Hall, the hot young First Team All-Star goalie who refused to distance himself from Lindsay.

Toronto owner Conn Smythe didn't even wait that long to punish Maple Leaf captain Jim Thomson. The Players' Association secretary was benched repeatedly throughout the season before he too was traded to Chicago. Even Doug Harvey, the league's top defenseman as well as the association's vice-president and most accomplished ringleader, was mentioned in trade talks before the Canadiens decided he was too valuable, as their five straight Cups would prove. He was traded in 1961.

The players' union responded in kind. In an effort to get the league to raise pension benefits and the amount of television revenue available to players, the Players' Association filed a suit in New York and Toronto accusing the league of failing to bargain in good faith. (In addition, it applied in all six NHL cities to be the legal collective bargaining agent for the players.) Three weeks later, it filed an antitrust suit, charging that the owners had "monopolized and obtained complete domination and control and dictatorship".

Before anything could be adjudicated, the Red Wings players voted in November 1957 to withdraw from the Players' Association. Their leverage gone, their spirit broken, their solidarity eroded through defections, the reeling union leaders desperately sought a compromise. But what they negotiated were terms of surrender.

It came on February 4, 1958, when the players agreed to drop their unfair labor practices litigation in exchange for small concessions: a $7,000 minimum salary, increased pension and hospitalization benefits, a slightly larger playoff share, moving expenses for a traded player, and affirmation of an injured player's right to judge his own fitness.

The following day, less than a year after it was formed, the NHL Players' Association was officially pronounced dead.

Nearly a decade passed before the team owners formally negotiated with a reconstituted players' union, the NHL recognizing the NHL Players' Association as the exclusive representative of the players in June 1967.

THE JACKIE ROBINSON OF HOCKEY

On January 18, 1958, Willie O'Ree made history as the first black player ever to play in the NHL.

YET EVEN WHILE DEBUTING with little fanfare for the Boston Bruins at the Montreal Forum, he "never gave it any thought that I had just broken the color barrier". For all he wanted to be was "just another hockey player". Instead he would forever be known as "the Jackie Robinson of Hockey" – an impossible legacy for anyone to live up to, let alone a 22-year-old called up as an injury fill-in. Like Robinson, O'Ree broke his sport's color line with grace and dignity; but unlike Robinson, O'Ree was an accidental pioneer integrating the last lily-white big league sport.

"I certainly don't consider myself a Jackie Robinson," O'Ree said then. "I'm aware of being the first and of the responsibilities, but I'm also aware that there have not been many colored players able to play hockey, that there has never been the discrimination in this game there was in baseball, and that I didn't face any of the very real problems Jackie Robinson had to go through."

Nor could O'Ree have anywhere near the impact on hockey that Robinson had in immediately opening baseball's door and spurring all other sports to integrate. In fact, O'Ree's 1958 debut barely broke the ice, lasting just two games before he was sent back down to the minors. But he was back in 1960-61 making the Bruins' roster as a speedy third-line winger.

He encountered blatant racism throughout a season in which he got four goals and 10 assists in 43 games. "People just wanted a piece of me, maybe because they thought I was different," he said, "so I had to defend myself. I wasn't going to be run out of any rink." Not even Chicago Stadium the night Eric Nesterenko taunted and butt-ended him into an ugly brawl.

O'Ree gained acceptance by standing up to the physical abuse and turning the other cheek to the racial slurs. Foes baited him and fans taunted him. Racial insults, notably absent in Montreal and Toronto, were a constant companion on US road trips to Chicago, Detroit, and New York. Ironically, he found American sanctuary only in the city that over the years has been the flash point for several incidents of northern racism – Boston. The Bruins not only embraced him, but signed him before the Boston Red Sox became the last major league baseball team to hire a black player.

His NHL career lasted only 45 games. He never made it back, largely because he had lost almost all his sight in his right eye when he was struck by a puck as an 18-year-old junior. He always believed that held him back more than his skin color. Yet he never stopped defying the stereotype while playing out his 23-year pro career in the minor leagues. For whereas baseball's integration merely confirmed what so many assumed about Negro Leaguers belonging in the majors, O'Ree faced the stereotype that blacks didn't belong in the game. Fully 13 years would pass before another black player followed O'Ree across the color line, and still more before a black had an impact as a star for minority youngsters to emulate.

Today, O'Ree serves as the NHL role model he never had growing up in New Brunswick while idolizing Quebec's all-black line centered by Herb Carnegie, the best black pioneer never to play in the NHL. In those days when the six-team NHL was all Canadian, hockey's all-white composition was attributed to cultural differences in Canada's tiny black population; but as expansion created more jobs, socioeconomic issues were raised to explain why minority progress remained glacial into the 1990s. Since the 1994 formation of the NHL/USA Hockey Diversity Task Force to promote grass-roots opportunities for economically disadvantaged youngsters, black participation has grown to the point where two dozen minorities played in the 1998-99 NHL season.

On January 18, 1998, the 40th anniversary of his breakthrough, O'Ree was hired as Director of Youth Development for the NHL/USA Diversity Task Force. Having come full circle, the man who broke the stereotype at the highest level is now inspiring kids to break it on a mass level.

"When I was your age, they called it a white man's sport because there were no blacks," O'Ree tells kids at clinics, "but that barrier is down. Today's barriers are equipment and ice time, and you gentlemen right here are the future.'

Cups and More Cups

ALL THAT SLOWED MONTREAL'S DYNASTY-IN-THE-MAKING were injuries to the likes of the Richards, Geoffrion, and Plante. Such injuries enabled the 1957-58 Red Wings to finish first for an unmatched eighth time in nine seasons behind Howe, whose fifth scoring title helped him win his third Hart Trophy as MVP. But the Canadiens recovered in time for the playoffs, dispatching the Rangers in five games in the semifinals, while the Wings were upset by the Bruins. With Rocket Richard exploding for a vintage four-goal performance in the 5-1 opener, the Canadiens cruised to a five-game victory over the Bruins – and captured the dynasty's second Cup.

On October 19, 1957, The Rocket became the first player in NHL history to score 500 goals, but less than a month later he suffered a career-threatening severed Achilles tendon. Then came the life-threatening injury suffered by Geoffrion on January 28, 1958. He was leading the league in scoring when he collided with teammate André Pronovost in practice, crumpling to the ice and telling teammates, "Somebody get me a priest." Geoffrion was rushed to a nearby hospital and given the last rites before major stomach surgery repaired a ruptured intestine and saved his life. The absence of Geoffrion and Richard underscored the Canadiens' depth: Dickie Moore, despite playing with a broken wrist for the final three months of the season, won the scoring title while leading the league in goals. Henri Richard was runner-up with four points less, but led the league in assists. So, in the absence of Maurice Richard as a postseason All-Star selection for the first time in 13 years, Henri Richard upheld the family honor as the First Team All-Star center. With the offense pouring in a record 250 goals, and with Plante winning his third straight Vezina and Harvey his fourth straight Norris, the Habs finished first by 21 points. The Rocket returned to lead them through the playoffs with 11 goals in 10 games. They swept Detroit in the semi-finals, then needed six games to polish off Boston in the final – and capture Cup No. 3.

Silver was a Canadiens' color, too.

By 1958-59, the Montreal machine was rolling in its drive to become the first NHL team ever to win the Stanley Cup four years in a row. Not even Rocket Richard's season-wrecking ankle injury could keep the Habs from running away with the regular season by 18 points. Moore won his second straight scoring title with an NHL record of 96 points, this time just ahead of Beliveau and his league-best 45 goals. Plante won his fourth straight Vezina. Harvey, though, lost his four-year grip on the Norris, but only because teammate Tom Johnson won it instead. The Canadiens needed just five games to beat the Maple Leafs in the final for Cup No. 4.

The 1959-60 season ended the same way it started – with the Canadiens making history. On November 1, 1959, after a blistering shot by Ranger Andy Bathgate gashed in his face, Plante repaired to the dressing room and emerged wearing a cream-colored mask that made him look more like a spaceman than an out-of-this-world goalie. Harvey reclaimed the Norris, but now there were new stars emerging to challenge the Habs' dominance, none of whom was more dynamic than scoring champion Bobby Hull. Plante would never need his new mask more than in the playoffs, with the Canadiens opening with a semifinal showdown against Chicago and Hull's supersonic shot. They shut down Hull and swept the Blackhawks behind Plante's two straight shutouts, then overcame the Maple Leafs in a four-game final to duplicate the Red Wings' 1952 feat of eight unanswered wins – and gained the dynasty's fifth Cup.

In the third game of the final, Rocket Richard scored what proved to be the final goal of his career. The following September, hours after he scored four goals in a training-camp scrimmage, he called a press conference to announce his retirement.

It was the end of an era. And the end of a dynasty.

JOHNNY **BOWER**

THE KID WHO WAS TOO YOUNG FOR THE Canadian army in 1939 – he sneaked in at the age of 15 – seemed too old for the NHL at 34. That's how old he was when the Toronto Maple Leafs finally drafted him. He had played a year in juniors, 12 years in the minor leagues, and a season with the woeful New York Rangers five years earlier. But it wasn't until his first season with the Leafs in 1958-59 that he made the NHL for keeps. That season a US immigration officer stopped him at the border for being "too old" to be a goaltender. Hardly. He wasted no time earning his nickname of "the China Wall". In 1960- 61, he earned the Vezina Trophy and First Team All-Star selection. The next three seasons, he backstopped the Leafs to three straight Stanley Cups. Then, joined in the Toronto net by Terry Sawchuk, Bower shared another Vezina in 1965 and, at 43, another Cup in 1967, the personification of the oldest team ever to win it all.

GUMP **WORSLEY**

LORNE WORSLEY, WHO GOT HIS NICKNAME AS A kid because of a resemblance to a comic-strip character, won the Calder Trophy as the 1953 NHL rookie of the year with the last-place New York Rangers. So competitive was that Golden Age of Goaltenders that the Calder got him a demotion to Vancouver of the WHL, displaced by Bower. He displaced Bower the next year and backstopped the Rangers for seven seasons until a blockbuster 1963 trade sent him to the Montreal Canadiens in return for Jacques Plante. The Gumper helped the Habs win the Stanley Cup in 1965, 1966, 1968, and 1969; in the third playoff run, he went 11-0 with six shutouts. Twice he shared the Vezina Trophy and he and Bower joined the trinity of Sawchuk-Plante-Hall as the Hall of Fame goalies of the Golden Age.

TORONTO
MAPLE
LEAFS

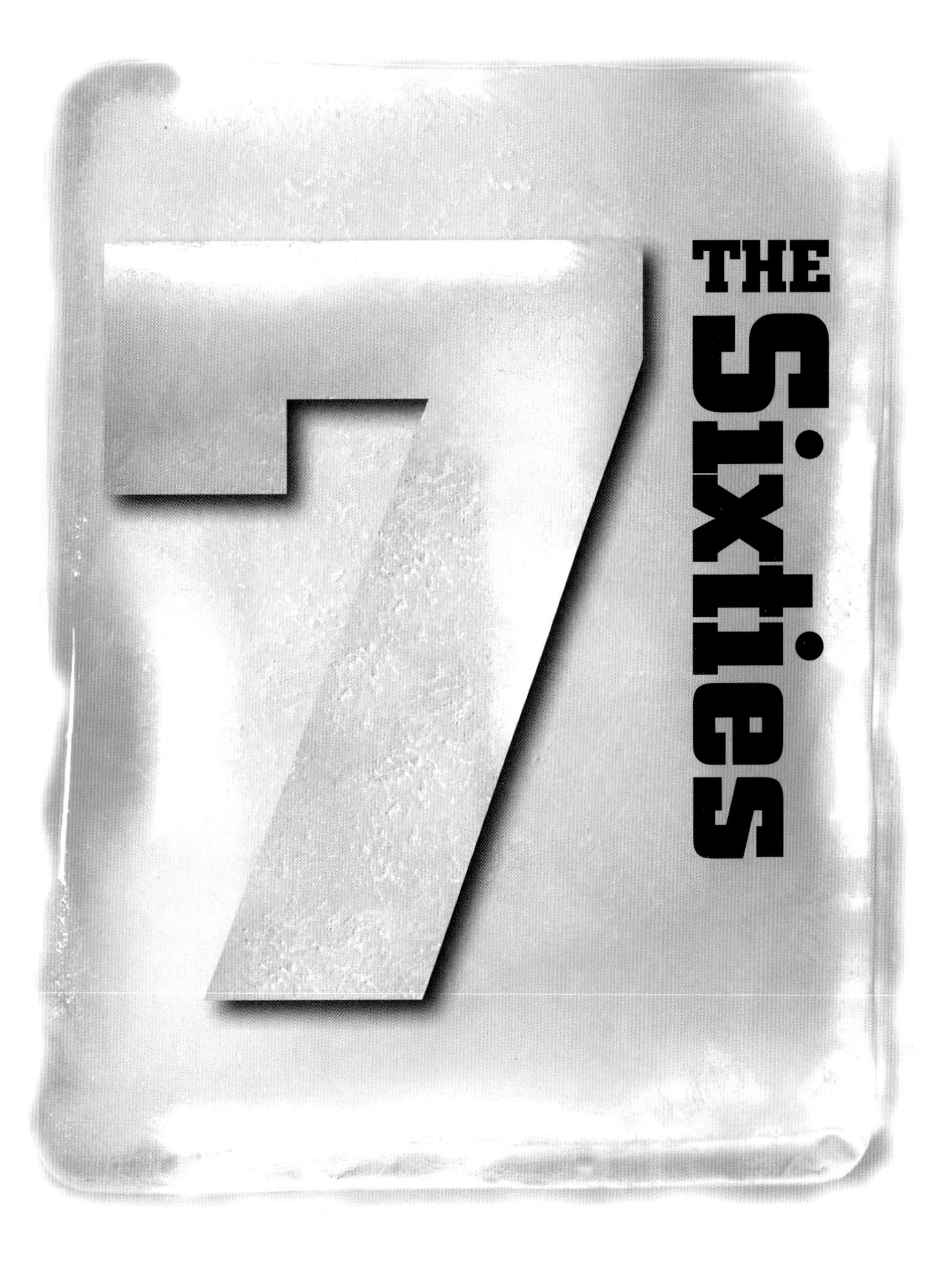

The Great Expansion

The irony and the history of the NHL in the 1960s is a very rich one. During a decade in which the league would prepare to double in size thanks in part to inexpensive and available air travel, the years 1960 to 1969 would be ruled by two teams just a train ride apart. The rivalry between the Montreal Canadiens and the Toronto Maple Leafs during this era was one of the fiercest in hockey, if not in all of sport.

Opposite page: Captain George Armstrong carries the Cup and ends an era in 1967.

THE 1967 EXPANSION OF THE NHL ADDED SIX TEAMS: THE Philadelphia Flyers, the Los Angeles Kings, the St. Louis Blues, the Minnesota North Stars, the Pittsburgh Penguins and the Oakland Seals. The move to double the size of the league came relatively late to the sometimes slow-moving NHL ownership. Minor-league hockey as well as professional football and baseball had already spread across the US by 1962, and teams were thriving all over California. The NHL could not ignore the massive revenue potential in these new population centers and in 1967 six new owners paid the NHL $2 million apiece to join the club.

But before all of that, the NHL club was still closed to outsiders. Beginning in 1960, Montreal won the Stanley Cup and would win it five more times in the decade. Toronto won three straight Cups from 1962 to 1964 before Montreal won it back in 1964-65 and 1965-66. But these two teams would meet in the finals only once during the decade, with the aged Maple Leafs pulling off a stunning upset in 1966-67 before Montreal finished the decade by winning in 1968 and 1969. Only the Bobby Hull/Glenn Hall Chicago Blackhawks could bring the Cup south of the 49th parallel. Make no mistake: these two teams – the pride of English Canada Maple Leafs and the pride of French Canada Canadiens – did not like each other. During their epic finals battle, Montreal's noted enforcer John Ferguson had just ordered dinner in a Toronto restaurant when the Maple Leafs' Eddie Shack entered and ordered as well. Ferguson, who despised Shack, among other Toronto players, threw down $20 before his steak arrived and stormed out of the restaurant. How could he eat in an atmosphere like that?

In many ways, the colorful jousting between these two teams was typical of the now-romanticized "Six Team Era", as clubs played each other 14 times a season, more than enough time to reignite heated story lines, if not a handful of fights, too. But this specific rivalry cooled enormously with the arrival of those six new teams in 1967-68, and the dilution of the schedule combined with the shrinking Maple Leafs' talent pool meant the end of another feisty era in the NHL.

STAN MIKITA

HIS STYLE WAS LESS DRAMATIC THAN THAT OF HIS teammate and fellow All-Star Bobby Hull. Mikita made his name early on as a surly 5-ft 9-in corner-cramming center who backed down from no one and who helped Chicago to the 1960-61 Stanley Cup in his first full season. He led the NHL in points in 1963-64 (89) and in 1964-65 (87), but also racked up more than 100 penalty minutes in four of his first six years, including a career-high 154 in 1964-65. His game evolved dramatically with experience and his penalty minutes plummeted to just 12 in 1967-68 when he became the first player in history to win the Hart Trophy, the Art Ross Trophy, and the Lady Byng Trophy all in the same season. And he did it all again in 1967-68, this time with just 14 penalty minutes. Mikita was also among the first to use a curved stick blade, which let him lift the puck off the ice with more speed and accuracy for most of his 22 years in Chicago. He remains the franchise's leader in games played (1,394), assists (926) and points

(1,467), and he won the Lester Patrick Trophy in 1976. As his game changed, so did his personality. These days Stan Mikita is a popular after-dinner speaker and the co-star of television commercials for IBM with Gordie Howe. He was elected to the Hockey Hall of Fame in 1983.

CROSS-ERA STAR

If there is one player who personifies the transformation of the traditional player of hockey's golden era to the marketable athlete of the modern era, it could very well be Tim Horton.

A NATIVE OF NORTHERN Ontario and the product of the Toronto Maple Leafs' old-school farm system, Horton joined the NHL club for good in 1952 and began an NHL career that would span 24 seasons and include four Stanley Cups, seven All-Star games, and many awards. His clean-cut look and affable smile made him popular with fans; his strapping physique, skating speed and puck handling endeared him to his coaches and teammates as well.

But just as he was making his name as a player in 1956, he broke his jaw and snapped his leg bone in a nasty collision against the New York Rangers that threatened to end his career. While he would return the following season as skilled as ever, he used his time off to prepare for a life after hockey, making off-ice business deals which would lead to his investment in a chain of doughnut stores bearing his name that thrive to this day.

Hockey was still his meal ticket, and he played the game as if he were a kid on a frozen pond. He liked to tell people he was paid to go to practice but that he played the games for free. The Maple Leafs won three straight Stanley Cups from 1961 to 1964 and another in 1967, and Horton eventually became Toronto's highest-paid player as well as the face of hockey in a time when games were being televised across both Canada and the US. His finest season may have been 1961-62, when he scored 38 points in 70 regular-season games and another 16 in 12 playoff games as the Leafs won the Cup.

Throughout his career, he was always one of the strongest players on his team, and he carried the puck with an ease most defensemen did not have. His strength was legendary and while he was known to toss bodies around during games, his most feared move was the Horton Hug, a massive squeeze that tied up many of the toughest players. "Horton's one weakness is that he hasn't got a mean bone in his body," said Toronto coach George "Punch" Imlach, who wished Horton had become more of a bruising enforcer. "If he had, they would have had to make a rule against him."

Earning $80,000 in 1970 for a struggling Toronto team, he was dealt to the New York Rangers and then to the Pittsburgh Penguins before he was reunited with Imlach, by then head coach in Buffalo. There, Horton, at 42, was a stable influence for the young Sabres players who voted him their team MVP in 1973.

"Tim was the greatest thing to happen to us because he was an on-the-job tutor," recalled former Sabres teammate Jim Schoenfeld, who went on to coach in the NHL. "It's something I think today's game misses sometimes because the older players are overlooked in favor of the younger guys and you don't have that veteran to share his experiences with you."

But Horton didn't finish two seasons with the Sabres. After playing against Toronto on February 14, 1974, he was driving back to Buffalo in his own sports car when police reports say he began to travel more than 100 miles an hour. The car veered across the highway's grassy median and flipped over several times, ejecting Horton and killing him instantly. He was 44.

Horton played the sixth-largest number of NHL games (1,446) and was a model of consistency, leading to his induction into the Hockey Hall of Fame in 1977. A small-town Canadian boy who grew up playing for English Canada's team, he began his career early in the six-team era and died when the game was reaching across North America. He combined celebrity with business sense as he built a successful off-ice career. And by the time he had reached his last years in the NHL, during which he had been traded to Pittsburgh, Horton had let his trademark crewcut grow and his shaggy sideburns fill out. He is at once remembered as a throwback to one hockey era and a witness to the birth of another.

Horton: "Not a mean bone in his body."

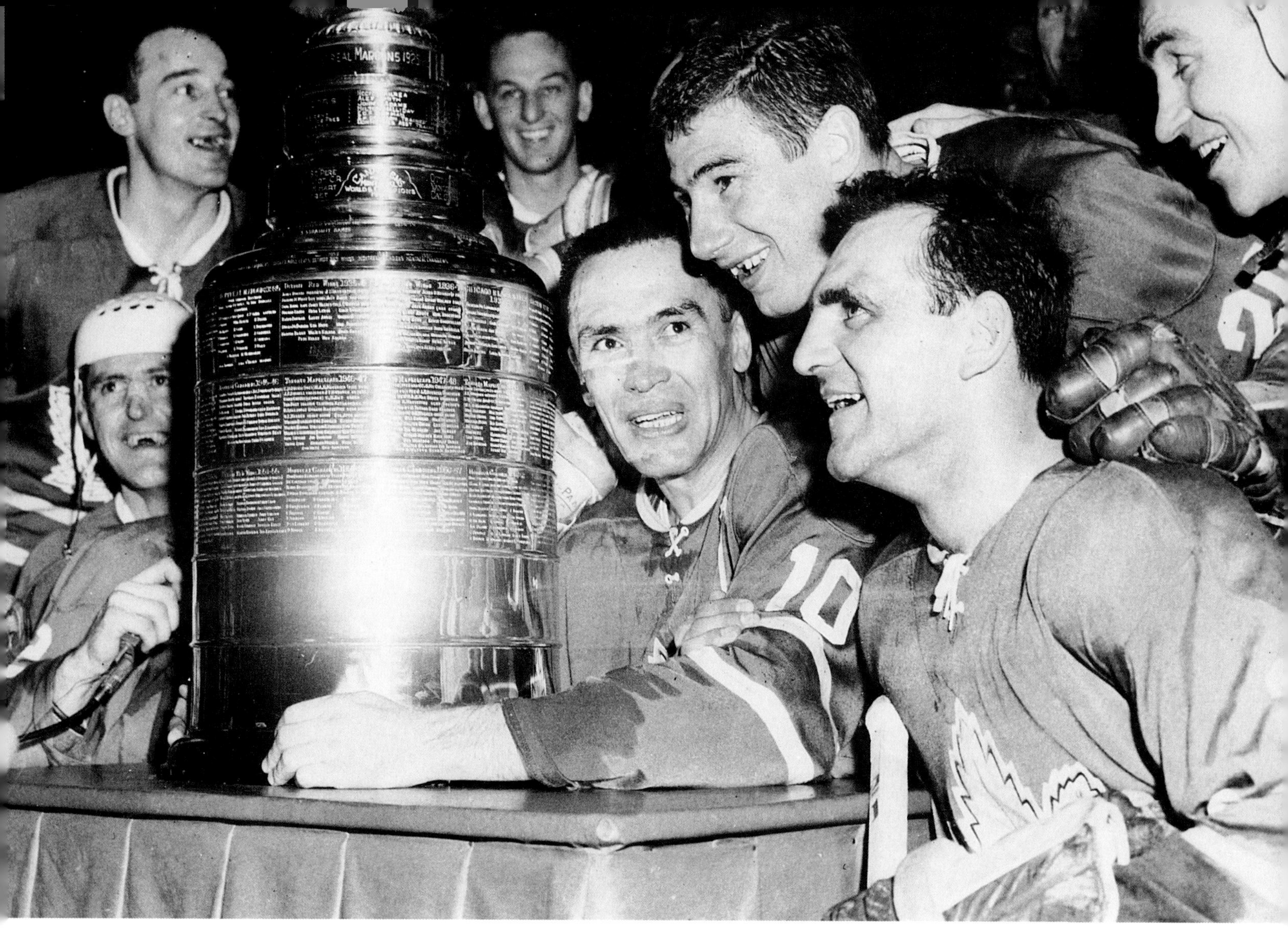

In 1962, George Armstrong (center), Bob Pulford and Bob Baun take a close look at their accomplishment; (opposite page) the Big M, Frank Mahovlich.

HENRI **RICHARD**

BEING THE BROTHER OF A LEGEND ALWAYS brings comparisons. But while Henri Richard was not as prolific at scoring as his big brother Maurice "The Rocket" Richard, the younger Richard used his skillful skating and playmaking to help the powerful Montreal Canadiens to a record 11 Stanley Cups (five in the 1960s) during his 20 NHL seasons. At 5 ft 7 in and nicknamed "the Pocket Rocket", Richard led the league in assists twice, for the second time in 1962-63, and made five of his nine All-Star Game appearances during the 1960s when he also won a Masterton Trophy. He was inducted into the Hockey Hall of Fame in 1979.

27
27
27
NORTHLAND

THE GOLDEN JET

Bobby Hull could hit like a tank and skate like a missile. He was a tough rumbler when he needed to be and a good-looking young man the rest of the time: an ambassador for the game who signed countless autographs and an outspoken critic of the league at times, too.

REPORTERS APPRECIATED him, fans adored him.

"He was the best advertisement hockey ever had," said Chicago coach Rudy Pilous about the man fans called the Golden Jet. "And could he ever shoot the puck."

Yes, there was that too. Hull and his 118-mile-per-hour shot never scored fewer than 31 goals in any season during the 1960s, and he was the first NHL player to score more than 50 goals in one season when he finished with 54 and a league-record 97 points in 1966. That was before the post-expansion explosion in scoring, too. A First-Team All-Star for eight of the ten seasons during the 1960s, he also won the Art Ross Trophy (1960, 1962, 1966), the Lady Byng (1965), the Hart Trophy (1965, 1966) and the Lester Patrick Trophy (1969).

But it was the shot that carried Hull to the top. Boosted in part by the curved stick blade which he and teammate Stan Mikita perfected, Hull's could test the best goaltender from anywhere inside the blue line and some parts beyond. Several goaltenders, including Toronto's Johnny Bower, claimed the puck coming off Hull's stick dipped and curved like no other, and opposing teams would do everything short of stitching a defender to Hull's jersey to slow him down. In the 1963 playoffs against Detroit, Hull scored twice in one game despite a separated shoulder. He then had his nose broken in the next game and played through that, too, with his eyes blackened and splints keeping his nose open. He bagged a hat trick in the seventh game.

And while Hull won only one Stanley Cup in 15 seasons with Chicago, he did help the Blackhawks dominate the regular season, his magnetism and full-ice rushes bringing fans streaming through the old Chicago Stadium turnstiles. He even got to play with his brother Dennis for eight seasons while he was there.

Then he stunned the NHL by accepting a $2.75 million deal with the Winnipeg Jets of the World Hockey Association, by far the biggest NHL name to jump to the new league. The move forced the NHL to ban him from participating in the 1972 Summit Series against the Soviet Union, but he would spend seven seasons in the WHA before the merger brought him back for two more years in the NHL. Had he not jumped, it's safe to say that the WHA's initial splash would have been reduced to a trickle. Instead, the league saw early success. "The World Hockey Association was great to me," Hull said years later. "But let's face it, I had that Blackhawks Indian head tattooed on my chest. Every time I put the jersey on for fifteen years, it was a trip. They were the greatest years in my life."

And if Hull never saw a shot he didn't like, he showed the same freedom with his words. He held out for more money in 1968 and eventually won $100,000 a year, one of several times he held out. Another time he stubbornly walked out of Chicago's training camp

Hull got his muscles the old-fashioned way.

He never saw a shot he didn't like to take.

because they wouldn't let his young son skate on the ice. Other times, he criticized the violence that had marred professional hockey in several outbursts, something he would continue to do even after his retirement in 1980. He yanked his son Bobby Jr. from the rough and tumble play of the Western Hockey League because his son wasn't learning anything and the fighting in games disgusted him.

His other son, Brett, plays for the Dallas Stars and won the league's Hart Trophy in 1991, making the two of them the only father-son combination to win the league MVP. Combined they have more than 1,100 goals in the NHL. But after a 22-year professional career which took him from raising cattle on an Ontario farm to earning thousands of dollars playing a game he loved, what people remember most about Hull is the laser-hot shot.

"When it hits you," goaltender Jacques Plante once said, "it feels like a piece of lead." There were 610 times in the NHL and 303 times in the WHA that it went in the back of the net. And it was golden.

THE DRAFT

Before the drafting of amateur hockey players became a made-for-television event held in state-of-the-art facilities in front of fans across the North America, the NHL's first Amateur Draft in 1963 didn't exactly excite the world.

IN FACT, IT DIDN'T EVEN excite the Chicago Blackhawks or the Detroit Red Wings, who chose not to use all of their choices, or picks as they were called.

That's mainly because the old system of NHL teams sponsoring minor-league teams to obtain the rights of amateur players was still the best way to collect talent. An NHL team would pay an annual amount of money to a junior team and secure the rights to any of the junior team's players. The Boston Bruins did this as late as 1960, when they paid $1,000 to secure the rights to a 12-year-old peewee team star named Bobby Orr.

Created during the 1962-63 season by NHL President Clarence Campbell, the draft was an effort to distribute the rising talent pool evenly, but sponsorship still continued until 1969, further restricting who was available to the professional clubs. Few future NHL stars emerged from the draft until sponsorship was discontinued altogether.

The first pick of the first draft was Garry Monahan, a 16-year-old member of the Toronto St. Michael Juveniles. Under the rules of the draft, the Montreal Canadiens paid his team $2,000 for the rights to Monahan, still the youngest player ever taken in an NHL draft as the minimum age rules set by the league fluctuated over the years.

In 1965, the league upped the minimum age to 18, restricting available talent even more, and only 11 players were chosen. Then, the following year, the New York Rangers mined a gem by picking the future Hall of Fame defenseman Brad Park, but this draft was shallow, too. In 1967, the six new expansion teams were granted the first six picks, but with the minimum age boosted to 20, the pickings were even slimmer.

The 1969 draft was an important one for two reasons. Firstly, with sponsorships out of the way, all available junior prospects of 20 years old and older were available to the 12 teams drafting. Secondly, Montreal exercised its cultural option, a special rule from 1963 that allowed the team to select annually up to two players of French-Canadian heritage to keep the French-Canadian flavor of the team. With the top two prospects being French-Canadian that spring, Montreal immediately took Rejean Houle and Marc Tardif. Stung by their own good deed, the rest of the league's general managers voted effectively to end the rule.

The history of drafting amateur talent is full of firsts. Tommi Salmelainen of Sweden was the first European-born player chosen when St. Louis made him the 66th pick in 1969. Taro Tsujimoto from Tokyo was the league's first Asian-born pick when Buffalo chose him as the 183rd, and in 1974, Philadelphia made Viktor Khatulev the first Soviet to be picked as number 160 in 1975. None of these players ever appeared in an NHL game, but this illustrated the NHL's expanding search for talent. With international players sprinkled throughout every roster in the 1980s, Sweden's Mats Sundin became the first non-North American chosen first overall when Quebec selected him in 1989.

Similarly, more and more American-born players were selected as high school and collegiate hockey got stronger. Neal Broten, the first American to score 100 points in an NHL season, was the first notable US player drafted when Minnesota took him 42nd overall in 1979. Five US stars were chosen in 1983's first round alone, and seven more became teams' top picks in 1986.

And as in any sports draft, there have been terrific late-round steals and first-round forehead-thumping oversights. The Flyers used their 17th overall pick on Bobby Clarke, who had scared away 16 other teams with his diabetes and small stature; Clarke is now in the Hockey Hall of Fame. The Los Angeles Kings mined Dave Taylor in the 15th round of the 1975 draft, and the undersized American went on to score 1,069 points, the most by any NHL player from a US college. And 87 of the 166 players chosen ahead of Theoren Fleury in 1987 never played in the NHL while the 5-ft-6-in, 160-lb seven-time All-Star has averaged more than a point a game over 10 seasons.

Through the 1970s and 1980s the draft had its fair share of growing pains. With the World Hockey Association poised to pluck players in 1972, the NHL held the next few drafts in secrecy, hoping to restrict the new league from offering deals to drafted players before the NHL teams could make their offers.

The event's name changed from the Amateur Draft to the Entry Draft when the WHA and NHL became one in 1979. The minimum age was set at 20,

although NHL teams could still select a 19-year-old player with the understanding that he either join the roster or return to his junior team.

In the growing quest for the best talent, NHL teams also continued to further chance picks by selecting players from Eastern-bloc countries despite the political instability of those nations. Montreal took the Soviet player Viacheslav Fetisov in 1978, but he couldn't come to the NHL until 1989, when New Jersey drafted him again, this time 150th overall. Teams took similar risks on Czechoslovakian players as late as 1989, when Hartford took Bobby Holik and Calgary chose Robert Reichel, at a time when turmoil in that country could have prevented them from leaving.

Through it all, the draft became an NHL gala. In 1980, 2,500 fans attended the first public draft, and today the annual proceedings are held in huge NHL arenas and televised internationally as wave after wave of new talent rolls into the league.

The decade opened with Montreal winning the Cup, the last of its five straight from 1956 and the final one of the great Rocket Richard's career. But then in 1961, stacked with Stan Mikita and Bobby Hull, and with the remarkable Glenn Hall in goal, Chicago upset Montreal in the semifinals and then beat Gordie Howe's Detroit Red Wings to claim Chicago's first title since 1938. In the preseason, Montreal's Maurice Richard, the symbol of the Canadiens' domination in the 1950s, retired after scoring four goals in an intrasquad game. Montreal's Bernie Geoffrion matched Richard's 50-goal mark with 50 goals and 95 points to win the Art Ross Trophy. These were still rowdy times in hockey. In 1960-61, a game between Boston and Detroit was delayed for 10 minutes during a wild fight. Later that season, Montreal charged that Toronto had shot at Henri Richard's head, and the younger Richard responded in another game by collecting 29 minutes in penalties. Chicago and Toronto dropped the gloves and then each other in March 1961, forcing police to enter the ice and restrain players.

Through it all, Hull matched the goal-scoring mark in 1961-62 (50 goals, 84 points) on the way to the Art Ross Trophy and the finals again. But despite an injury to Toronto's veteran goaltender Johnny Bower after four games, the Maple Leafs beat the Blackhawks in six and the Maple Leafs' stranglehold on the title began. In the same season, the original Hockey Hall of Fame was opened in Toronto and even there the Montreal rivalry was evident. The ceremonies included each team raising a team flag outside the door, and Montreal's and Toronto's representatives scurried to get their banner up first.

Toronto beat Detroit in five close games in the 1962-63 finals, too, but in the semifinals they played even better. Using his sprawling style, Bower posted two shutouts against the Canadiens and allowed just six goals in five games to send their rivals packing. The incidents of stick-swinging continued as did a trend of players assaulting referees. Geoffrion was suspended for five games after he flung his stick and gloves at an official.

The more things change, the more they stay the same. In 1963-64, Montreal pulled off a big trade which included sending goaltender Jacques Plante to New York and bringing in goaltender Gump Worsley. Toronto got Andy Bathgate and Don McKenny in a seven-player deal with New York. And for the first time since the best-of-seven playoff format was installed in 1939, all three playoff series went to seven games. Even so, the Maple Leafs beat Detroit again in a dramatic seven-game finals that featured an unfortunate break in Game 6. Toronto trailed 3-2 when Bob Baun's ankle was broken by a Detroit shot. "I went off and asked the doctor, 'What can we do?' And he said, 'Well, we can tape it and freeze it and see what happens.' So we did." Baun took to the ice again in overtime just in time to make a steal and score the game-winning goal. He skated again in the deciding seventh game, too.

It is never easy to fill a legend's shoes, and the early days of the NHL had plenty of legends. But when Sam Pollock stepped forward to replace Frank Selke as managing director of the Montreal Canadiens' ongoing dynasty on May 14, 1964, the transition seemed to be a perfect fit. Known as a demanding coach, Pollock fit the mold in Montreal, where winning was the norm and losing was not tolerated. "If you didn't do it," said defenseman Jacques Laperriere, "it didn't matter who you were. You were gone."

By maneuvering through the growing player draft and making clever trades with unsuspecting opponents, Pollock would use his background as a scout to build an unmatchable string of NHL championships that extended well into the 1970s. "He'll deny it," said noted hockey reporter Red Fisher, "but anyone who was around at the time – and I was – knows that Sam Pollock ran the National Hockey League." So, too, did his teams. The Canadiens took the 1965 Cup after knocking out Toronto in the semifinals and Chicago in the finals, and Jean Beliveau was named the first winner of the Conn Smythe Trophy, awarded to the top player in the playoffs each season.

EDDIE **JOHNSTON**

ONE OF A KIND AND THE LAST OF A kind, Johnston never took a break in 1962-63, becoming the last goalie to play all 4,200 minutes of a 70-game season in goal. And while that was a long season for the last-place Bruins, Johnston was part of the Bruins' 1970 championship team, which included goaltending partner Gerry Cheevers and the scoring punch of Phil Esposito and Bobby Orr. In 1970-71, he notched a 30-6-2 record as Boston roared to a 57-14-7 team mark. The Bruins won another Stanley Cup in 1972, thanks in part to his 1.86 goals-against average in the playoffs and his gaudy 6-1 postseason mark. After that season, he was sold to Toronto, then on to St. Louis and Chicago before he retired with 32 shutouts and a career record of 234-257-81.

ALEX **DELVECCHIO**

MAYBE IT'S SOMETHING IN THE DETROIT WATER, BUT next to teammate and linemate Gordie Howe, no one has played more than Delvecchio's 1,549 NHL games. When he retired in 1973, his 825 assists and 1,281 points ranked him behind only Howe on the all-time list. A three-time winner of the Lady Byng Trophy, Delvecchio captained the Red Wings from 1962 until the end of his career and was part of a record-setting line with Howe and Frank Mahovlich, which scored 118 goals. Before becoming the team's leader, he was part of Stanley Cup champion teams in 1952 and 1954, and he starred as the Red Wings won their last Cup for more than 40 years, hitting the post before he scored seven goals and eight assists to help win a third title in the 1955 playoffs. In the 12 playoff games of 1965-66 which ultimately ended with a loss to Montreal in the finals, his smooth passing helped him notch 11 assists. Nicknamed "Fats" for his pudgy face, he was elected to the Hockey Hall of Fame in 1977.

The End is at Hand

AFTER YEARS OF TALK AND CONSIDERATION, THE LEAGUE announced on February 9, 1966, that it would expand to 12 teams for the 1967-68 season. The announcement came as Chicago's Bobby Hull was tearing up the league's nets on his way to NHL records in goals (54) and points (97). Players around the league looked forward to an expanded market and salaries. While anticipation grew, however, the old ways still ruled and Montreal won it all again in similar style. After dumping rivals Toronto in a six-game semifinal, the Canadiens garnered another six-game Cup victory over Detroit, despite the strong playoff run by the Red Wings' goalie and Conn Smythe Trophy winner Roger Crozier. In that same 1965-66 season, the league tried to crack down on stick swinging by threatening $200 fines, which did chill the anger on the ice.

Teams approached the 1966-67 season knowing it was the end of an era, but the season wound up being remembered as the beginning of another era, too. Bobby Orr joined the league in 1966-67, beginning a career that would revolutionize the defenseman's position, as he was the third-highest scorer on the veteran Bruins team. The season was capped off by one of the most classic Stanley Cup battles, as Toronto stunned Montreal. In six games, both teams countered with good goaltending and solid defensive play before Toronto took the last championship of the Six Team Era. "In fact, we knew it would be our last whack at the Cup," said Toronto's Red Kelly.

While Montreal had Pollock, Toronto had George "Punch" Imlach, who at his best was a masterful hockey motivator and at his worst an unpopular and stubborn man. Both were fiercely protective of their teams, especially when they went head to head. Between periods of the 1967 series, players were interviewed on television. Imlach told TV producers that his player had to be on in the first three minutes of the intermission and Pollock demanded the exact same time slot in a competition for top billing.

Imlach helped build the Leafs into a hockey powerhouse as Toronto made the playoffs in 10 of Imlach's first 11 seasons, including winning four Stanley Cups. But his

LAST DAYS OF AN ERA

The expansion of any sports league usually brings with it new faces, an excitement for the future, and the pronouncement of a "better tomorrow".

BUT THE TORONTO MAPLE Leafs and their fans still cherish their 1967 Stanley Cup in part because the team did it with old faces, a longing for tradition, and a yearning for immediate redemption.

Losers of the 1966 Stanley Cup, the Maple Leafs limped through the 1966-67 regular season to finish third, well behind first-place Chicago and just off the pace of two-time champions Montreal. Each of those teams had young, brilliant stars of the day while the Maple Leafs were riding on the efforts of two goalies over 38. If North Americans perennially love an underdog, this Toronto team was theirs to embrace.

Toronto was a mix of old players (Johnny Bower, Frank Mahovlich) and young ones (Jim Pappin, Brian Conacher, Pete Stemkowski). George "Punch" Imlach, the team's dictatorial and quirky coach for three previous Stanley Cup victories, had a knack for working miracles, but this team seemed too patched together even to finish the regular season. Throughout, various players were injured and the team played inconsistently. After bickering publicly with several veteran players, the demanding Imlach saw his team go without a win for 11 straight games and he was hospitalized for stress and exhaustion.

"Punch can be a hard man to work for," said Tim Horton, the Leafs' veteran defenseman who was once forced by Imlach to attend practice on the day one of his daughters was born. "But if you do things his way, you're going to win the Stanley Cup once in a while."

If it was a wild time for the Maple Leafs, it was also an anxious time for hockey in general. Attendance was climbing and the expectation of the 1967 league expansion had players expecting better salaries and owners even better profits. A typical game became a rugged experience with plenty of clutching and grabbing, although now fans watched it all behind safety glass at most arenas. Also typical of this era were the fierce rivalries between teams: Chicago didn't like Detroit;

The 1967 Leafs. The oldest team to win the Stanley Cup. But the team didn't adapt to the changes coming.

New York never liked Boston; and, as seen in this series, Montreal and Toronto were forever rivals. Thankfully, four years before the series, Maple Leaf Gardens had built separate penalty boxes for visiting teams. Before that, fighters had to share!

Entering the playoffs, Chicago was the team to beat. Loaded with the 52-goal scorer Bobby Hull and the 97-point scorer Stan Mikita, Chicago seemed invincible. But goaltender Terry Sawchuk led the Maple Leafs to a stunning series victory in six games, setting Toronto up for an all-Canadian final in Canada's centennial year. Toronto was still such an underdog that space had already been built for the Stanley Cup trophy at the exposition hall in Montreal.

But unlike the game in later eras, the dominant characters in the NHL of the 1960s were coaches like Imlach and Montreal's Toe Blake. Before this series, the Toronto coach played mind games with Montreal's rookie goaltender Rogie Vachon, telling reporters the Canadiens can't win "with a Junior B goaltender". Blake was a force himself, running the team from behind the bench like a conductor.

But while Vachon was better than Junior B, Toronto's goaltenders were Grade A. Toronto's own tandem of the ageless Bower and Terry Sawchuk would prove to be the difference. Still, the rookie Vachon shut them down 6-2 in the series opener. The Maple Leafs, behind Bower, took the second game 3-0, stuffing Montreal's high-powered offense again and foreshadowing the rest of the series. It was in the third game where goaltending stood out: Vachon faced 60 shots and Bower faced 54, but Bob Pulford's overtime game-winner put Toronto up, 3-2.

Montreal won the next game 6-2, again beating Sawchuk, to even the series 2-2. With Bower missing with a groin injury, Sawchuk would muffle the Canadiens with a 4-1 victory in Game 5 and a 3-1 victory in Game 6. Pappin, who had scored just 32 points in 1966-67, led all playoff scorers with 15 points in 12 games, but it was the smothering defense – typical of any good team in that era – that kept Toronto in it. "The checking was so close," said Montreal's Jean Beliveau, "we felt like we each had a twin."

That was the last of the glory days for the Toronto Maple Leafs, the oldest team to win the finals, and it was also the end of the six-team era. Toronto did not make the playoffs the following year and have gone more than 30 years without reaching the finals. Montreal began a streak of title contentions that may never be matched. Although Imlach made several headline-grabbing trades in 1968, Toronto sputtered and he was fired.

Montreal, however, capitalized on the burgeoning draft and built for the present and the future. Other Maple Leaf veterans soon left in trades or through the expansion draft. The Canadiens continued their smooth transition from year to year for the next decade. And for all of hockey, the 1966-67 season was the last of its kind.

CARL **BREWER**

A FREE SPIRIT WHO ALWAYS SPOKE HIS MIND IN an age when many players feared management, Brewer was one of the pillars of the defense-minded Maple Leafs' title teams of the early 1960s. But his ongoing battle with Toronto coach Punch Imlach led to his strike in 1963 and his first retirement in 1965. With the help of the future players' union head R. Alan Eagleson, Brewer won back his amateur status and played for the Canadian national team in 1966 before playing overseas. He then returned to sign with Detroit in 1969 and finished his career with the Toronto Toros of the WHA. In the NHL, Brewer never scored more than four goals in a season, but he did log more than 100 minutes in penalties in five seasons, his career-high coming with 177 in 1964-65. Ironically, Brewer became one of the loudest and most active opponents of Eagleson.

New Clubs, Old Faces

BUT ABOVE ALL, THERE WERE MORE GAMES. EACH TEAM now played 74 games, and with six new clubs, the league schedule grew from 210 games to 444. Attendance had reached something of a plateau before expansion, as 2.5 million attended in 1960 compared to 3.3 million in 1967. But in the following three seasons, attendance leapt to more than 5.4 million, 5.9 million, and 6.4 million.

The Blues continued to make news as the most challenging first-year expansion team, luring goaltender Jacques Plante out of retirement to team with veteran Glenn Hall in net. Then, Red Berenson turned heads by scoring six goals in one game for St. Louis, which finished on top of the West Division. But while the regular season showed change, Montreal beat Bowman and the Blues again in the finals.

In the following season of 1969-70, Boston and Montreal each made history, one for the better and one for the worse. Montreal did not qualify for the playoffs in the East Division despite earning more points than any team in the West Division. Emboldened by Orr and Esposito once more, Boston won the Stanley Cup for the first time since 1941. The Bruins knocked off New York in six games and then swept four games from powerhouse Chicago and standout rookie goaltender Tony Esposito, who had 15 regular-season shutouts. Orr, who became the first defenseman to lead the league in scoring with 120 points, completed the series sweep of St. Louis by scoring a dramatic overtime goal.

ALAN EAGLESON

For better and for worse, the pace of the growth of hockey between the late 1960s and the 1990s can be directly attributed to the ambitious son of a factory worker named R. Alan Eagleson.

AS A YOUNG LAWYER FROM Toronto, Eagleson had proved himself to be a defender of players' rights when he helped settle an AHL player strike sparked by the mistreatment of players. And when he negotiated Boston's initial $13,000 salary offer to the teenaged Bobby Orr into a record $75,000 two-year deal in 1966, other NHL players took note. On December 28, 1966, his quiet meetings with the rosters of every team culminated with what would be the first meeting of the NHL Players' Association (NHLPA).

As executive director of the NHLPA, he quickly got the Board of Governors to recognize the group as the players' official bargaining agent, and the average salary grew from $7,500 to $10,000. He was credited with shaking loose the long-frozen salary structure and leading the players into the post-expansion era before becoming the star player on international hockey's center stage.

As the driving force behind the thrilling 1972 Summit Series, only he had the power to convince both the league and its players that the series would benefit everyone. And the players' loyalty for Eagleson was never more evident than in the series' decisive eighth game. When the red light took too long to light after an obvious goal by Team Canada, Eagleson went berserk at the referees, and Soviet police began to escort him roughly from the arena. Canadian players Peter Mahovlich and Gary Bergman led the charge as the entire Canadian team flew over and flailed at the police, freeing their spirited representative and getting him to the safety of the Canadian bench. Once there, Eagleson was even more fired up and shot the mostly Russian crowd an internationally recognized one-finger salute before Canada rallied to win. He was Canadian hockey as much

But while the decade's championships were ruled by an elite group, the general history of the league at this time was made up of some remarkable moments, too. Some of them wound up in record books while others simply show how the league was quietly evolving step by step. In 1960, Gordie Howe became the first player to score 1,000 career points and later that season set a playoff record for career assists. Almost directly in between those two events, a boy named Wayne Gretzky was born. Howe, an affable but hard-nosed player, remained the face of professional hockey for the next 20 years before Gretzky's arrival in 1979.

Chicago's Glenn Hall was one of several seemingly ageless goaltenders sprinkled throughout the league during the 1960s, remnants of an era when players stuck around forever. Hall, who was awarded a station wagon by the Chicago franchise upon playing his 500th straight game in goal, ended his streak at 502 (or 33,135 minutes) in 1962, although he would play for the rest of the decade. Toronto's Bower similarly played beyond the usual age and only retired when his arthritis slowed him down.

Modifications in the game occurred, too. Earlier in the decade, the league mandated that plastic guards be put on the back of players' sharp skates to limit the chance of injuries. In 1961, penalty shots had to be taken by the player against whom the foul was committed. But the faceoff rule of 1964 had a bigger impact. Previously, players taking a faceoff could just bull through their opponent, leaving the puck for a teammate to collect. But with contact limited by the new rule, players had to become more adept at challenging for the puck and flipping it out by themselves. The ice surface itself saw a series of changes at the faceoff circle hashmarks, and the center red line turned into a checkered red line in 1964, too.

as any non player could be.

But as his NHLPA reign continued, his deals would seem quirky. In 1975, the league and the union avoided a work stoppage by agreeing to a five-year collective bargaining agreement that included the players' acceptance of a new free-agent clause. The key portion – which helped teams far more than players – said that when a player finished his contract with one team, he couldn't play for another until his old team was compensated by his new team, either in cash, players and/or draft picks.

In exchange, the players received a richer pension plan and the owners' approval to play in the Canada Cup, Eagleson's international tournament similar to soccer's World Cup. But the extra money that poured into the players' new pension plan essentially came from the Canada Cup, effectively gaining the players nothing from that phase of the bargaining agreement. In an obvious conflict of interest, Eagleson, the player agent and defender of union rights, officially represented the NHL in all international hockey negotiations.

Even odder, in 1977 the Cleveland Barons were on the brink of folding in the middle of the season when the NHL and NHLPA teamed up to loan the franchise $1.3 million. Years later players questioned whether these moves were less peacekeeping missions on Eagleson's part and more signals that he was working too close to protect the interests of owners.

The foundation was shaking but it took more than a decade for Eagleson's power to erode completely. In 1980, Orr charged that Eagleson had kept secret a lucrative offer from the Boston Bruins which would have kept him with the team he loved. Others, led at one point by Boston's Mike Milbury, began to accuse their own union leader of cozying up to league officials.

Eagleson was eventually forced out as NHLPA's head in 1991. His demise became inevitable because of two forces: one was an investigation conducted by the *Lawrence Eagle-Tribune*, a suburban daily in the Boston area. Following some conversations he had at a reunion picnic for former Bruins, the *Eagle-Tribune*'s sports editor, Russ Conway, began looking into all the benefit packages these players said they had never benefitted from. This small newspaper devoted incredible resources to get the story. The other force was an earlier investigation conducted at the request of several players by the former head of the pro football players' union, Ed Garvey. His report was devastating. By the time these two forces were finished, the face of hockey was changed. Eagleson resigned in 1991.

Voted to Canada's parliament in the 1960s and loved by NHL players through the early 1970s, Eagleson quickly fell from grace. The players who had defended him so staunchly packed a Boston courtroom and later one in Toronto to see their former leader plead guilty to a two-country indictment and be led off to an Ontario jail. They cheered his demise. He paid a $1-million fine and served five months of his 18-month sentence before entering a work release program. He was kicked out of the Canadian Sports Hall of Fame and forced to resign from the Hockey Hall of Fame. It is believed that Eagleson is the only person ever to have to leave a sports hall in which he was enshrined.

REVOLUTIONARY

Bobby Orr's meaning to the NHL can be stated simply. Many people have tried so hard to explain just what Bobby Orr meant to the NHL, but one of the most importants thing you need to know about his career is this: His skills changed the game of hockey forever.

In a time when sports fans need to know – demand to know – who is No. 1, Orr greatness is simply assumed. He didn't play as long as Gordie Howe, score as often as Wayne Gretzky, or win as many uch as Guy Lafleur, and yet he is easily ranked in the Top 3 of among the greatest players of alltime. for revamping how hockey teams score goals.

One of the last great players to come out of the sponsorship system before the draft pipeline opened up, Orr was just 12 years old when Boston scouts came across him playing in Parry Sound, Ontario. Soon after he was playing in the Ontario Hockey League for for the Bruin's affiliate in Oshawa, Ontario, as a 14-year-old star and destined for Boston Garden ...

He signed a stunning $70,000 NHL contract in 1966 and the phenom from Parry Sound, Ontario immediately showed the future to Boston and the rest of the NHL. The signing was an important moment for both the Bruins, who got a badly needed star, and for Orr, who employed a little-known attorney named R. Alan Eagleson to negotiate a contract far beyond the then-average pay. The deal would spur Eagleson to help form the players's union so off the ice and on, Orr was making history.

The face that changed the game; as an Oshawa Junior.

Then came the revolution, which would soon be televised. Up until Orr's arrival, defensemen were rarely focal points of their team's offense and were mainly burly enforcers. Toronto's Tim Horton had strong offensive skills when necessary, and Montreal's Doug Harvey and Chicago's Pierre Pilote directed their team's attacks. But Orr was the focal point, a solid defender who could race down the ice and either pass off, shoot or create a diversion. And he was quick enough to get back on defense if it didn't work.

He won the Calder Memorial Trophy in 1966-67 with 13 goals and 41 points, despite missing several games to an injury early in the year. In the 1968-69 season, Orr scored 21 goals to break the record for scoring as a defenseman and help Boston set new NHL team records for goals (303), assists (497), and points (800). That season foreshadowed the Bruins' Stanley Cup sweep over St. Louis in 1970, as Orr not only won the first of eight James Norris Trophies, but was also named a First Team All-Star in 1968 and 69.

Here is another thing you need to know about Orr: The Bruins called his hockey sticks "wands" for the magic he performed with them. On May 10, 1970, and in St. Louis, Orr scored the game-winning goal in a 4-3 overtime victory to complete a four-game sweep of the Blues for the Stanley Cup title, the city's first hockey championship since 1941. The moment, chosen as the "Greatest Moment in Hockey History" a few years ago, and captured in several famous photographs, shows Orr diving through the air, nearly parallel to the ice, arms outstretched in the glory of victory a second after the goal. "Bobby was the god of Boston hockey at the time," teammate Ed Westfall said. "So it was only right that he got the winner."

Here is another phrase so many use when discussing Orr: "If only his knees had stayed healthy." In his second season he took a hard hit that tore up

Even without his familiar No. 4, Orr had a style and ability that was unmistakable.

his left knee, requiring the first of six knee operations. He missed the historic 1972 Summit Series against the Soviet Union.. But despite even creakier knees, he played in the 1976 Canada Cup and was one of the best on the ice. After scoring a career-high 46 goals in 1974-75, he limped through just 10 games the following season before a bitter contract dispute ended his career with Boston.

As a free agent with Chicago, he hoped to rejuvenate his career, but knee injuries kept him to just 26 games over two seasons before he retired in 1978. He finished his 12-year career with 270 goals and 915 points in 657 games, three league MVP awards and two scoring titles. And as much as people marvel at what Orr was in his prime, most also wonder what he could have been if he had been healthy. Would his love for the game have carried him to 20 years? Would he have scored twice as many goals? Would Boston have won more than two Stanley Cups?

More than 20 years after he played his final game, he remains the idol of NHL players, many not born when he stoped playing. So what is it about this player, who played so little and meant so much? It must be attitude. For here is another sentence you can associate with Orr:

"If I had to do it all over again, I would do it the same way."

His words, not ours.

And then there was the curved stick. Cherished by players like Hull and teammate Stan Mikita, the curved stick allowed players to create more lift on their shots. The league struggled to find a happy medium, restricting the blade to 1½ inches in 1968, then to 1 inch in 1969, and to ½ inch in 1970. Other players, like Toronto's Dave Keon, played on with the traditional flat blade, mainly because the curved stick limited a player's backhand shot.

People made news, too. Billy Reay began his run as the most successful coach with one team when Chicago hired him in 1963. Toe Blake, Montreal's leader through the 1960s, had coached 500 wins with Montreal, something you wouldn't see with the revolving door of coaches in later decades.

Things were happening for the first time everywhere. Ulf Sterner became the first Swedish-born player to play in the Canadian-dominated NHL, albeit for just four games as a New York Ranger. In 1966, Bill Gadsby became the first player to play 300 games with three different teams – Chicago, New York, and Detroit, while Los Angeles called up the oldest rookie in the NHL when it let 37-year-old Jim Anderson skate for seven games, scoring his first and only goal in his final outing. There was another first as well, this time a tragic one: Bill Masterton became the first fatality in a hockey game when he smashed his head on the ice after a bodycheck in 1968.

There was more glory on the ice, too. During this decade, goal-scoring numbers exploded, thanks in part to the gifted shooters named Hull, Esposito and Howe, but also because expansion somewhat weakened defenses. In 1960, half of the NHL teams scored more than 200 points and three players cracked 80 points. By 1969, each of the original six teams scored more than 230 goals, with Boston leading the way at 303. Nine players from four different teams broke the 80-point mark. The league's changes were well underway as Vancouver and Buffalo joined the NHL the following season. Montreal's organization was prepared for the new way of hockey, and it would show in the next decade. Toronto's organization was not prepared, and that would show as well. The rest of the league saw an opening and each made their move, with the new expansion club Philadelphia building a reputation as a title contender. The tightly knit group of six was now a gathering of twelve, and the intense pursuit of the Stanley Cup was now spread across four time zones, too.

RED **BERENSON**

BERENSON AND THE NO. 6 WILL FOREVER BE linked together. One year after the NHL expanded to 12 teams in 1967, Berenson, playing for the St. Louis Blues, became the first expansion team player to crack the league's top 10 scoring club as he notched 35 goals and 82 points. This was the same year Phil Esposito, Bobby Hull, and Gordie Howe each shattered 100 points, but Berenson tied with notable scorer Jean Beliveau and came ahead of Frank Mahovlich (78 points). In this same season, Berenson did what none of the others ever did: he scored six goals in an 8-0 victory against Philadelphia, another NHL expansion team. Berenson is one of only seven scorers to net six goals in one game, and he is the only one to pull off the feat while playing on the road. Following his retirement in 1978, he coached St. Louis until 1982, then moved on to coach the University of Michigan, where he had starred before joining the Montreal Canadiens in 1962.

BILL MASTERTON

Like so many young Canadian men, Bill Masterton lived with the dream of playing in the NHL. Like no one before him or since, Masterton died as a result of injuries suffered on the ice in his first and final NHL season.

In a sport that combines the power of massive bodies moving furiously across hard ice on razor-sharp skates with wooden sticks, it is may seem remarkable that only one player has ever died from his injuries. Masterton, a 29-year-old center for the first-year expansion Minnesota North Stars, was a six-foot, 189-lb journeyman who had come out of retirement to take another shot at the NHL. His work ethic helped him reach that goal, and heading into what would be his final game on January 13, 1968 against the visiting Oakland Seals, things had looked good for both him and his new team. Masterton had scored 4 goals and 8 assists in 39 games for North Stars, who led all of the other five expansion teams in the NHL's Western Division.

It was the first period and Masterton, skating up the ice at full speed, passed the puck off to his right just as two Oakland Seals defenders converged on him. Ron Harris checked him into Larry Cahan and Masterton flipped backwards, smashing his head on the ice. It's unknown whether Masterton was knocked out by the hit or the fall. Either way, he would never awake again.

"I was standing ten feet away and you could hear the explosion," referee Wally Harris said. "He was checked hard, but I'm sure it wasn't a dirty play," said Minnesota coach Wren Blair. "He was hit so hard that I'm sure he was unconscious before he fell." His wife Carol was at the game and saw workers wheel her husband off the ice. His parents were listening to the game on the radio from their home in Winnepeg, Manitoba. All of them rushed to Masterton's side at the hospital, but the injuries were massive and he died 48 hours later, leaving a widow and two children. The North Stars would lose the next seven games, finish fourth, and lose in the playoffs.

His injury and resulting death were chilling reminders of how dangerous the game of ice hockey could be. The accident prompted some players to begin, reluctantly, to wear helmets. It took the NHL until the 1979-80 season to decree that anyone who came into the NHL from that point on had to wear a helmet, and the last player to play without one was Craig MacTavish, who retired in 1997. Some players enjoyed the freedom from any restriction a helmet might cause, while most others felt it was a sign of weakness to don the sort of protection that could have helped save Masterton's life.

During his life, Masterton had played two years of juniors before entering the University of Denver, where he played well enough to win the National Collegiate Athletic Association's championship tournament MVP. Ironically, he wore a helmet all through college. He spent two more years in the minor leagues, leading the American Hockey League's Cleveland Barons with 82 points in 1962-63, then he retired, returned to school, and eventually settled into a life as a contracts administrator with a Minneapolis company.

Masterton returned when the NHL expanded from six teams to twelve in 1967. His work ethic and maturity caught Minnesota's Coach's eye and he became the first player to sign with them. Masterton told reporters then that Minnesota was the only team he wanted to play for because it let him stay at home and having worked out and coached hockey during his time off, he said he felt in good enough shape to make another run for the NHL.

"Because he had a habit of giving everything he had for every second he was on the ice, Bill was the type of player who didn't have to score a lot of goals to help a club," Coach Blair said.

Shortly after Masterton's death, towards the end of 1968, the Professional Hockey NHL WWriters' Association presented the League the Bill Masterton Trophy, to be awarded annually to the NHL player who best exemplified perseverance, sportsmanship and dedication to hockey. Since 1968, the winners include Hall of Famers Bobby Clarke, Lanny McDonald and Mario Lemieux among others.

It seems an appropriate award. Before Masterton reported to the North Stars' first training camp, there was some speculation that he would need to spend his first season in the minor leagues. Even so, he told reporters why he came back to play for the team in the city he now called home. "I had to give it a try," he said. "Once you're in hockey, you always wonder if you can play with the best."

Enter the Great One

Wayne Gretzky didn't sneak up on anybody. A phenomenal player seemingly since he laced on skates for the first time, Gretzky had been making headlines from the moment he scored 378 goals and 139 assists as a 10-year-old in one season of youth hockey.

Opposite page: The decade began with Gordie Howe meeting a 10-year-old record-breaker named Gretzky.

As a junior player, he flew through the competition. And as an 18-year-old who weighed 165 lbs soaking wet and after a heavy meal, he led the upstart World Hockey Association in scoring.

Still, it wasn't quite clear if the kid they had dubbed The Great One since the fifth grade would prosper at the highest level of professional hockey. If NHL watchers weren't impressed by the polite kid from Brantford, Ontario, the kid who had signed autographs as a 12-year-old peewee star was certainly awed by the NHL. "When they play the national anthem, I'm probably going to get butterflies," he told a reporter the day before his first game in Chicago. "Wednesday is going to be a special day in my life."

It turned out to be not only a special day for Gretzky, but also a turning point for the NHL, which had recently absorbed Edmonton and three other teams from the other league. Gretzky's wondrous scoring ability, combined with his graceful passes sparked by exceptional vision, were a far cry from the grinding, physical style of hockey which opened the decade in 1970. From employing a markedly different style of offense to the now obligatory appearance of players' last names on their jerseys, the game itself changed dramatically, sometimes unexpectedly and unwillingly, but mostly for the better.

Following the initial expansion season of 1967, scoring across the league increased dramatically, with players cracking the 100-point barrier with regularity. And it was during the 1969-70 season when Bobby Orr showed the NHL and the world that NHL defensemen could score, too. With his assist in a 3-1 victory over Toronto on April 5, Orr clinched the Art Ross Trophy as the first (and still the only) defenseman ever to lead the league in overall scoring (33 goals, 120 points). Also, Minnesota's Charlie Burns made quieter history by becoming the last man to be a player-coach in the NHL, and goaltender Tony Esposito, younger brother of Phil, notched 15 shutouts in his rookie year for Chicago.

***Image everlasting:* Orr flies past Glenn Hall and the Bruins have won the Stanley Cup.**

But the game as it was being played in the early part of this decade was a physical, violent game, marred by intimidation during the action and bench-clearing brawls in between.

Boston and Philadelphia built championship teams that beat you both with goals and with their fists, and not necessarily in that order, and other teams felt compelled to copy them if only to survive. This included two new teams (the Buffalo Sabres and the Vancouver Canucks) who joined the league for the 1970-71 season.

After winning the Stanley Cup in 1970, the Bruins posted another record-shattering season but fell short of a second Cup. Esposito (76 goals, 152 points) led the league, Orr (37 goals, 102 assists) was second and Boston teammates John Bucyk (51 goals, 65 assists) and Ken Hodge (43 goals, 62 assists) finished third and fourth. As a team, the Bruins scored 399 goals, 108 more than the next team, and notched an NHL record 57 team wins. But the NHL's second-best goal-scoring team was Montreal,

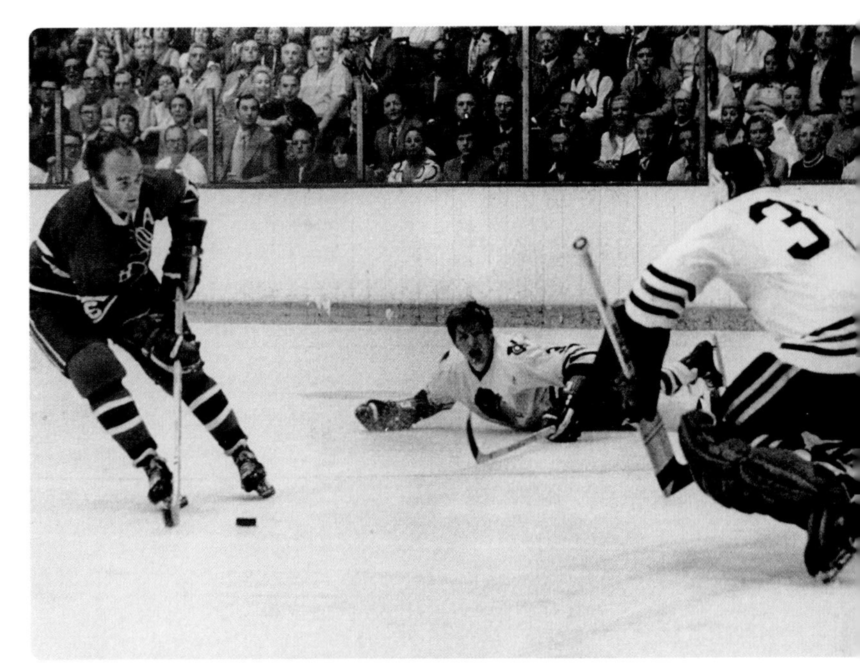

Henri Richard finished his career with 11 rings.

GERRY **CHEEVERS**

RUSSIAN GOALTENDING LEGEND VLADISLAV Tretiak called Cheevers the greatest goaltender he had ever seen, but Cheevers never made an All-Star game and never won the Vezina Trophy. Traded by Toronto as a rookie, Cheevers manned the goal for Boston's Stanley Cup champion teams in 1970 and 1972, but he is remembered today for the eerie mask he wore depicting stark black stitches painted in places where pucks would have cut his face. His jump to the WHA left Boston ailing in the net, but his return and his playoff savvy helped the Bruins make it to the finals against eventual champion Montreal in 1976-77 and 1977-78. Retiring in 1980, he coached the Bruins for more than four seasons before his induction in the Hockey Hall of Fame in 1985.

BREAKING THE POINT BARRIER

Phil Esposito was a blue-collar player who led a wild and crazy hockey career which made the most of his imposing presence on the ice.

HE HAD A HUGE APPETITE for life and an unquenchable thirst for victory and competition. But above all else, Esposito was one of the greatest goal scorers ever to play in the NHL.

The son of a northern Ontario nickel miner and older brother to eventual NHL Hall of Fame goaltender Tony Esposito, Phil Esposito didn't take hockey seriously until later in his junior career, and he eventually joined the powerful Chicago lineup with Bobby Hull and Stan Mikita. But Chicago's 1966-67 regular-season title dissolved into a collapse against Toronto in the semifinals. An immediate round of changes included trading Esposito, who disappointed everyone by not scoring in the six-game debacle against the Maple Leafs. There were no disappointments in Boston. Esposito only went on to win five scoring titles (including four straight), two Hart Trophies and two Stanley Cups for the soon-to-be "Big, Bad Bruins".

But at a time when NHL scoring numbers were soaring, Esposito didn't just set new marks, he blew up old ones. He set a new NHL scoring record in 1968-69 with 126 points, the first time anyone scored more than 100 in a season. (There were three 100-point scorers that season, including 41-year-old Gordie Howe). Then Esposito shattered Bobby Hull's record for single-season goals with 76 in 78 games in 1970-71. He was never afraid to shoot either, and still holds the NHL single-season record for shots with 550 that season. "I see him taking all those shots and I wonder why his arms don't fall off," said Montreal goaltender Ken Dryden.

With his long dark hair, bushy sideburns and broad shoulders, Esposito merged his emotions and skills to embody the very grit that set North American hockey apart. He could fire the puck hard or feather it soft or hammer an opponent for position near the crease, where he dominated the slot. In his then-record 152-point season in 1970-71, he had 76 goals but also 76 assists as he teamed with Bobby Orr and the rest of the Bruins to become one of the most potent offenses in league history.

And he could strike fear into other opponents, too. In the 1972 Summit Series against the Russians, Esposito cross-checked Russia's instigator Boris Mikhailov, but from the penalty box, the beefy Bruin pointed at the Russian, then nodded, and then twice swept his forefinger across his throat in a slitting motion. Then, as his Canadian teammates clearly recall, their fiery leader mouthed to his Russian counterpart, "Me and you, me and you." This was in Moscow during the height of the Cold War; Esposito finished with two goals in that series-clinching eighth game.

"The Soviets did everything they could to intimidate us," said Esposito, who originally considered sitting out the series after the 1972 Stanley Cup. Instead, the team's assistant captain – and self-appointed spiritual leader – led all scorers with seven goals and 13 points. "They tried to aggravate us off the ice, but the fact that we could intimidate them on the ice won it for us." And that carried over to his NHL game as well.

Fun-loving and beloved, Esposito knew a good time when he saw it, and he saw plenty of it in Boston. Players wanted to play with him, not against him. Former teammate Walt McKechnie saw that first hand: "Phil Esposito is the best team leader I ever played with. He took me and made me feel as important as Bobby Orr." Without Esposito, who had injured his knee, the Bruins were knocked out of the playoffs in 1973. That didn't stop his teammates from removing a hospital door from its frame, wheeling him out of the hospital, down to the post-season party, and back to the hospital later that night.

But if he was loud and boisterous on the ice, he could be overwhelming off it, and Boston management didn't expect him to accept his lessening role on the ice as he grew older. He was traded to New York as part of a 1975 blockbuster deal which brought Brad Park to Boston. Esposito, who loved Boston and who earlier had turned down a lucrative World Hockey Association offer, was hurt. "There should be a rule protecting veterans from trades after a player has been with a team five or seven years," he said, showing both his loyalty and naïveté at the same time. Even so, he reported to New York and led them in scoring four years straight, even carrying them to the finals in 1979. He retired in 1981 with his 717 goals and 1,590 points, second at the time only to Gordie Howe.

But he hardly slowed down. Twenty years after winning one of their championships (when one Bruin dumped a pitcher of beer over the Boston mayor's head at a civic party for the team), every member of the Stanley Cup-winning Bruins team attended a reunion party. "I think we had more fun at the reunion than we had at the championship party," Esposito said.

THINKING MAN'S GOALIE

Ken Dryden has been called cerebral, articulate and scholarly, hardly words typically used to describe an NHL goalie.

BUT DRYDEN, A HALL OF Fame goaltender who led the Montreal Canadiens to six Stanley Cup championships and finished his career with a record of 258 victories, 57 losses and 74 ties for a league-record .758 winning percentage, was anything but typical in his success as a goalie. It's his life beyond the statistical register which makes Dryden one of the more fascinating players in the league's history.

Drafted by Boston in 1964 before his 17th birthday, he turned down the Bruins and instead enrolled at Cornell University, an Ivy League school not known for producing hockey players. At Cornell, he earned his degree while becoming a three-time All-American between 1966 and 1969.

After his senior year, Montreal drafted him and soon uncharacteristically made him the No. 1 goalie throughout the 1971 Stanley Cup playoffs, having played just six games late in the regular season (and winning them all). Tall for a goalie at 6 ft 4 in, but remarkably agile and mature in the crease, he replaced the struggling Rogie Vachon and then faltered briefly himself in the quarterfinals against burly Boston. Montreal lost the first game 3-1 and trailed 5-1 in Game 2 before winning 7-5. But Montreal and Dryden weathered the storm to oust the heavily favored Bruins in seven games, as Dryden allowed just 26 goals on 260 shots. He then led the Canadiens past Minnesota and Chicago to capture the Cup. His 12-8 playoff record earned him the Conn Smythe Trophy as the MVP of the playoffs. The Calder Trophy, as the League's top rookie, did not come until the next season.

Ken Dryden: a very different goalie.

Dryden also went on to play against the Soviet Union in the legendary 1972 Summit Series. He cherished that opportunity because it afforded the curious goalie a chance to travel overseas. During that experience, he watched the Soviets dynamic style of hockey, complete with seamless transitions from offense to defense, and accurately predicted then that it was the future of the North American game.

Then, at the peak of his game, he sat out the 1973-74 season in a contract dispute and worked as a legal clerk in Toronto so that he could finish his law degree from McGill University in Canada. More remarkably, he returned to the Canadiens the following season and from 1976 to 1979 helped Montreal win four straight Stanley Cups against some of the most talented teams in NHL history.

His finest season was in 1975-76, when he went 42-10-8, with eight shutouts and an average of 1.81 goals against. Playing on the most dominating teams of that era, he went 12-1 in the playoffs, scattering 25 goals across 13 games.

Two years later, as quick as he had come back, he retired at the age of 31, further illustrating his different style. So many hockey players stay as long as they can; Dryden left after less than eight NHL seasons despite the fact that Montreal offered several times to renegotiate his contract.

After his hockey career, he moved his family to England. Long before returning to the NHL in 1997 as the president of the Toronto Maple Leafs, Dryden produced hockey documentaries and wrote books including *The Game*, a rich, articulate and insightful look into the lives of professional hockey players. In the book he elegantly contemplates issues such as exorbitant athlete salaries, the celebrity of sports and the tensions of the game itself. He makes keen observations on the nature of fans and, quoting the poet W. B. Yeats and the author Bertolt Brecht among others, captures his introspective life with the championship Canadiens, weaving in both the beauty of the competition and the drudgery of the life of a professional athlete.

"It is hockey that I am leaving behind," Dryden wrote of his retirement. "It's 'the game' I'll miss."

GUY **LAFLEUR**

LAFLEUR BLOSSOMED IN THE JUNIORS AND GAVE NHL fans a taste of what was to come when he became the first rookie to score three goals in a game three times in one season. He defined the marquee player: The No. 1 draft pick in the 1971 Amateur Draft, he became a French-Canadian idol on Quebec's bigger stage. After three tough seasons, he blossomed to score 53 goals and 119 points in 1974-75 and was well on the way to becoming the youngest player to reach 400 goals and 1,000 points in NHL history. While racking up a Montreal record, Lafleur was also part of five Stanley Cup champion teams and won the Art Ross Trophy (1976, 1977, 1978), the Hart Trophy (1977, 1978), and the Conn Smythe Trophy (1977). After retiring in 1985 and being elected to the Hockey Hall of Fame in 1988, he returned to play briefly for the New York Rangers and then the Quebec Nordiques.

The Bruins' Esposito, Orr and Cheevers helped Boston dominate the early 1970s.

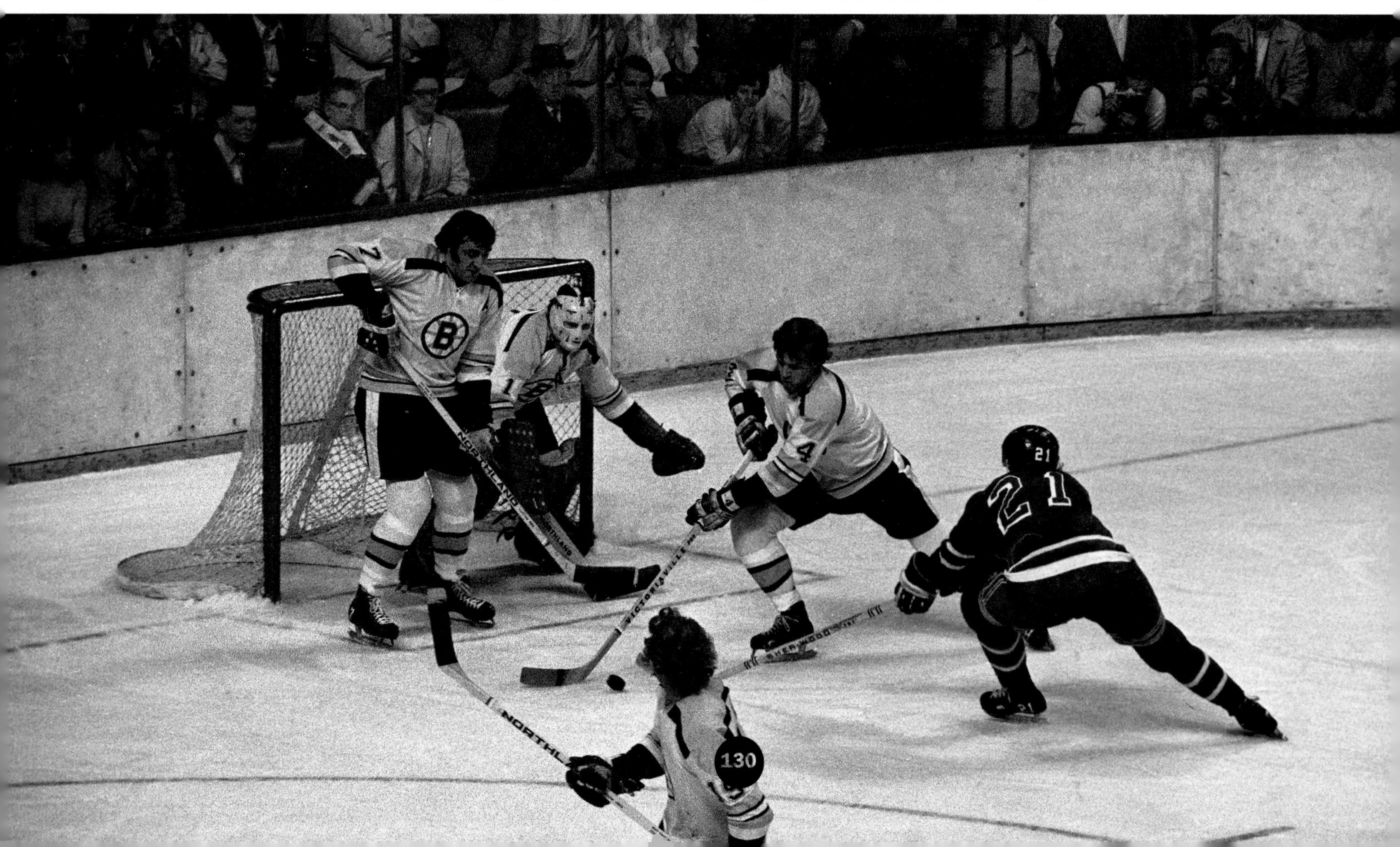

and combined with the red-hot goaltending of a remarkable rookie, Ken Dryden, the Canadiens stunned the Boston dynamo in seven and went on to win the Stanley Cup over Chicago in a seven-game Final. Earlier that season, Dryden had become a part of a much smaller NHL footnote as he and his goaltending brother Dave became the first brothers to face each other in a game.

Boston would be back in 1971-72 as Esposito and Orr finished first and second in NHL scoring. The Bruins, bolstered by their own Hall of Fame goaltender Gerry Cheevers, knocked the New York Rangers out of the finals as Orr became the first ever two-time winner of the Conn Smythe Trophy, awarded to the MVP of the playoffs.

This season also marked the first for rising young stars whose scoring would help attract attention to the league, and more importantly, distract many observers from the brawls. Detroit's Marcel Dionne scored 77 points, a new record for rookies, and Montreal's Guy Lafleur notched three hat tricks in the season, the best showing for a rookie in the modern era.

But Boston's domination was short-lived, no thanks to the emboldened WHA and the deteriorating and gimpy knees of Orr. Cheevers was one of several key Boston players who jumped to the new 12-team league, and while Esposito led the NHL in scoring again, Orr suffered the first serious knee injury that eventually slowed his once-dashing game. It was a painful, unfulfilling experience for Boston, made even more so when Esposito became, in 1975, the first player to break 100 points in six straight seasons. Orr won the Norris Trophy for the league's best defenseman a record sixth time in 1973, but Boston couldn't keep the winning teams together. In 1973, Montreal beat Chicago for the title as Canadiens legend Henri "the Pocket Rocket" Richard broke Red Kelly's record for career playoff games with 164 appearances. That same spring, journeyman goaltender Andy Brown would become the last player to play goal without a mask.

MARCEL **DIONNE**

UNLIKE SO MANY OF THE SCORING GREATS, Dionne, the third most prolific point scorer in league history (1,771 points), never won a Stanley Cup. Playing in the shadows of others was something familiar to Dionne, who was drafted by Detroit in 1971 after Montreal picked Guy Lafleur. He set a rookie record with 77 points, but finished third in the voting for the Calder Cup. He did take the Lady Byng Award twice, once in 1974-75 when he racked up 121 points behind Boston's tandem of Bobby Orr and Phil Esposito. And he played in Los Angeles before Wayne Gretzky made that chic. He scored more than 50 goals in half of his 12 seasons there. His only scoring title and Art Ross Trophy came in 1979-80, when he had 137 points and 53 goals. But he was still overshadowed by Gretzky that season, as the 19-year-old tied with Dionne on points and won the Hart Trophy. Dionne was elected to the Hockey Hall of Fame in 1992 and is still the Kings' all-time leader in points (1,307), goals (550), and assists (757).

MEETING AT THE SUMMIT

The games meant nothing and the games meant everything. The revered Canadian players were confident and then they were relieved.

THE SOVIET UNION TEAM was unknown and evil, and then it was instructive and perhaps even revered.

The 1972 Summit Series pitted a team of Canadian NHL stars against the Soviet Union's national team, an eight-game summer exhibition which most North American fans expected their stars to utterly dominate. Instead, the well-conditioned Soviets used a crisp, fluid attack that nearly won them the series and surely won them the respect of hockey purists everywhere. "It's the one thing you have to learn in hockey," said Serge Savard, who played on the NHL team expected to win easily. "If you're not scared of losing, you're not going to win. And when we started that series, we didn't have that fear."

Organized by then-NHL Players' Association executive director Alan Eagleson, the series was scheduled for four games across Canada followed by four games in Moscow, and the Canadians took a punch in the nose when the Russians skated away with a 7-3 win in Game 1 in Montreal. Canada took the next game 4-1 in Toronto, thanks to goalie Tony Esposito, but Russian goalie Vladislav Tretiak, who played every minute of every game, virtually stood on his head to force a 4-4 tie in Winnipeg. If Game 1 stung Canada a bit, Game 4 shocked the team and the nation even more as the Russians led all the way in a 5-3 win in Vancouver to lead the series 2-1-1 before the venue shifted continents to Moscow.

Following that loss, Canada's Phil Esposito fired back at the fans who booed his team, saying, "To people across Canada, we're trying our best." Esposito, who finished the series leading the team with seven goals and 13 points and was the squad's emotional leader throughout, said: "I don't think it's fair that we should be booed." The impromptu scolding bonded the Canadian team, but more trouble loomed as four players,

No one could know how the sport would change as a result of the 1972 Summit Series.

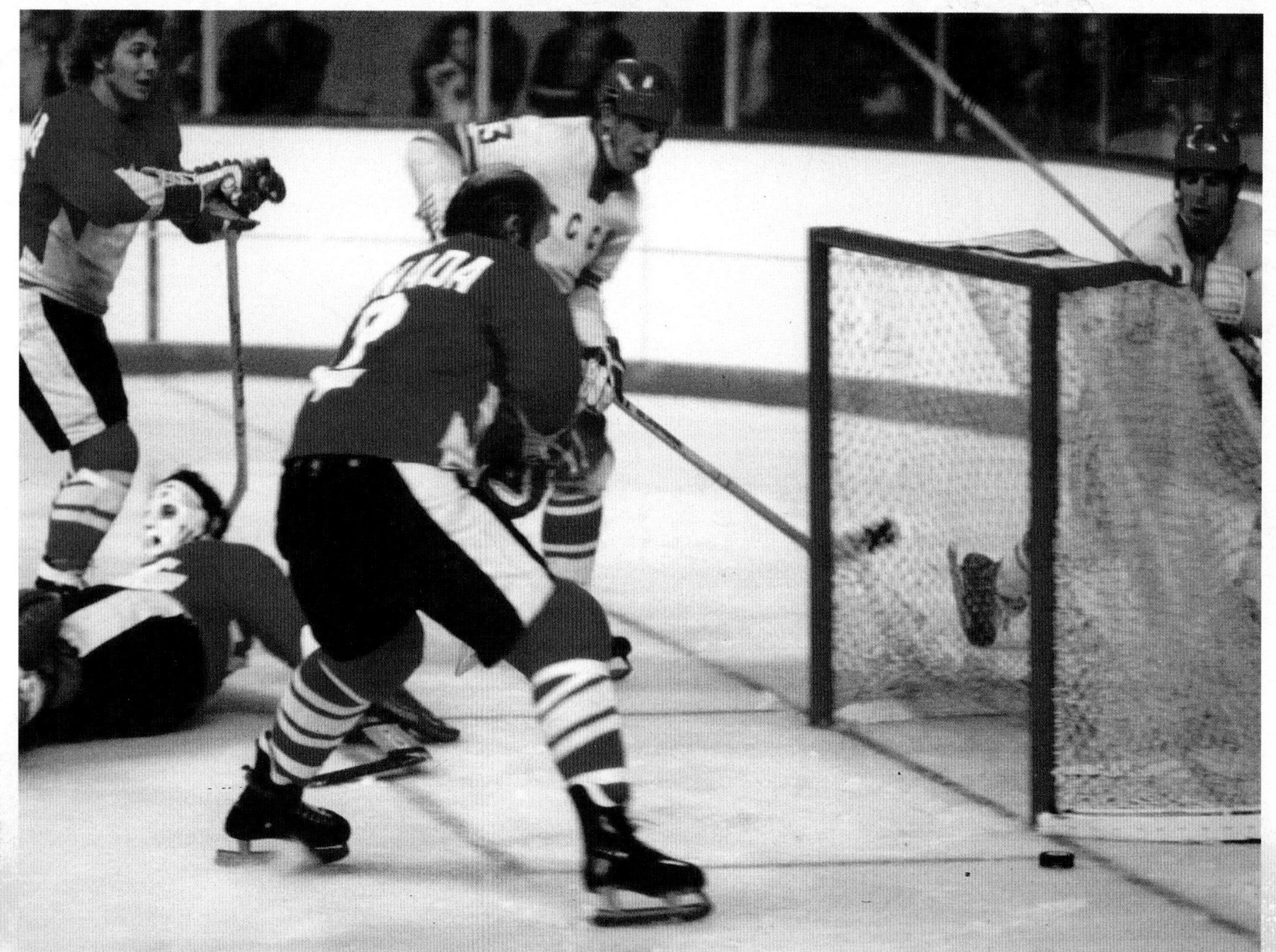

including the Rangers' Vic Hadfield, left the team because they weren't getting ice time. Still, Canada led Game 5 in Moscow before the Russians poured in four goals to win 5-4 and lead the series 3-1-1.

Then the momentum changed. Canada won the next game 3-2, and with two goals by Esposito and the second game-winning goal of the series for Paul Henderson, Canada won again, 4-3. "I can't recall any games that I've been at where you can just feel the tension. And it keeps building up," said broadcaster Foster Hewitt, who covered all eight games. The fear Savard described was back, and the series was tied 3-3-1.

In the finale, Russia led 1-0, but Esposito tied it. Russia led again, 2-1, before Brad Park tied it. The Russians moved ahead 5-3 in the second period, but Esposito scored again in the third and Yvan Cournoyer nailed an Esposito rebound to tie it 5-5 with 7 minutes 4 seconds left to play. Several thousand Canadian fans who made the trip to Moscow to witness the game through the wire mesh screens surrounding the old Luzhniki ice arena chanted, "Da, Da, Ca-na-da, Nyet, Nyet, So-vi-et!"

Then Paul Henderson took his place in hockey history. Henderson, who had slipped and fallen moments before, collected yet another Esposito rebound and fired it at Tretiak, who blocked it nicely. But this time, Tretiak was down, and Henderson slipped his own rebound up and into the net, thus driving the date September 28, 1972, into the memory of an entire nation, including an 11-year-old boy named Wayne Gretzky who had skipped school to stay home and watch the game on television. They heard Foster Hewitt's call: "Henderson has scored for Canada."

"I still talk about that goal 300 days a year," Henderson recalled years later adding that every Canadian he meets tells him exactly where they were and what they were doing when he scored. "And the thing about it: they felt a part of it. They always say 'We'. They don't say, 'You did this.' We as Canadians did it."

The 6-5 win gave Canada a 4-3-1 series but the final results were a fascinating mix of jubilation, relief, and later, profound curiosity. Goalie Ken Dryden, who started four of the eight games, described the 1972 series as a chance for the Soviets and their dazzling style to hold a mirror up to the rough-edged Canadians to show what hockey looked like. "And the message in the mirror was undeniable," Dryden wrote. "They were heading in the right direction and we were not."

Tretiak, who would go on to coach many of today's top NHL goalies, described the Russians' style in 1972, but he could have been forecasting the look of the NHL in the 1980s and 1990s as well. "The NHL players fired many hard slapshots, but we thought that was inefficient. We used short, quick passes to create a high-percentage on goal. To us, the man without the puck was the most dangerous because he could go to an open area and receive a pass."

Vladislav Tretiak (20) never played in the NHL, but he's in the Hall of Fame.

The Broad Street Bullies

THEN THE CLOUDS DARKENED, THUNDER ERUPTED, AND along came the Flyers, who showed no mercy in their quest for championships. If the Bruins were big and bad, the Flyers were bigger and worse. They were dubbed the "Broad Street Bullies" because their home arena was on Broad Street and their home-grown toughness let them bully anyone who dared take the ice against them. In the NHL in the mid-1970s, intimidation won. In 1973-74 Bobby Clarke, who had scored 104 points the season before, led the Flyers with 35 goals and 87 points and pulled the tough guys past the New York Rangers in seven games during the semifinals. In the Stanley Cup finals, the young Clarke faced a less-than-nimble Orr and the Flyers became the first expansion team to win the NHL crown by taking the Bruins in six games. It took the Flyers only seven seasons from expansion to The Cup. A look at the statistics and one also sees that Philadelphia collected more than 1,700 penalty minutes, far more than any other team.

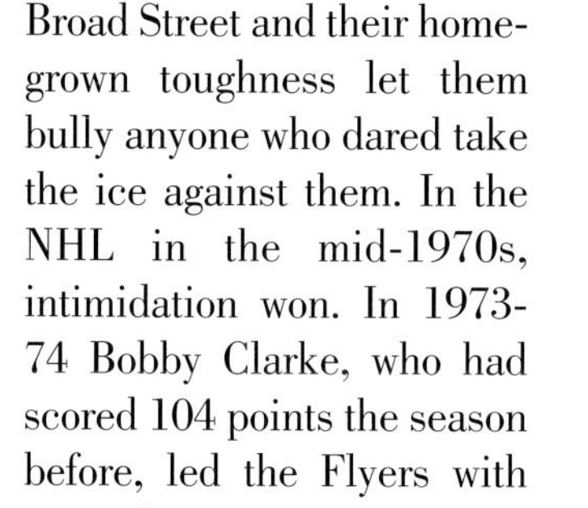

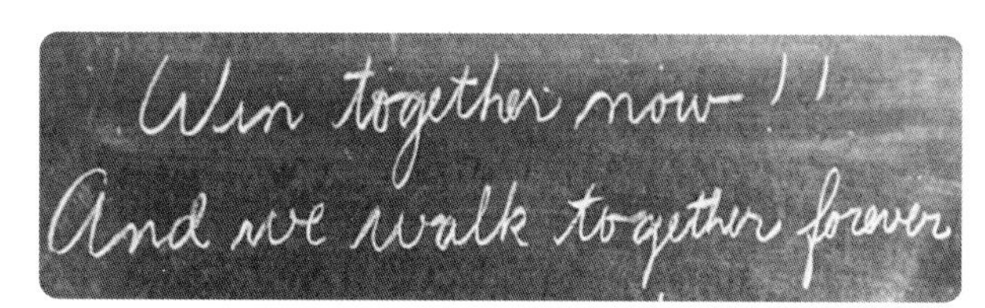

One of Coach Fred Shero's inspirational messages.

The Flyers continued their rough ways the following season. This was a franchise that played an exhibition against the touring Soviet Union Red Army team and nearly body-checked the Russians into forfeiting midway through the first period. There were never any apologies. Team owner Ed Snider objected to writers who called the Flyers' home ice "the cradle of licensed muggings", among other things. "I don't think we played as rough as some of our

BOBBY **CLARKE**

PLAYING HIS ENTIRE CAREER IN THE CITY WHERE they filmed the movie *Rocky* seems appropriate for this consummate underdog who never gave up on the ice. Clarke dominated his junior league in scoring, but teams shied away from him partly because he was small but mainly because he was diabetic. However, the gritty player was the first one from an expansion team to score 100 points in a season. He then led the hard-charging Flyers to the 1974 and 1975 Stanley Cups, playing ferocious defense and cunning offense. During his 15-year Flyer career, he proved his durability and dexterity by winning the Bill Masterton Trophy (1972), the Hart Trophy (1973, 1975, 1978), the Lester Patrick Trophy (1980) and the Frank J. Selke Trophy (1983). He also made eight All-Star games and was elected to the Hockey Hall of Fame in 1987.

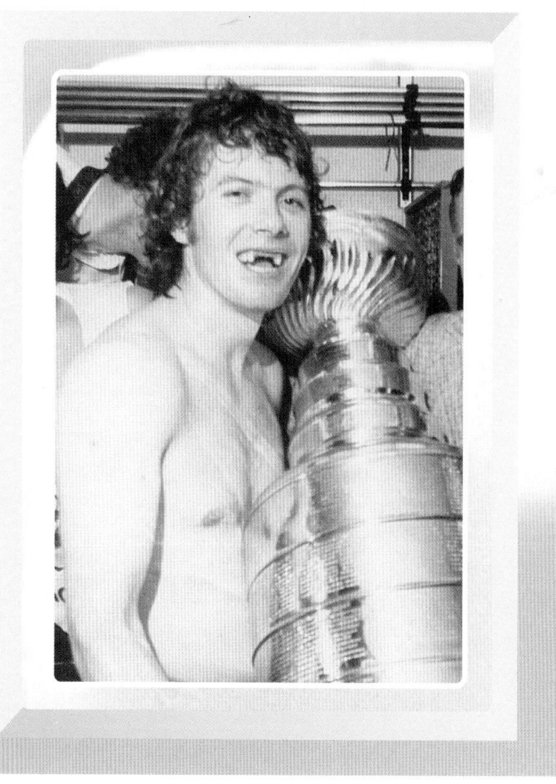

The Broad Street Bullies: A team only teammates could love.

league games," Snider said, questioning the writers' rights to criticize his team. "If they don't like our style, they don't have to come to the games." The Flyers' Dave Schultz was more creative in his description of the Flyers' over the years. "Hockey is a contact sports," Schultz said. "It's not the ice follies." Schultz still holds the single-season record for penalties with 472 in 1974-75.

It's no coincidence that that was also year the Flyers won their second straight Stanley Cup by thumping Buffalo in the finals, once again with help from an unlikely source, the singer Kate Smith. The season before, Smith's rendition of "God Bless America" (used in lieu of the "Star-Spangled Banner" to open the game) was almost as much of a crowd-pleaser as the Flyers 1-0 win in Game 6. And she returned to sing the song on the home ice of one of the most physical teams in NHL history. The 1974-75 season was also the first for two more teams: the Kansas City Scouts and the Washington Capitals, who would play in the first NHL arena to have an instant replay screen on the scoreboard. The Scouts played only two seasons before the franchise shifted to Colorado on its way to its current post in New Jersey.

But the Flyers weren't the only ones leaving scars on the game as well as on their knuckles. The St. Louis Blues and New York Rangers dropped the gloves and collected 246 penalty minutes between them, then a league record for two teams in one game. Other incidents were occurring almost daily. Chicago's Stan Mikita and Boston's Orr slashed at each other with high sticks in one game. In another, Boston's Dave Forbes was ejected and suspended for 10 games after deliberately jamming Minnesota's Henry Boucha in the face with the butt end of his stick.

It could be reasonably argued that these kinds of bloody incidents kept the league from enjoying the kind of revenue growth other professional sports leagues were seeing. While hockey has always been a big draw on Canadian television, there weren't the kind of lucrative US national television deals which funded the coffers of professional football and baseball. In 1976, the 15 American teams split $2 million in TV revenue from a limited national television deal, or roughly $135,000 a club. The Canadian teams fared better since television drew more fans in Canada, a country with one-tenth as many viewers.

Attendance was leveling off as well. During the 1971-72 regular and playoff seasons, 8.1 million people attended a combined 582 games. After a spike in the 1973-74

season, when the league expanded schedules to 80 games, it drew just 8.4 million in 1978-79 despite playing 725 games. Ironically, fans who attended games had to grow accustomed to the changes television brought to the game, including extended commercial breaks for sponsors which upset the usual rhythm and flow of the action. It was a likely combination of the ugly scenes and the lack of widespread TV exposure that kept the game from growing as much as its rivals of professional football and baseball did.

Changing Times

THERE WERE SIGNS OF CHANGE ALL OVER – SLOW CHANGE, but still transformation. The World Hockey Association, which began play in competition with the NHL on October 11, 1972, had brought teams and rules changes to their own games that increased scoring and somewhat freed up skaters. Even the 1972 Summit Series, pitting the Soviet Union's skillful national team against an overconfident Team Canada, showed the world that the fast-paced, highly disciplined European style could often skate circles around the North American's dump-and-chase-and-dig style. In addition to the third-man-in rule in 1971-72, the league decreed three seasons

TIGER IN A BOX

As the 22-year-old pugilistic enforcer of the Toronto Maple Leafs, Dave "Tiger" Williams was asked about his past. Was it true that he punched out a high school teacher he didn't like, one with horn-rimmed glasses? "That's a lie," Williams told the reporter. "He wasn't wearing horn-rimmed glasses."

TO KNOW DAVE "TIGER" Williams is to know that the colorful left winger never dodged a question and rarely dodged a fight. As one of the most recognized – and reorganized – faces in hockey during the brawling days of the 1970s, Williams was consistently among the league leaders in penalty minutes, eventually setting the NHL all-time record with 3,966 penalty minutes over his 14 pro seasons.

Fighting has always been a part of the game in varying degrees. But unlike fights in the late 1980s and 1990s between helmeted fighters, the battles of this era were more brutal, none more so than the Wayne Maki v. Ted Green incident of 1969. Maki of St. Louis clipped Boston's Green in the head, forcing skull chips into Green's brain and requiring extensive surgery and the insertion of a steel plate. And this was in an exhibition game.

So when people recount the physical 1970s, they remember them as gory but charming, turning first to the teams that won. The Philadelphia Flyers took two Stanley Cups as "the Broad Street Bullies", chief among them Dave "the Hammer" Schultz, who still holds the NHL record for most penalty minutes in a season (472). Then they point to the "Big, Bad Bruins", who checked and shoved their way to two Stanley Cups at the beginning of the decade. (For the Bruins, it didn't hurt to have Bobby Orr, either.)

But while Williams never got

Tiger Williams doing his work near the net. He never met an opponent he liked.

his name on the Stanley Cup, he did have his name etched in the police blotter, winning a different kind of fight. In an attempt to crack down on fighting in the NHL, Ontario Attorney General Roy McMurtry began bringing criminal charges of assault against visiting hockey players skating outside the rules at Maple Leaf Gardens. He had arrested six other NHL players when Williams's stick left a gash in Pittsburgh's Dennis Owchar's head that needed 22 stitches.

There was no penalty on the play and Williams maintained it was accidental, but for the first time McMurtry brought charges against a home-team player. That also brought a backlash from Canadians who enjoyed seeing visitors prosecuted but balked at charging one of their own. Williams, the last player ever arrested by McMurtry, was acquitted a year later and took it in his stride, noting that he had missed a game to be in court. "We might have won last night if I had been able to play," Williams shrugged as he left the courthouse.

With the Tiger, it was always a matter of not liking his opponents. After refusing to participate in the traditional handshake after the Flyers had eliminated Toronto in the 1977 quarterfinals for the third straight year, Williams had his sportsmanship questioned by no less than NHL President Clarence Campbell. Campbell fired off a letter to Toronto team owner Harold Ballard that was far more elegant than Williams's style of play. In it, he said, "I would hope that [Williams] could be made to appreciate that Maple Leaf players do not behave in a manner that offends their fans." You could almost hear Williams giggle and snort; the next season he earned 351 penalty minutes, the second-highest total of his career.

Despite being the poster boy for bad behavior, one of Williams's lasting marks (aside from his flattened nose) was his ability to pick his spots. At times he would goad less combative players to throw them off their games, and at other times he'd take on anyone who fancied having a piece of him.

Like the league which was trying to grow through an era marked by bloody games and bench-clearing brawls, Williams always talked about shedding the tag of being just "a goon". He did finish his career with 241 goals and 513 points, scoring a career-high 35 goals and 62 points with Vancouver in 1980-81, his only All-Star season.

But penalties were always what the Tiger did best. In 1986-87, his second-to-last season, he played in all 76 games and racked up a career-high 358 minutes in the regular season, and another 30 over five postseason games. "I want people to remember Tiger Williams as more than just a punch in the mouth," he said.

The 1977 Canadiens won most of the hardware and most of their games.

later a minor penalty for any penalized player who didn't proceed directly to the bench. And in 1976-77, any instigator of a fight was penalized with a major and game misconduct penalty, a move clearly aimed at thwarting goons.

And while fights and violence brought attention in 1974-75, seven players scored more than 100 points for the first time in league history. One of them was Orr, who would miss the opening of the next season with his fourth knee operation. Another was Lafleur, who played for a team that had traditionally favored scoring over fighting.

Bleu, blanc, et rouge is French for "blue, white, and red", the colors of the Canadiens, but they may well have been the colors of the Stanley Cup trophy itself during a good chunk of NHL history. From 1964-65 to 1978-79, Les Habitants virtually took up residence in the finals, making the championship series 11 out of 15 seasons and winning the Cup 10 times. The names of the players who lifted the Cup for Montreal read like a Hockey Hall of Fame mailing list: Beliveau, Tremblay, Richard, Mahovlich, Dryden, Robinson, Gainey and Lafleur. But while they won it in 1971 and again in 1973, the most impressive portion of this streak came with four titles between 1976 and 1979 when Lafleur and the Canadiens, coached by Scott Bowman, went 16-3 in finals games, never once being pushed to seven games.

The Canadiens of the late 1970s may have been the most dominant team in NHL history, if not in all sports for a four-year period. The team lost just three times at home and then won 12 of 13 playoff games in 1976 (4-0 in the finals against defending champion Philadelphia). And then they made just three roster changes for the next season and they got better.

In 1976-77, the Canadiens disappointed their home fans only once at the Montreal Forum, going an astonishing 33-1-6. Overall, Montreal was 60-8-12. Then the team won 12 of 14 playoff games in 1977 (4-0 in the finals against Boston) to capture the Cup.

The hockey world was noticing that skill, class and speed could be as successful as grit, brawn and intimidation.

In those four seasons, the Montreal Canadiens won four Cups, and 12 straight playoff series, losing only 10 playoff games. Their regular-season record was an incredible 229-46-45. They lost only 14 times at the Forum. The team showcased nine future Hall of Fame players and two Hall of Fame geniuses, coach Scott Bowman and general manager Sam Pollock.

Consistency breeds success; all nine of those players and the coach were there for all four Cups. Pollock retired after the 1978 Cup. Even the team trainers remained the same. And Lafleur was clearly the symbol of the times, scoring a then-record 50 goals in six straight seasons on the way to becoming the youngest player to score 400 goals and 1,000 points. A small Stanley Cup footnote: 1977 was the first year any player playing in 40 regular season games for a championship team would have his name engraved on the Stanley Cup. Previously, only playoff-eligible players were awarded that honor.

UPSTARTS START UP

All Gary Davidson wanted when he founded the upstart World Hockey Association was more hockey in North America. Instead, in seven years, the WHA wound up affecting the way professional hockey was operated by the venerable NHL forever.

ALMOST IMMEDIATELY, new teams and new money lured star players away and forced the older league to look seriously into expanding again into different cities. The biggest move occurred when the Winnipeg Jets signed the Chicago Blackhawks' fan favorite Bobby Hull in a $2.5 million long-term deal, much more than any NHL player was making at the time. Bernie Parent, a big-name goaltender, signed with the Philadephia Blazers. Others who jumped included Derek Sanderson, Ted Green and J. C. Tremblay. And later, the WHA lured Frank Mahovlich, among others.

But big signings could only sustain so much interest. The league scored a national television deal, but that disappeared after a year. You could win a lot of bar bets by asking for the seven WHA championship teams, (New England, Houston, Houston, Winnipeg, Quebec, Winnipeg, and Winnipeg) and many of the new teams suffered low attendance. NHL owners expected the league to fold easily, but it sustained itself by creating just enough new interest in the game each year. Next to convincing Hull to join the inaugural season, the WHA's biggest coup was signing Mark and Marty Howe, Gordie Howe's sons, then convincing the retired NHL great to come play with them in Houston.

But while the WHA went anywhere that would have its teams, it didn't have the kind of stability that came with the NHL's more cautious approach. Over the seven seasons, the WHA had 27 versions of teams, many moving from city to city. The Ottawa Nationals played one year in Ottawa before two in Toronto as the Toros. Then the Toros moved south of the border (far south) and became the Birmingham Bulls, Alabama's first and still only big-league team.

Bobby Hull with a new hairline and a new uniform jumped to the WHA.

By taking many shots and hoping some stuck, the WHA did encourage the NHL to scramble and stake out some territory with a second team in New York (the Islanders) and one in Atlanta (the Flames). And when the day arrived to merge, the NHL plucked four markets where the WHA had been pioneers with a good degree of success: Edmonton, Hartford, Winnipeg and Quebec. Edmonton had a then-state-of-the-art Coliseum. The WHA also had the foresight to explore markets in Denver, Calgary, Ottawa, and Phoenix; today each of these cities call themselves NHL towns, too.

Was WHA hockey as good as the NHL brand? Not quite. Already past his prime, Bobby Hull ripped up the league for 77 goals in 1974-75. Hull's teammate Anders Hedberg scored 51 goals in 49 games. But there were other contributions, the most lasting being the scouting and signing of European players. WHA teams aggressively acquired players from the European hotbeds of hockey, Sweden and Finland; and they took some risks with underage players, including a well-known but undersized center named Wayne Gretzky. Others were future NHL stars, such as Mark Messier and Mike Gartner. These moves prompted the NHL to break down and draft younger. too. And there were wild times including one game between Indianapolis and Cleveland in

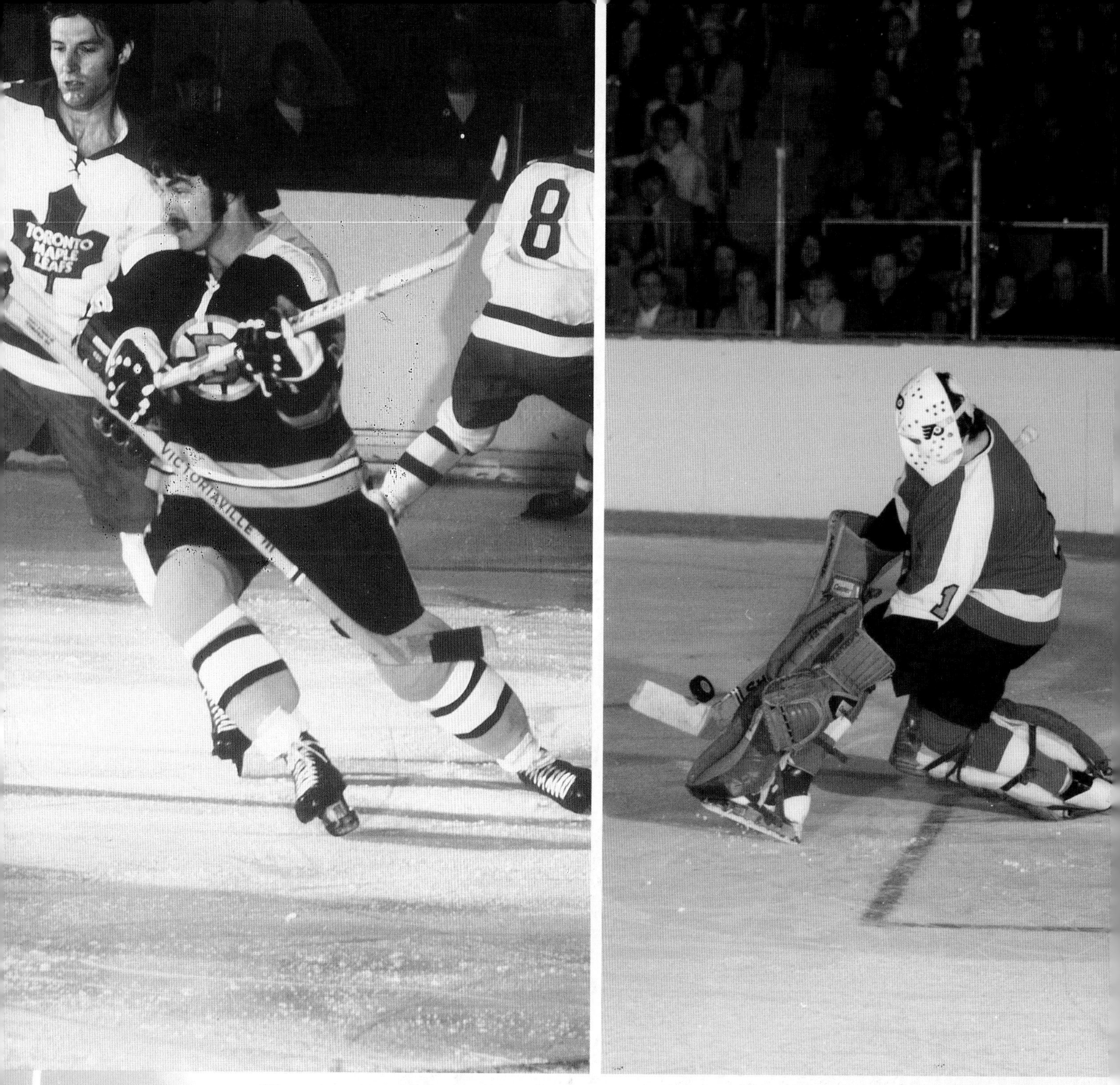

Other successes of WHA recruiting efforts were Derek Sanderson (left) and Bernie Parent.

which the coaches duked it out during an on-ice brawl.

In 1973 there was a secret plan to merge the two leagues, the WHA looking to capitalize on the NHL's shock that the WHA had survived and the NHL looking to attract more money. But the pact failed. In 1978, there was a plan to merge six WHA teams with the NHL for a $2.9 million entry fee per team, but those plans fell through when a group of owners killed the deal. However, the following year, WHA president Howard Baldwin, Philadelphia Flyers owner Ed Snider, and NHL president John Ziegler realized the financial losses for both sides were too great to go on. The four strongest WHA teams joined the league, thus ending the war and creating a 21-team NHL which lasted until the moves to the US Sun Belt more than a decade later.

A Genius of a Coach

IN THAT CASE, CALL SCOTT BOWMAN A PROFESSIONAL engraver. Much of the Canadiens' success can be attributed to the Montreal coach who had grown up with the game as a junior coach and an NHL assistant in Montreal.

Having led St. Louis to three Stanley Cup finals, he took over the Canadiens in 1971 and burned his discipline into this well-drilled team. Bowman, who boosted his total to eight Stanley Cups with stints in Pittsburgh and Detroit, was often despised by his players. Still, they knew enough to realize they needed to follow Bowman's theory of moving the puck to the open man. "The reason they were so good was because they were so unselfish," Bowman recalled years later.

Scott Bowman early in his coaching career.

And so they were again in 1978, when the Canadiens won 12 of 15 playoff games, including a 4-2 series win in the finals against Boston. The biggest potential barrier to the Canadiens' continued reign seemed to lurk off the ice, as team owners Edward and Peter Bronfman sold the team for $20 million to the Molson family, owners of Canada's popular brewery. Sam Pollock, the construction chief credited with building the Montreal dynasties, retired, and the team seemed to be aging. Still, Montreal tasted the title once more before the close of the decade. Then the end of their reign came all at once. Dryden, Jacques Lemaire and Yvan Cournoyer each retired, and Bowman, miffed at being passed over for Pollock's job, left for Buffalo.

Montreal took the headlines, but there were more subtle changes which made the league look much different from the way it had in the 1960s, an era lovingly referred to by hockey fans as "old-time hockey". During the 1970s the Toronto Maple Leafs began a slide which depleted the once-proud organization of talent and stability and left them floundering for most of the decade. The Leafs still had stars in the 1970s, such as Darryl Sittler and Lanny McDonald, but the days of competing for the Cup seemed over. When Bobby Hull jumped to the WHA's Winnipeg Jets, Chicago lost its main drawing card and felt its Original Six pride bruised. The Kansas City franchise moved in 1976 to Denver, where they would be known as the Colorado Rockies before moving once more in the 1980s. The Kansas City shift was the first franchise relocation since 1934, when the Ottawa Senators became the St. Louis Eagles on their way to becoming defunct. The Scouts' move signaled some changing demographics as well as some flawed ownership. That same year, the California Golden Seals jumped to become the Cleveland Barons, and in 1979 financial burdens forced the team to merge its roster with the Minnesota North Stars. With the WHA in a state of flux each season, six of the teams applied for entry into the NHL but were turned down. Three others – Phoenix, Calgary, and San Diego – folded just one season after Denver and the Minnesota Fighting Saints had collapsed as well. At one point, there were as many as 32 teams in both the NHL and WHA, depleting the talent pool and playing less-than-perfect hockey.

THE TEN-POINT GAME

When Toronto team captain Darryl Sittler scored an NHL-record 10 points against the Boston Bruins on February 7, 1976, he was asked if he had done anything out of the ordinary the day before to get ready for the game.

NO SPECIAL MEALS, HE said, no special practices, no special superstitions. "Well, my son fell in the mud while I was babysitting him," he told reporters afterward. "Other than that, nothing different."

The talented Maple Leafs center played a once-in-a-lifetime game which hockey players only dream about, as he scored six goals and four assists in a 11-4 win against the Boston Bruins, staking his place in hockey lore and driving a rookie goalie from the NHL all at once. It is still the most points any NHL player has scored in a game (10 others have scored 8) and it is still talked about on rinks throughout North America.

And never mind the shoddy babysitting. There were no indicators that Sittler was set to go off either. Coached by the animated Don Cherry, the Bruins were riding a seven-game winning streak heading into Maple Leaf Gardens. Sittler, having been publicly scolded by Maple Leafs owner Harold Ballard, had just one point in his previous eight games.

Against Boston, he dominated every period. He had two assists in the first period as Toronto went ahead 2-1. The first was a long pass threaded right to the stick of teammate and friend Lanny McDonald. In the second period, he would have what many would consider a great game: three goals and two assists to teammate Borje Salming. But he was not done. He would score another hat trick in the final period. The ninth point, a 40-ft wrist shot, broke the existing record held by several players, including Maurice Richard. The tenth seemed like fate.

"Look at my face on the tenth point when I tried to pass in front and it hit (Boston's) Brad Park's skate and went in," Sittler recalls. "The smile and the shrug say it all."

Sittler: the only man to reach double figures in a game.

Playing against Minnesota the night following the 10-point game, Sittler had one assist and one shot which glanced off the post. Hockey is like that. Still, the 10 points turned out to be 10 percent of the 100 points he would score for the entire season, one that included two more stunning outings for the Kitchener, Ontario, native. He tied a league record with five goals in one playoff game against Philadelphia, then scored the overtime winner in the Canada Cup series later that autumn.

But for every hero, there seems to be a victim. Dave Reece, a rookie goaltender for the Bruins, let in every one of the goals that fateful February 7 night. With veteran goaltender Gerry Cheevers back from the World Hockey Association, this would be the rookie's fourteenth and final NHL game. Reece, who would toil in the minors before retiring, learned to joke about the game that left him with the nickname "the Human Sieve". He told one writer who called on the anniversary of the game that Sittler's terrifying scoring streak didn't leave any scars. "I wake up in the middle of the night screaming," Reece said, "but it's not that bad."

Sittler wound up a little bit better off than that. Elected to the Hall of Fame in 1989, he scored at least 36 goals in eight of his 12 Toronto seasons to become Toronto's all-time scorer with 389 goals and 916 points. For his career, he amassed 484 goals and 1,121 points.

LIKE HIS 6-FT 4-IN, 225-LB FRAME, EVERYTHING Robinson did seemed to be big. Teamed with future Hall of Famers Serge Savard and Guy Lapointe on defense, he helped Montreal to six Stanley Cups in 14 seasons and eventually made the playoffs in an NHL-record 20 straight seasons. His 227 playoff games rank him second on the all-time list as well. Dubbed "Big Bird" for his size and curly hair and supposed resemblance to the Sesame Street character, Robinson's agility and defensive prowess earned him two Norris Trophies (1977, 1980), but it is his control and restraint which made him one of the best defensemen ever to play the game. Despite playing in an era of defenders raised to brawl and instigate fights, he never posted more than 76 penalty minutes in any season. He was elected to the Hockey Hall of Fame in 1995.

LARRY **ROBINSON**

Breaking Records

PLAYERS OTHER THAN THE CANADIENS MAY NOT HAVE BEEN winning titles, but they were still making their marks. Ian Turnbull set an NHL record for defensemen with his five goals in a 9-1 win over Detroit in 1977, carrying the torch that had been passed by Orr. Having played his final full season in 1975, the one-time Boston hero limped through three more years with Chicago before retiring in 1979. Even goaltenders were getting into the action. New York's Billy Smith became the first goaltender to be credited with a goal when he was the last Islanders player to touch the puck before Colorado's Rob Ramage put it into his own empty net on November 28, 1979. Smith was already well known for his combativeness, earning the nickname "Battling Billy" and amassing 54 penalty minutes in 1978-79. One player saw more hockey than anyone, as Doug Jarvis played his first NHL game for Montreal on October 8, 1975, to begin an NHL-record streak of 964 games over 12 seasons. Jarvis never missed a game during his entire career.

And the evolution of the hockey stick continued with simplicity being overtaken by customization. During the 1970s, rules would allow the stick to shrink to 2 inches from 2½ inches. The curve of the blade, which allows players to lift the puck more easily on a shot, was restricted and set at 1 in. Standard-issue sticks had become personal items and carpentry tools used to shave the sticks down became a staple in any equipment trainer's domain.

But with all the domination of the Canadiens, and with all the intimidation of the Bruins and Flyers, and with all the infiltration of new hockey cities, no event from the 1970s will be as well recalled as one that happened in the last weeks of the decade. The 1970s ended with a turbulent drama which evolved into the opening act for another era.

While the New York Islanders were preparing to begin a run that would equal Montreal's reign of four Stanley Cups, Wayne Gretzky was taking to the ice and shuffling his skates as a nervous teenager in Chicago Stadium on October 10, 1979. The most prolific scoring career in the history of the NHL would start quietly enough as Gretzky passed the puck to teammate Brett Callighen, who then fed Kevin Lowe for one of the Oilers' goals and Gretzky's first assist. Edmonton lost 4-2, but the new teams and added games brought more than 3 million more fans to the NHL arena. The Great One's many surprises had only just begun.

TOO MANY MEN

Near the end of the raucous 1970s, the league's history added another wonderful little tale about a team which, in one sense, tried too hard.

THE FACT THAT THE CRUCIAL point of the story wasn't caught on tape just adds to the luster of the telling of the tale. The game in which it occurred illustrates two different playing styles facing off for the last time in this decade.

It happened to Boston in the semifinals of the 1979 Stanley Cup playoffs, during the Bruins' attempt to return to the championship glory of the early 1970s. Leading 4-3 in the third period against the three-time and defending champion Montreal, the Bruins were whistled for having too many men on the ice. Montreal scored on the power play and then took the victory in overtime.

"It was my fault," Boston coach Don Cherry said.

"I was numb, not mad," Boston defenseman Brad Park recalled years later. "It wasn't until two days later that I started to rehash what happened, why it had happened."

"I've never seen a team try so hard, give so much, come so close and not get a victory," Boston goaltender Gerry Cheevers said on the night that Montreal's Guy Lafleur made the most of good fortune and banked it off the post to swing the game's momentum back to the champions. Soon after, Boston – the hockey team and the city – openly wept.

Pairing the elusive Canadiens against the gritty Bruins was also a match between two very different styles of play. In the 1970s, an earlier incarnation of the Bruins and then the Philadelphia Flyers used intimidation and brawn to bull their way to championships. In contrast, Montreal had earned its reputation (and five titles since 1970) as a skillful and elusive team, one that could move the puck at will and pluck the opponents' puck at any time.

Both styles were entertaining and endeared each team to its city and its fans. Montreal's players were perceived as dashing figures, marquee players who drew as much attention as Hollywood movie stars at a time when athletes were becoming national celebrities.

The 1978-79 version of the Bruins was seen as a group of entertaining, working-class grunts, throwbacks to the days when the "Big, Bad Bruins" helped start the trend of winning hockey through intimidation. The year after losing this game to Montreal, three Bruins would receive severe suspensions for going after fans harassing them from the stands. Part of the continuing trouble stemmed from the league's sluggish attempt to curb the violence that marred games early in the decade, forcing star player Marcel Dionne to say, "If the owners don't clean up this sport, I'll quit. What's the league waiting for, somebody to die out there?"

Before the 1975-76 season, the league mandated that only team captains could discuss a ruling with an official, a move which curtailed some of the constant bickering and stalling that slowed the game. The next season the NHL adopted the third-man-in rule, which would eject from the game any player interfering in an ongoing fight between two other players. It was the first real admission that fighting was a problem.

For most of the seventh game of that 1979 Montreal-Boston semifinal series it seemed as if Boston's over-achieving "Lunch Pail Gang" would pull off the upset for their first win in Montreal in nine tries. Using tight checking to bottle up Lafleur and Co., Boston led 3-1 in the third period when Guy Lapointe beat goaltender Gilles Gilbert to cut the score to 3-2. Boston's Rick Middleton silenced the Forum with a goal to put the Bruins up 4-3 with 3 minutes 59 seconds to play, but in the rush to clamp down on the Canadiens' potent attack for the remaining minutes, too many Bruins hopped onto the ice. The violation actually went unnoticed for several seconds before linesman John D'Amico made the call. Lafleur scored on the ensuing power play and Boston, rattled by the error, saw Yvon Lambert redirect a pass just past Park to net the winner for Montreal.

Don Cherry says people would approach him for years afterward to say that penalty cost them small side bets. "I answered, 'Gee, I really feel sorry for you. When we lost that game, it cost me my job.'" But hockey teams can be awfully close-knit groups of men, and Cherry had a team that loved to stick together. The penalty itself was away from the puck and thus was not captured by the unforgiving eye of the main television camera; using multiple camera angles to track every movement on the ice and the bench was still years away. Cherry knows who committed the penalty, but vows never to tell any one. "When guys on that team get together for beers," Cherry said, "they never talk about it. It's just too painful."

Giving Guy Lafleur (opposite) a power-play chance helped end the Bruins' chances.

A European Invasion

The Iron Curtain was still fully draped in the summer of 1980, when the greatest player in Czechoslovakia made a daring break for freedom – and the NHL. In a scene befitting *Mission: Impossible*, 23-year-old Peter Stastny, along with his pregnant wife and younger brother, Anton, were whisked out of the country.

Opposite page: Peter Stastny broke through the Iron Curtain and the exodus began.

UNDER THE GUISE OF A SCOUTING TRIP – AND THE COVER of darkness – Quebec Nordiques owner Marcel Aubut and chief scout Gilles Leger aided the Stastnys in their flight. As with any spy thriller, there were anxious moments: the brothers became temporarily separated in Innsbruck in Austria, before boarding a plane for Amsterdam en route to their final destination: Canada.

The covert operation made international headlines at the time, as did other news involving Peter Stastny over the years. And some 18 years later he made more news, when he was inducted into the Hockey Hall of Fame. "I didn't hesitate when I got the chance to play in the NHL," Stastny said. "I wanted to have the challenge to compete against the best players in the world."

Not only did Stastny compete, he thrived, finishing the 1980s as the NHL's second leading scorer, behind Wayne Gretzky.

A year after arriving in Quebec City – a season that saw Peter Stastny win the Calder Trophy – the brothers raised about $30,000 to pay for bribes to get their older brother, Marian, out of Czechoslovakia. The trio played together with the Nordiques, even on the same line, for the 1984-85 season, after which Marian Stastny signed with the Toronto Maple Leafs as a free agent.

Europeans playing in the NHL were nothing new in 1980 – the first one dates to the 1940s – but their appearances were rare. And the defections of the Stastny brothers contributed to the first mass wave of Europeans (via defections or otherwise) to head to the NHL. The World Hockey Association's seven-year run in the 1970s started the flow of Europeans to North America, with the prime sources being Finland and Sweden.

As the 1990s end, the NHL has more of a European flavor than at any time previously, not only because players from throughout the continent appear on team rosters, but also because the style of play has taken on more of a European tone.

And today, Europeans are among the best players in the league, with a pair of Czechs, Buffalo Sabres goaltender Dominik Hasek and Pittsburgh Penguins right wing Jaromir Jagr, considered the best players in the NHL.

Borje Salming of Sweden became the first European to star in the league, beginning by playing with the Toronto Maple Leafs in the 1973-74 season and ending with the Detroit Red Wings in 1989-90. At first, Salming was a target of other players – physically and verbally – because of his heritage. Canadians believed Europeans played a 'softer' brand of hockey – many still believe that – but Salming proved himself. Three times he was an All-Star and twice the runner-up for the Norris Trophy. His career culminated with his entry into the Hall of Fame in 1996.

The first team to tap into European talent in earnest was the Winnipeg Jets of the World Hockey Association. The Jets made a splash in 1974 when they signed star Swedes Anders Hedberg and Ulf Nilsson, who then played alongside an NHL defector, Bobby Hull, who was born in Ontario. After winning two Avco Cups with Winnipeg, Hedberg and Nilsson signed with the New

GLENN **ANDERSON**

ANDERSON WAS A MAINSTAY DURING THE Oilers dynasty of the 1980s, winning five Stanley Cups before capturing a sixth with the New York Rangers in 1993-94. He totaled 498 goals and 601 assists and is among the all-time leaders with 93 playoff goals. He played for the Canadian Olympic team in 1980, in the 1984 and 1987 Canada Cups, and in Rendez-Vous 1987.

HE DID IT HIS WAY

Viacheslav Fetisov of the Soviet Union was among the world's great defensemen in the 1980s, able to take out the finest of onrushing forwards with a thundering check.

BUT ONE BY ONE, SOME OF Europe's top players began to pass him by. These players, however, weren't eluding Fetisov on the ice; they were defecting from their countries to get to the NHL, leaving Fetisov behind.

Fetisov could have defected himself, but he chose to do something most hockey players would not have done. He chose to stay in the Soviet Union. He chose to challenge the Communist party to change the system. He chose to fight for his freedom. He chose the path of most resistance.

"I want to open doors for others – not just hockey players," Fetisov said. And he did. But not before he was nearly given a one-way ticket to Siberia.

Fetisov finally arrived in the NHL with the New Jersey Devils in the summer of 1989, by which time he had become one of the Soviets' all-time greats. By the age of 24, he was captain of the Central Red Army. Seven years later, he was an NHL rookie.

Fetisov played six seasons in New Jersey, but was traded to the Detroit Red Wings just two months before the Devils won the Stanley Cup – by sweeping the Wings. Fetisov and Detroit would get their Cup two years later, and another the year after that. Those titles capped a career which long ago had overflowed with honors, both team and individual.

The Stanley Cup was a just reward for Viacheslav Fetisov.

Beginning as a 17-year-old in 1975-76, Fetisov played 13 seasons with the Red Army club, which won the league title during every one of his final 12 years there. He was a First-Team All-Star nine times and he was twice player of the year. Three times he won the Gold Stick Award as Europe's top player. His teams won gold medals at seven World Championships, two Olympics and one Canada Cup. He was one of the select Soviet "Honored Masters of Sport" and, because of his hockey exploits, a major in the Red Army.

A man with such a résumé in the Free World would have had wealth and fame beyond imagination. Fetisov had only the fame. He lived in a barracks outside Moscow for 11 months a year, sharing a room with another player and spending more time with his teammates than his girlfriend Ladlena (now his wife). The barracks were fenced in, with soldiers patrolling the one exit – like being a prisoner.

"No, worse," Fetisov said. "Sometimes prisoners get out. This was total control. When you're 18, you're so ambitious you don't care about much else, just hockey. You live in barracks all year, it's OK. But later, you see life is too short to be a robot."

Players in the Eastern Bloc were defecting, beginning with the Stastny brothers, in 1980. Politically, ever so slowly, things began to change. Glasnost came into being. Early in 1988, Fetisov was awarded the highest honor that can be bestowed upon a Soviet citizen, the Order of Lenin. At that time, military leaders told him that he soon would be free to leave the Soviet Union, and thus join the NHL.

Fetisov had been drafted by the Montreal Canadiens way back in 1978, then went back into the draft and was picked by New Jersey in 1983. The Devils had given him an opportunity to defect in early 1989, when the Red Army team was in the United States playing NHL clubs. But Fetisov chose to go home, to gain his freedom his way.

The promises of the military leaders, however, were empty. So, just a couple of weeks after deciding not to defect when in the United States, he declared that he would no longer play for the Red Army. Fetisov and his wife were threatened with banishment to Siberia. His coach, the famous hockey czar Viktor Tikhonov, called him a traitor. Some of his teammates believed it. But three months after he left the team, Igor Larionov – who later would play with Fetisov in Detroit – led a bunch of players who went on television before the World Championships and said that if Fetisov didn't play, they wouldn't either. Fetisov played.

Still, he was not free to go. It was long believed that it was unconstitutional for Soviet soldiers to sign contracts. Fetisov hired lawyers who proved the constitution had no such restrictions. Mikhail Gorbachev, knowing the West was watching to see if he would be true to his vow for reform, let the Fetisovs leave. They boarded a flight for New York. "Until the plane took off," Fetisov said years later, "I didn't believe it would happen."

York Rangers in 1978, with their contracts generating the most noise: two-year deals worth $1 million apiece.

Another Swede, Pelle Lindbergh, was among the top goaltenders in the world in the early 1980s and the first from Europe to thrive in the NHL. A junior star at home before signing with the Philadelphia Flyers in 1981, Lindbergh won the Vezina Trophy in 1984-85 and took the Flyers to the Stanley Cup finals that season. But soon after, on November 10, 1985, he was killed when he drove his car off the road.

For a long time, for obvious reasons, it was easier for players in the Nordic countries, as opposed to those in Eastern Bloc nations, to jump to the NHL. But players from countries under Soviet influence were still being drafted, and they did trickle across the Atlantic. Czech Michal Pivonka defected to join the Washington Capitals in 1986 and Alexander Mogilny defected after leading the Soviet Union to the World Junior Championship in 1989, signing with the Sabres.

The dominant team of the 1980s, and one of the greatest the NHL has ever seen, was the Edmonton Oilers. The Oilers won the Stanley Cup five times in seven seasons: 1984, '85, '87 and '88 with Gretzky (and again in 1990, after Gretzky had been traded to the Los Angeles Kings). While other teams, the Montreal Canadiens, most notably, had great success over a longer period, the Oilers of the 1980s had dominant players at each position whose careers stretched well into the 1990s, long after each had left Edmonton.

A Legend in His Own Lifetime

Yes, the Oilers had the game's greatest player in Gretzky – and a number of other Hall of Famers-to-be, most notably Mark Messier – but they also played a style of hockey not seen before in the NHL. It was breakneck offense, accentuating skating and the need for open ice. It was a style which Oilers coach Glen Sather had first witnessed watching midget hockey in Finland and Sweden in the 1970s, when Edmonton was still in the WHA.

"They were teaching kids the fundamentals of the game," Sather said. "But they were also teaching them about switching lanes and creating open ice."

Sather sought supreme skaters who could play that style, including the greatest scoring defenseman of all time, Paul Coffey, and a bevy of Europeans, including

Jari Kurri and Esa Tikkanen lift the Cup (left); Mark Messier as a young and successful Oiler.

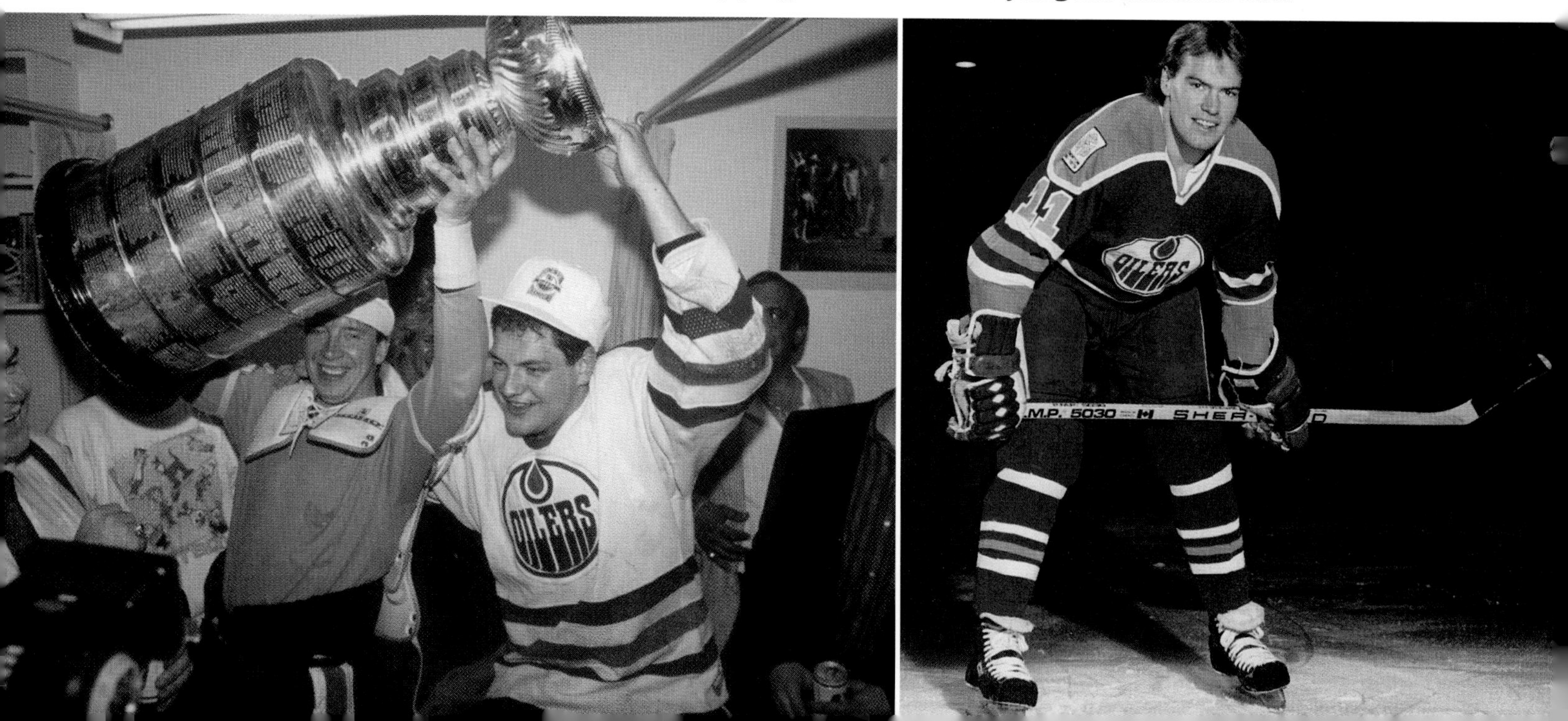

BRENT **ASHTON**

ASHTON, A LEFT WING, HAD A MORE THAN adequate NHL career, playing in nearly 1,000 games (998) while scoring 284 goals and 629 points. The fact that he did it with eight teams after being traded an NHL-record eight times makes him noteworthy. Ashton began play with Vancouver in 1979-80 and was traded in 1981 to Winnipeg, for whom he didn't play before being dealt to the Colorado Rockies (also in 1981), and then to Minnesota (1983), Quebec (1984), Detroit (1987), Winnipeg again (1988), Boston (1991) and Calgary (1993). He left the NHL after the 1992-93 season.

Finland's Jari Kurri and Esa Tikkanen. Kurri is the NHL's all-time leading scorer among Europeans, with 1,398 points; Peter Stastny is second, with 1,239.

The centerpiece of the Oilers was Gretzky. Sather needed creativity to play the European style, and said, "I knew he was probably the most creative player who had skated in the NHL. He had tremendous peripheral vision."

Gretzky totaled 46 goals and 110 points in his first pro season, in the WHA in 1978-79. Gretzky did not turn 18 until January 26, 1979. Then the Oilers and three other WHA clubs were absorbed into the NHL, and many people in the established league salivated at the thought of "The Great Gretzky" coming to strut his stuff with the big boys.

"Everywhere I went they thought I'd get killed because of my size," said Gretzky, who was 5 ft 11 in and 170 lbs at the time, when he was still only 18. "I heard a lot of talk then that I'd never get 110 points like I did in the WHA."

The critics were partly right – it took Gretzky 13 sea-

DINO **CICCARELLI**

NEVER DRAFTED BECAUSE OF A KNEE INJURY which threatened his career before it had even begun, Ciccarelli is one of nine players to score 600 goals, finishing the 1998-99 season with 608. He scored a rookie-record 14 playoff goals in leading the North Stars to the Cup finals in 1981. He also played for Washington, Detroit (reaching the finals again in 1995), Tampa Bay and Florida. Most of Ciccarelli's goals were the result of his persistence around the net, a persistence that cost him hundreds of facial stitches and numerous injuries.

MIRACLES DID HAPPEN

It was soon after the 1980 US Olympic team had beaten the vaunted Soviet Union – to this day, it is no less stunning that *the Americans beat the Soviets at hockey*.

US CAPTAIN MIKE Eruzione said: "Right now, I'm a little confused. Everything happened so fast. I don't think you can put into words what this means. But I know this, we can't forget we've got one game left. I'll be dammed if I'll let them get lazy now. We're one more day away from a dream."

Or, what has become more commonplace in US sports vernacular, a miracle.

Before a patriotic and frenzied crowd in Lake Placid, NY, the Americans followed up their 4-3 stunner over the Soviets two days later, on February 24, with a gold-medal-winning 4-2 win over Finland. Talk about Super Sunday.

This was a group of kids which came together six months earlier and was charged with battling veteran-laden powerhouse nations. And, less than two weeks before the 13th Winter Olympics commenced, it didn't look good. That's when Team USA was thumped 10-3 by the Soviets in New York.

The Americans were seeded seventh in the 12-team tournament, and right off the bat had to face a tough Swedish team in their opener. But they tied with Sweden with 27 seconds left, then surprised gold-medal contender Czechoslovakia 7-3 and were 4-0-1 when they ran into a rematch with the Soviets.

Team USA had won Olympic gold in 1960 but virtually nothing since. The Soviet Union had won virtually everything since then, including 21 straight Olympic matches and all four gold medals.

Somehow, coach Herb Brooks saw it fit to tell his players before the game that "the moment is yours".

Down 2-1, the Americans tied the score with a goal from Mark Johnson with one second left in the first period, after which the Soviets made a curious move, substituting Vladimir Myshkin for their star goaltender, Vladislav Tretiak.

The Soviets took a 3-2 lead into the third period, on Alesandr Maltsev's goal at two minutes 18 seconds of the second, before Johnson evened things again on a power play at eight minutes 39 seconds of the third. Eighty-one seconds later, the unbelievable occurred when Eruzione connected for the eventual winner. (Eruzione means "eruption" in Italian and in the stands his father said, "I almost slapped my wife off her chair.")

But there were still 10 minutes to go, and the Soviets were in control everywhere except on the scoreboard.

"I stressed we must stay with our system and our tactics," Brooks said. "I've seen too many teams back off from the Soviets. We were getting kind of antsy, we started to dump the puck, we were starting to panic, and we had to calm them down."

Goaltender Jim Craig, who will always be remembered for being draped in the American flag following the gold-medal victory, was a wall down the stretch, in all facing 39 Soviet shots (the Americans managed only 16).

Said Brooks: "Craig told me yesterday, 'You wait, wait till tomorrow, coach. You haven't seen it.'"

In large part because of Craig, there was a tomorrow for the Americans, who went on to battle Finland. They trailed in that game as well, by 2-1 entering the final period.

During the intermission, all Brooks told his players, according to defenseman Mike Ramsey was, "We've been a third-period team all year. He just said, 'Suck it up and do what you've done all year.' We knew that, and we did it."

Just 25 seconds in, Phil Verchota tied the score. Then at six minutes five seconds, Johnson assisted on Rob McClanahan's goal. For good measure, Johnson connected shorthanded with three minutes to go, and the gold medal was secured.

"If anybody in here is surprised we won the gold, let me know," Craig said. "Every time it was big, we played like 20-year veterans."

Actually, the whole world was surprised, from the 8,000 flag-waving fans chanting, "We want gold, we want gold" during the game, to Vice President Walter Mondale, who congratulated the victors personally after the game, to President Jimmy Carter, who did likewise on the telephone, to the Team USA players themselves.

"This is the team of destiny; you can't explain what's happened here," said defenseman Bill Baker. "It just happened."

Mike Eruzione (center) scored the goal and waved the flag at Lake Placid.

WHERE THEY WENT

There were 20 players on Team USA and 13 went on to play in the NHL, with widely varied success.

THE SQUAD'S BIGGEST stars were defenseman Mike Eruzione and goaltender Jim Craig. Eruzione retired after the Games, believing nothing could match the Olympics. Craig spent three lackluster seasons in the NHL. On the flip side were forwards Neal Broten, Mark Johnson, Mark Pavelich and Dave Silk, and defensemen Dave Christian, Ken Morrow, Jack O'Callahan and Mike Ramsey, all of whom played at least seven NHL seasons.

"The moment is yours," Coach Herb Brooks said.

Broten may have had the most success individually, scoring 105 points for Minnesota in 1985-86. He won a Stanley Cup with New Jersey late in his 17-year career. Morrow went right from the Olympics to the New York Islanders and promptly contributed to their four consecutive Stanley Cups. Ramsey played 17 seasons, mostly with Buffalo. Johnson played 11 seasons. His father, Bob, who coached the 1976 Olympic team, coached Pittsburgh to a Stanley Cup.

As for the 1980 coaches, Herb Brooks coached the New York Rangers and New Jersey in the NHL and even coached the French Olympic team in 1998. Craig Patrick, his assistant on Team USA, was coach and general manager of the Rangers and now is general manager of the Penguins.

JARI **KURRI**

THE FINN IS THE HIGHEST-SCORING EUROPEAN player in NHL history – the longtime Oilers standout totaled 1,398 points and 601 goals. Kurri was an eight-time All-Star and won five Stanley Cups with Edmonton. He was traded to Los Angeles in 1991 and went to the finals again with former teammate Wayne Gretzky and the Kings in 1993.

sons before he scored as *few* as 110 points. In 1979-80, 137 points later, Gretzky tied with Marcel Dionne for first place in the league's 1979-80 scoring race as a rookie. Gretzky won the first of his nine Hart Trophies that season. He then won the next seven scoring titles, setting standards which may never be reached again: 92 goals in 1981-82, and 163 assists and 215 points in 1985-86.

But despite the individual glory for Gretzky, his arrival into the NHL coincided with the arrival of another one of the great teams of all time, one that certainly kept the Oilers from at least one more Cup. The New York Islanders won the first of their four successive Stanley Cups in 1979-80, making the Oilers the victims in their final championship in 1982-83. In that series, Gretzky, who after winning his third Cup had already won three Art Ross Trophies and four Hart Trophies in his four NHL seasons, was limited to four assists as New York swept Edmonton.

But the Oilers were not disheartened by that sweep. In fact, Gretzky opened the next season by scoring in 51 straight games (yes, another record), reaching 61 goals and 153 points by January 27, 1984, the last game of the streak. That season, he and his teammates never let up, trouncing the Islanders in five games in a finals rematch, going 15-4 in the postseason.

"We've matured together," Gretzky, by then 23, said of the Oilers, among them Conn Smythe winner Messier, star goaltender Grant Fuhr, Coffey and Kurri. "Most of us are pretty young guys. Now that we've made the breakthrough, the best is yet to come." Indeed.

In 1984-85, Edmonton won again, with Gretzky adding the Conn Smythe to his trophy collection, after dispatching the Lindbergh-led Flyers in another five-game finals. But while Gretzky kept tacking on the honors – he notched his 1,000th NHL point in his 424th game to shatter the mark that Guy Lafleur needed 720 games to set – some new competition arrived: a hotshot who had broken all of Lafleur's Quebec Major Junior Hockey League records, Mario Lemieux. Lemieux scored 100 points for the Pittsburgh Penguins in winning the Calder Trophy and he began to bring the Penguins franchise back from its expected demise.

Also that season, the Capitals' Bobby Carpenter – dubbed "The Can't Miss Kid" on a cover of ***Sports Illustrated*** magazine and drafted third overall out of St. John's Prep in Massachusetts – became the first US-born 50-goal scorer, connecting for 53 in his fourth NHL season, at the age of 21. "This is a remarkable achievement for a guy who has come out of high school and really had to grow up in the best league in the world," Washington Coach Bryan Murray said. Carpenter, however, would never score as many as 30 goals again, although he had a more than respectable career which continued to the end of the 1990s with the New Jersey Devils.

On the night Gretzky scored his 1,000th point, December 19, 1984, the Sabres' Scotty Bowman won his 691st regular-season game in a coaching career with St. Louis, Buffalo and Montreal, supplanting Dick Irvin in the record book as the all-time leader.

THE SUTTER **BROTHERS**

Duane, Ron and Darryl Sutter.

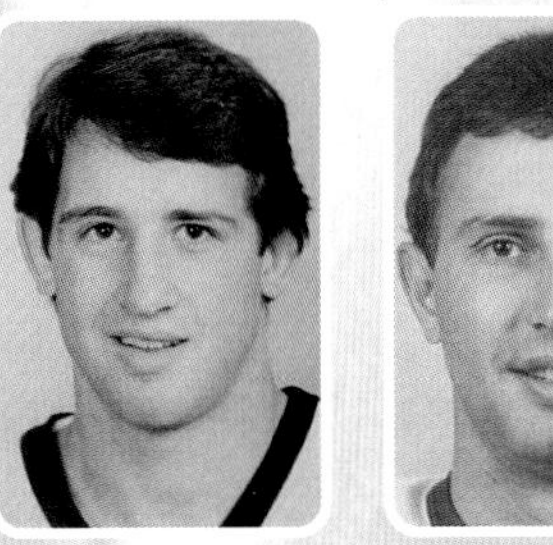

Rich, Brent and Brian Sutter.

THERE WERE SIX IN ALL, WITH BRIAN Sutter the first to play in the NHL, in 1976-77. The others were Darryl, Duane, Brent, Rich and Ron. Brent and Duane were part of the Islanders dynasty, with Brent winning three Cups and Duane four. Brent had the most successful playing career of the sextet, scoring 363 goals and 829 points. Brian and Darryl also coached in the NHL. On October 30, 1983, four of them played in the same game, with Brent and Duane skating for the Islanders and twins Ron and Rich, who were rookies, skating for the Flyers.

GRANT **FUHR**

FUHR WAS IN GOAL FOR THE FIRST four Oilers' Cups, winning the Vezina Trophy in 1988. He also played for Toronto, Buffalo, Los Angeles and St. Louis, for which he set an NHL record for games by a goaltender in a season, 79, in 1995-96. He was the first black player to take on a superstar's mantle in the NHL.

THE HARD WAY

There are so many ways to score goals. Shooting forehand, shooting backhand. From the crease, from the blue line. While on a power play, while shorthanded. Off a defender, off a post. Between a goaltender's legs, over his shoulder.

THROUGH THE COURSE OF NHL history, goals have been scored every way imaginable, and in many ways unimaginable. But, before December 31, 1988, never had so many been scored in so many ways by one man on one night.

With the new year lurking, Mario Lemieux did something that not only had not been done before, but few if any people had ever even considered occurring: He scored at even strength, shorthanded, on a power play, on a penalty shot and into an empty net.

The New Jersey Devils became part of the answer to a trivia question after Lemieux accomplished the improbable against them in the Pittsburgh Penguins' 8-6 win at Civic Arena.

Of course, just scoring five goals is enough of a rarity. It's been accomplished less than 30 times in NHL annals. Lemieux has done it twice.

In the first period that night, it certainly looked as if Lemieux could score five, or maybe even more. He connected early, four minutes 17 seconds into the game, against Devils goaltender Bob Sauve. This one came at even strength. A tad later, at seven minutes 50 seconds, he beat Sauve shorthanded. Then he did it again at 10 minutes 59 seconds, this time on a power play. If Lemieux had stopped there, it would've been quite a game: a hat trick with each goal scored a different way.

In the second period, with Chris Terreri now in goal for the beleaguered Sauve, Lemieux was awarded a penalty shot. Could there be anything more unfair to a goaltender than Lemieux with a penalty shot? It was no contest, and at 11 minutes 14 seconds of the period, Lemieux had a fourth different type of goal.

Lemieux was held in check until the very end. With the Penguins holding a 7-6 advantage, the Devils pulled their goalie and Lemieux scored into an empty net, with just one second remaining in the game. "He put the puck through his legs, he made some twirls. The things he did out there were amazing," said Rob Brown, who assisted on Lemieux's first goal. And, by the way, Lemieux assisted on the three Penguins goals he didn't score, giving him his second eight-point game of the season. He went on to win the scoring title for the second successive time, with 199 points (85 goals, 114 assists).

Lemieux, who at the time was 23 and much more shy than he is today, chalked up his historic effort simply to being fresh because he had been excused from practice the day before.

People have called Lemieux's five-goal performance hockey's equivalent to hitting for the cycle. But that doesn't do it justice. A better baseball analogy might be hitting four home runs: one with the bases empty, a two-run shot, a three-run drive and a grand slam. And, no, it's never been done.

DENIS **POTVIN**

THE CAPTAIN OF THE ISLANDERS FOR ALL FOUR OF THEIR Cups, Potvin was elected to the Hall of Fame in 1990. During his 15-year career, Potvin broke Bobby Orr's career goal and point records by a defenseman (only to be overtaken by Paul Coffey). He played in the All-Star game nine times. His older brother, Jean, was a teammate with the Islanders, and played on the first two Cup-winning clubs. Potvin was the first choice in the 1973 Amateur Draft and won the Calder Trophy in 1974 and the Norris Trophy in 1976, 1978 and 1979. Every NHL game he played was with the Islanders.

Record Setting

Gretzky scored those record 215 points in 1985-86, outdistancing Lemieux by 74, but the Oilers hit the one pothole on their road to four Stanley Cups in a five-season span. The Oilers were eliminated in a game in which one of their young defensemen, Steve Smith, scored into his own goal.

The next season, when Edmonton regained the championship, Smith, who had handled his mistake with dignity and maturity, was given a place of honor in the on-ice parade with the Cup. In 1986, the Canadiens won their record 23rd Cup in an otherwise desultory decade for the Original Six – the only Cup recorded by any of them this decade. A 20-year-old goaltender, Patrick Roy, became the youngest Conn Smythe winner, outperforming another rookie goaltender, Mike Vernon, whose Calgary Flames had ousted Edmonton in the second round.

On April 2, 1986, one of Gretzky's teammates, Coffey, broke Bobby Orr's record for goals by a defenseman in a season. A spectacular end-to-end dash featuring Coffey splitting the two Vancouver Canucks defensemen before deking goaltender Wendell Young highlighted his 47th goal of the season.

"It was as if he said, 'I may as well do it the right way,'" said his coach and general manager, Glen Sather. Coffey would score one more in a year that culminated with his second straight Norris Trophy.

Earlier in the season, two more of Orr's records were eclipsed, each by the Islanders' Denis Potvin. Potvin scored his 916th point and 271st goal, both tops for a defenseman. Eventually, Coffey would shatter both of those marks.

Normalcy was restored in the 1986-87 season, which concluded with another Oilers championship (and the customary Gretzky scoring title, 183 points). Edmonton did have a slightly longer path to the finals, though, as the NHL expanded the first-round series to the best of seven, from the best of five.

Two events stood out during the season, both for their longevity.

On December 26, 1986, Doug Jarvis of the Hartford Whalers played in his 915th consecutive game, overtaking Garry Unger as the NHL's all-time Iron Man. Jarvis's streak ended soon after, at 964 games, and, amazingly, encompassed his entire career. He began play as a Canadien on October 8, 1975, and, after a stint with the Capitals, ended as a Hartford Whaler on October 10, 1987. En route, Jarvis won four Stanley Cups in Montreal and one Selke Trophy in Washington.

Jarvis, a 5-ft-9-in, 170-lb center, said, "It's an individual thing, a sidelight," but Gordie Howe, someone who knows a bit about longevity after an NHL career which spanned a record 26 seasons, countered: "It's an unbelievable record. I can't believe the guy went that long without catching a cold."

While Jarvis took 12 years to accomplish his task, the Islanders and Capitals made their mark on the 1986-87 season in six hours 15 minutes. Beginning at 7:40 on a Saturday night in Washington, the teams took the ice for Game 7 of their first-round playoff series and didn't get off till 1:55 on Easter Sunday morning. Pat LaFontaine connected at eight minutes 15 seconds of the fourth overtime to give New York a 3-2 victory and end the longest game in 44 years, the fifth longest in history. It also completed the Islanders' comeback from a 3-1 series deficit, making them only the third club to do so.

In 1987-88, Gretzky missed significant time because of injury (16 games), for the first time in his eight-year NHL career. It cost him his lock on the Ross and Hart trophies. Instead, Lemieux, in his fourth season, emerged to take both honors. He totaled 168 points (to Gretzky's 149) and 70 goals (to Gretzky's 40).

Even though Gretzky was healthy for the postseason and Edmonton did win the Cup again, the season marked the beginning of the end for the Oilers dynasty. Coffey was not part of this title; he was involved in a contract dispute at the start of the season and was traded to Lemieux's Penguins.

Gretzky notched his 1,000th assist during the season, as did Marcel Dionne, now with the New York Rangers, to join Howe in that select group. Dionne also became the third player in history to score 700 goals, behind Howe and Phil Esposito.

One of the marquee events of 1987-88 took considerably less time to accomplish. Just a matter of seconds, in fact. With time winding down at the Spectrum on December 8, and the Flyers holding a 4-2 advantage over the Bruins, Philadelphia goaltender Ron Hextall lofted a puck out of the zone – down the ice – and into an empty Boston net. Never before, in any of the previous 40,218 NHL games, had a goaltender scored by shooting the puck into the goal. "I don't mean to sound cocky," said Hextall, "but I knew it was just a matter of time before I flipped one in."

DR. OVERTIME

When the Montreal Canadiens won their 23rd Stanley Cup in 1986, it was a stunner, the most unlikely championship for the NHL's most remarkable franchise. But, if we all knew then what we know now about their goaltender, the title run wouldn't have seemed so far-fetched.

PATRICK ROY WAS 20 years old at the time, a self-described "scared" rookie who was less than two years removed from being a nothing-special third-round draft pick after a rather poor junior career with Granby of the Quebec League. Today, Roy is the most accomplished playoff goaltender ever. And in playoff overtimes, he's even better.

Roy's regular season numbers are quite good – with 46 career shutouts, fourth all time in wins and headed for number one as soon as next season – but the postseason is his time to shine.

"Playoffs are playoffs," Roy has said countless times in his career.

"When I start a season, I always focus myself for playoffs, think about playoffs, do everything for playoffs. When playoffs come, the concentration is there."

When a guy says "playoffs" three times in one sentence, take that as a hint that they're important to him.

At the start of the 1985-86 season, the Edmonton Oilers, the new beasts of Canada, were coming off their second straight Cup victory. The Canadiens were coming off a second-round playoff exit, with someone named Steve Penney as their top goaltender. Montreal's Cup drought was fully expected to continue through a seventh season, which would make it the club's longest dry run in more than four decades.

The Canadiens still had Larry Robinson and Bob Gainey, but it was a rebuilding year of sorts, as eight rookies made their debuts during the season. Montreal finished second in the Adams Division and seventh overall in the NHL, and Roy had a respectable season, 23-18-5 in 47 games with a 3.35 goals-against average as he supplanted Penney.

But, as the man said, playoffs are playoffs. The Canadiens swept the Boston Bruins in three straight games (Roy allowed six goals), then beat the Hartford Whalers in seven (13 goals allowed). Roy's overtime brilliance started to shine, as the Canadiens won Game 7 with rookie Claude Lemieux's goal five minutes 55 seconds into overtime. Montreal then handled the New York Rangers in five games (nine goals allowed), including another overtime won by Lemieux. Montreal was in the Cup finals for the first time in the decade, and Roy's goals-against average was under 2.00.

Now, the Canadiens did get a break in that they didn't have to face any of the four teams that finished ahead of them in the Wales Conference. And they seemed to get an enormous break when they met Calgary in the finals, after the Flames had ousted the Oilers in the second round. But Calgary was the Campbell Conference's second-best squad.

In the first all-Canadian finals since 1967, the Flames won the opener, then the Canadiens won Game 2 in overtime, with yet another rookie, Brian Skrudland, scoring the fastest overtime goal in playoff history, nine seconds in.

Montreal won the next three games to secure the Cup, and Roy won the Conn Smythe Trophy with a 15-5 record and 1.92 goals-against average. Like Jacques Plante and Ken Dryden, Roy had led the Canadiens to the Cup as a rookie.

The Flames and Canadiens met again in the 1989 Finals, with the Roy magic missing that round. Calgary won in six games. The next time the Canadiens were in the Finals, in 1993, Roy turned in his most impressive performance. He went 16-4 with a 2.13 goals-against average. But even more remarkable were his 10 consecutive overtime wins. He easily won the Conn Smythe after the Canadiens took the Cup by knocking off Wayne Gretzky and the Los Angeles Kings.

One round earlier, the Canadiens had beaten the New York Islanders in five games, winning one game in overtime and another in double overtime. "He was just about unbeatable in that series," defenseman Uwe Krupp, then with the Islanders, recalled a few years later. "I believe it got to be a factor on our team. We weren't able to exploit his weakness – we just weren't able to score goals on him."

By the 1995-96 season, the one in which Roy had angrily exited Montreal via one of the biggest trades in franchise history, Krupp and Roy were teammates in Colorado. Roy led the Avalanche to their first Cup and his third, capping the title with a stirring 63-save, triple-overtime shutout of the Florida Panthers which completed a four-game sweep.

"I'm not tired at all," Roy said after he improved his postseason overtime mark to 28-8 with his eighth playoff shutout.

Today, Dominik Hasek of the Buffalo Sabres is largely considered the best goaltender in the game. Hasek has won four

Patrick Roy is always in position to make a "routine" save, especially in overtime.

Vezina Trophies and even two Hart Trophies. And he certainly shone for the world to see in the 1998 Olympics. In the semifinals, Hasek outdueled Roy in a shootout as the Czechs eliminated Canada en route to the gold medal.

Hasek certainly is the more spectacular of the two, flopping on the ice and flailing his arms and legs to make some surreal saves. But Roy, a classic butterfly goaltender, rarely if ever displays such acrobatics. He is always in position to make a "routine" save.

Roy has three Vezinas, and played much of his career when offense was more prevalent than it is today. Roy finished 1998-99 with 412 regular season wins and, at the age of 34, clearly within reach of front-runner Terry Sawchuk (447).

But no matter what he does for the rest of his career, Roy will always be remembered for the playoffs. His 110 postseason wins are far and away an all-time best, and his overtime play may never be equaled. He is 33-10 in playoff overtimes.

When asked what his overtime philosophy was and why he was so successful in sudden-death play, Roy said simply, "I realize the next goal is the end of the game."

Yellow Sunday

THE 1988 PLAYOFFS WERE TROUBLED ONES, WITH TWO incidents causing great difficulty. In the first, a dispute among the New Jersey Devils, the League and on-ice officials resulted in a one-game walkout by the officials assigned to the Devils-Bruins playoff series. Replacements had to be found, and they were, but the two linesmen had to work the first period in yellow practice sweaters. The night is forever known as "Yellow Sunday". In the finals, the ancient Boston Garden electrical system gave way during a steamy Game 4. The game was suspended and the series returned to Edmonton, where the Oilers wrapped up their sweep on home ice. But the world was starting to shake under the Oilers dynasty.

In the offseason, the unthinkable happened: Wayne Gretzky was traded. On August 9, 1988, Gretzky was shipped to the Kings in a move that he said he had requested to be closer to his wife, Los Angeles actress Janet Jones, but which others claimed was necessitated by Edmonton owner Peter Pocklington's financial trouble.

Kings owner Bruce McNall sent an estimated $15 million to the Oilers, along with Jimmy Carson, Martin Gelinas and first-round draft picks in 1989, 1991 and 1993. Los Angeles also received Mike Krushelnyski and Marty McSorley.

The Oilers slumped to third in the Smythe Division, while the Kings rose to second, setting up a first-round playoff showdown. Edmonton raced to a 3-1 series lead before Los Angeles rallied to win three straight in a stirring reversal. But Gretzky's playoff magic ended there, as the Calgary Flames swept the Kings in the next round en route to becoming the final Stanley Cup champion of the decade.

While the 1980s ended with what seemed to be the demise of the Oilers dynasty, the decade had begun with the emergence of the dynastic Islanders. General Manager Bill Torrey, along with Coach Al Arbour, had put together a remarkable nucleus, with center Bryan Trottier, right wing Mike Bossy, goaltender Billy Smith and Potvin – Hall of Famers all – the core of the four successive Stanley Cup triumphs.

Islanders fans will always recall that first final series against the vaunted Flyers, who had finished first overall during the regular season after putting together the longest unbeaten streak in NHL history, a 35-game blitz (25-0-10) that shattered the standard of 28 set by Montreal in 1977-78.

Bob Nystrom scored the most famous goal in Islanders history, at the unforgettable time of 7:11 of overtime, to give New York the series in six games.

That game also was noteworthy because it was the last Stanley Cup or regular-season game on US network television until 1993.

That was an unfortunate turn of events for the growth of hockey in the US. With the gold-medal-winning US men's team attracting international adulation and coverage, the sport could have experienced a growth spurt. There were attractive teams, like the Islanders and Oilers, and brilliant players like Gretzky, Messier, Trottier, Stastny and Dionne. But the spotlight unfortunately focused on other sports.

Few players ever burst into hockey consciousness as the goal-scoring wizard Bossy did. In 1980-81, he was at his best, scoring 50 goals in the first 50 games to equal Maurice "Rocket" Richard's accomplishment of 38 years earlier (the next season, Gretzky would merely score 50 in the first 39 games). Bossy finished with a league-best 68 goals. But it was Gretzky who won the scoring title with 164 points, breaking Esposito's mark of 152 in 1970-71, and the assist crown with 109, topping Bobby Orr's record 102, also accomplished in 1970-71.

The Islanders defeated Gretzky and the Oilers in the Cup quarterfinals before making it two straight titles by downing the upstart Minnesota North Stars.

A year after the Flyers had set the all-time unbeaten mark, the Winnipeg Jets did the opposite, going a record 30 games (0-23-7) without a victory.

THE GREAT TWO

There will never be a singular sports moment more memorable to Canadians than Paul Henderson scoring in the final minute to win the Summit Series against the Soviet Union in 1972.

BUT STACK TOGETHER three down-to-the-wire games, then throw in the world's two best players united for the first time, and the 1987 Canada Cup rightfully earns a special place in the history of international competition.

It was the third Canada Cup of the decade and, apart from this being the rubber match after the Soviets won in 1981 and the Canadians won in 1984, it brought together Wayne Gretzky and Mario Lemieux. It is rare that two of a sport's all-time greats play together, much less in the prime of their careers.

Gretzky and Lemieux were on the same team throughout the six-nation tournament taking place in August and September of 1987, but it wasn't until the Canadians had lost the opener of the three-game finals against the Soviets that Coach Mike Keenan fully linked his two biggest superstars.

They had skated together only intermittently through the round-robin portion of the event. Keenan had said it would be counterproductive. But after the Soviets captured Game 1 of the finals, 6-5 on Alexander Semak's goal five minutes into overtime at the Montreal Forum, the coach reconsidered.

With a pair of great goal scorers equally adept at passing, Gretzky decided how the two players would operate. "On two-on-ones," he told Lemieux, "you take the shots."

As Gretzky explained: "I wanted him shooting because he's got those awesome wrists. He could snap a puck through a refrigerator door."

Faster than you could say "Whirlpool", the tandem clicked. Lemieux scored Canada's last three goals of Game 2 at Hamilton, Ontario's Copps Coliseum – including the winner 10 minutes 6 seconds into double overtime to finish another 6-5 game – with Gretzky assisting on all three. "He has a vision of the play," said Lemieux, "which is absolutely exceptional."

In the final game, also at Copps Coliseum, the Soviets raced to a 3-0 lead after only eight minutes. But the Canadians rallied and the match was tied at 5 late in the third period. That's when Gretzky broke in and delivered a brilliant pass to Lemieux, who snapped a wrist shot over the left shoulder of goaltender Sergei Mylnikov with one minute 26 seconds left to set off a celebration for the Canadians.

"As I skated in," Lemieux said, "I saw that the top shelf was open. I was just trying to find a hole." It was Lemieux's Canada Cup-record 11th goal of the tournament, four of which were game-winners and nine of which came on assists from Gretzky. He finished with 18 points to Gretzky's 21.

Controversially, Gretzky was named the tournament's most valuable player. Incontrovertibly, the sport's two best players put on a stellar show.

In photo left, Gretzky celebrates Canada's victory over Soviet Union in the 1987 Canada Cup; the scoreboard at right tells the story.

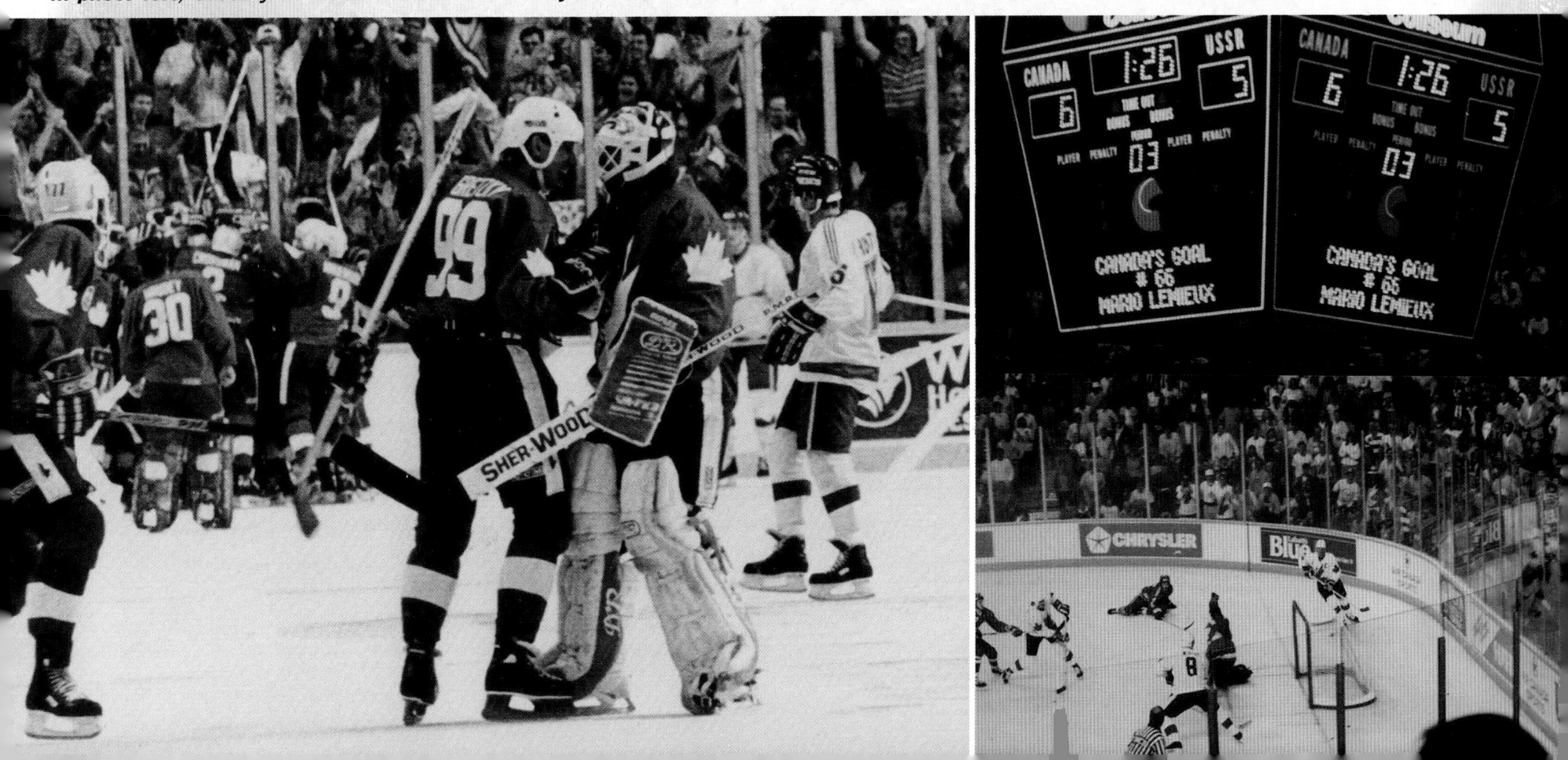

JIM SCHOENFELD

A GRITTY DEFENSEMAN WHO PLAYED MOSTLY with Buffalo in the 1970s, "Schoney" perhaps will best be remembered for an incident when he coached New Jersey. Upset at the officiating in Game 3 of a 1988 second-round playoff series against Boston, Schoenfeld yelled at referee Don Koharski after the game and then bumped him near the locker rooms. Schoenfeld was suspended, but the Devils got a court injunction to let him coach Game 4. The regular on-ice officials refused to work the game and off-ice officials were used. The Bruins won the series in seven games.

Geographical Changes

IN 1981-82, THE LEAGUE REALIGNED ITS TEAMS BASED ON geography. In the postseason, clubs faced division foes at the start, unlike the previous format in which the top seed played the 16th, No. 2 faced No. 15, etc. And opening-round series became the best of five, instead of the best of three.

That new format provided the Islanders with their toughest test en route to a three-peat right off the bat, in Game 5 against Pittsburgh. Playing at Nassau Coliseum, the Penguins took a 3-1 lead into the third period. But Mike McEwen scored with five minutes to play and John Tonelli connected about three minutes later to force overtime. Six minutes 19 seconds into overtime, Tonelli scored again.

After that, it was easy pickings for New York, who swept Vancouver in the finals to become only the third club to win at least three Stanley Cups in a row, joining Montreal and Toronto.

Just 11 days after the Islanders' victory, the Denver-based Rockies were sold and moved to New Jersey, becoming the Devils. That left another geographic void for the league, with no clubs between St. Louis and Los Angeles. Just two years earlier, the NHL had lost its only team in the South, when the Atlanta Flames moved to Calgary. In the 1990s, many of the geographic holes were filled in.

In 1982-83, the Islanders became only the second franchise with at least four consecutive titles (the Canadiens did it twice, 1956-60 and 1976-79). Despite Bossy registering his sixth 50-goal season in a row, tying Lafleur's mark, and his third successive 60-goal effort, a record which Gretzky would eventually break, the Islanders slumped to a sixth-place overall finish in the regular season. But they regrouped as true champions do, sweeping aside Edmonton for the last of their championships.

Of the decade's two dynasties, the Oilers are generally regarded as the premier entity. The Islanders had strength and flash in Bossy, Trottier and Potvin, but they were viewed as more workmanlike than the high-octane Oilers. Edmonton is the only club in history to score 400 goals in a season, and the Oilers did it five times (1981-82 to 1985-86), including the record 446 in 1983-84.

And, of course, the Oilers had Gretzky.

At the end of the decade, the NHL experienced a certain symmetry, with its past and present converging. The decade began with Gordie Howe returning to the NHL for one last season, skating for the Hartford Whalers in 1979-80 with his sons Mark and Marty on one memorable night, the three Howes lined up as a line to take the opening faceoff against

BRYAN **TROTTIER**

TROTTIER WON SIX STANLEY CUPS OVER HIS 18 NHL seasons, four with the Islanders in the early 1980s and two with Pittsburgh in the early 1990s. In 1978-79, he won the Art Ross and Hart trophies and in 1980 was the Conn Smythe winner. He totaled 524 goals and 1,425 points and was inducted into the Hall of Fame in 1997.

MIKE **BOSSY**

BOSSY SCORED 50 GOALS IN HIS FIRST NINE seasons, topping 60 five times, and failed to hit 50 only in his final season, 1986-87, after which he retired with a chronic back injury. He scored the Cup-winning goal in two of the Islanders' four titles (1982 and 1983) and won the Conn Smythe Trophy in 1982. A seven-time All-Star, Bossy totaled 573 goals and 553 assists in a career that culminated with his entry into the Hall of Fame in 1991. He won the Calder Trophy as the top rookie and was a three-time Lady Byng winner for gentlemanly play.

Howe's longtime team the Detroit Red Wings. And of course, that was Gretzky's first NHL season. By the end of the decade, Howe had long ago hung up his skates, stopping in 1980, just short of his 52nd birthday. But in 1989, the game's past, Howe, met its present, Gretzky. And it came with Gretzky's current team, the Kings, playing his former club, the Oilers, in his old rink, Northlands Coliseum.

On October 15, 1989, with Howe among the many NHL luminaries in attendance, along with Gretzky's family and friends and more than 17,000 fans, Gretzky tied his boyhood hero's all-time mark of 1,850 points with a first-period assist. Howe had been traveling with the Oilers in anticipation of Gretzky surpassing his point total, but it appeared this night would end with them tied, as the game wound down to the final minute. Gretzky, however, scored a goal with 53 seconds left to tie the score and overtake Howe.

After an on-ice ceremony in which Howe took part, the game resumed. It went to overtime and, naturally, Gretzky scored the winning goal.

"I don't know who writes his scripts," said Howe. "But they're doing a tremendous job."

"An award such as this takes a lot of teamwork and help and both teams here today definitely have a part of the 1,851," Gretzky said. "It's only fitting that it happened here. But Gordie's still the greatest in my mind."

Mark, Gordie and Marty Howe as Whaler teammates.

In 780 games spanning 11 seasons, Gretzky had 642 goals and 1,210 assists; in 1,767 games spanning 26 seasons, Howe totaled 801 goals and 1,049 assists. The all-time scoring mark was the 53rd of 61 records which would belong to Gretzky by the time he retired.

"He did it in true Gretzky fashion," said Messier, who during the ceremony presented his close friend with a diamond bracelet with 1.851 carats in the shape of "1,851". "He got the tying goal, then the winner in overtime. He has done that once or twice before."

SUDDEN VICTORIES

On November 10, 1942, the New York Rangers beat the Chicago Blackhawks in overtime 5-3. (Yes, the score is correct.) Eleven days later, the NHL discontinued regular-season overtime games because of World War II.

FORTY YEARS LATER, WITH the sports fan's mind-set far different than it had been back when (everybody loves a winner) the league made a move to end the glut of ties which had permeated the game. For the 1983-84 season, the league resumed regular-season overtime play, this time with a five-minute, sudden-death format.

The previous season, the Minnesota North Stars and Washington Capitals each tied 16 of their 80 games – one-fifth of their seasons. The season before that, the North Stars tied even more, a full quarter of their 80 games. There were more kissing-your-sister jokes than – well, you get the picture.

The first sudden-death game after the resumption of overtime came on October 5, 1983, with the Detroit Red Wings and Winnipeg Jets unable to decide things. It was not until three nights later that an overtime goal was scored. And it took the masters of extra play, the four-time-defending Stanley Cup champi-

The Great One and Mr. Hockey together again after Gretzky sets the scoring record.

on New York Islanders, to show everyone how it was done.

The Islanders defeated the Capitals 8-7 at the Capital Centre on Bob Bourne's power-play goal at two minutes. New York had rallied from a 5-1 deficit to tie the score twice in the third period, both on goals by Bob Nystrom, the last with 56 seconds left in regulation.

"I forgot about the overtime thing," said Nystrom, whose overtime goal in Game 6 against the Philadelphia Flyers in 1980 gave the Islanders their first Cup. (Overtime has always been a part of the playoffs.) "I thought we could go home with the tie, but hey, we'll take the victory." The Islanders had gone 10-2 in overtimes during their four-year Cup run.

In 1982-83, 17 of the 21 clubs had at least 10 ties. In 1983-84, only seven reached double digits. The record for ties in a season by one team is 24, by the Philadelphia Flyers in a 76-game season in 1969-70.

The NFL began using sudden-death overtime in regular season games in 1974, while the NBA and major league baseball always played till a winner was decided.

In the old days, hockey overtimes lasted 10 minutes and weren't sudden death, hence the Rangers' two-goal victory over the Blackhawks. It also was possible for both clubs to score in overtime.

The NHL eliminated overtime because of the tight train schedules during World War II. Extra play could mean a missed connection.

As one of the final rules changes before the NHL heads into the next century, the league decided following the 1998-99 season that too many teams were again satisfied with a tie. Beginning with the 1999-2000 season, each team gets a point for a tie in regulation and then they play the five-minute overtime to try to gain the second valuable point. But that's not all. To give the added period sustained offense, the teams will skate four-on-four. Around the time in the early 1980s that overtime was reintroduced, the Edmonton Oilers were so proficient at four-on-four hockey that they revelled in sending a man to the penalty box along with an opponent. Talk about an even-strength disadvantage.

NHL

A Cool Game for the Sun Belt

On August 9, 1988, Wayne Gretzky was traded south, and he took the NHL with him. When Gretzky left his beloved Edmonton for Los Angeles, he said it was "a good career move". He also said it was "an opportunity to help the game of hockey".

Opposite page: Wayne Gretzky says goodbye after 20 seasons, 61 records and millions of memories.

When Gretzky was traded to LA, hockey had room and reason to grow in the West. His Kings reached an improbable Stanley Cup final in 1993.

HOCKEY PURISTS, AND MANY CANADIANS, MAY HAVE cringed, not only about Gretzky leaving the country in which he was a national treasure, but also about what Gretzky was alluding to. It was obvious. For the NHL to be spoken of in the same sentence as the NFL, the NBA and Major League Baseball, it had to have what those leagues had: a prominent place in the United States. It needed increased exposure on US network television. It needed to expand its fan base. Gretzky coming to America, especially to a major market that still was new to hockey, was the best way – maybe the only way – for the NHL to gain that exposure.

In 1988, the NHL was made up almost exclusively of northern and eastern cities. Los Angeles was the only remotely southern city in the 21-team league. The closest clubs to the Kings geographically were the Vancouver Canucks, 1,200 miles to the north and in another country, and the St. Louis Blues, 1,800 miles and two time zones to the east. With 16 clubs qualifying for the playoffs, many people, even those in cities that had franchises, paid little attention to the regular season. And come the playoffs, the NHL in the United States was limited to a cable TV audience.

But Gretzky instantly made hockey cool in Hollywood, with the stars coming out to see the Kings the way they did to see Magic Johnson's Los Angeles Lakers. And what's cool in Hollywood often becomes cool throughout the United States.

This was the dawning of the Age of Aquarius for the NHL, when things were going to change rapidly, and drastically. Many forces began to work at once, with the Gretzky trade the fulcrum. The NHL was about to join the NFL, the NBA, and MLB in the big leagues. And with all the splendor and benefits of growth, the detriments came too.

In the 1990s, the NHL underwent a phenomenal facelift. The second network TV deal of the decade is about to commence – with ABC joining its cable sidekick ESPN in giving the league unprecedented broadcast coverage. Where Los Angeles had been the only Sun Belt team at the beginning of the decade, by 2000 there will be nine. And a decade which began with a Stanley Cup between the northernmost city, Edmonton, and the first US-based team, Boston, ended with a parade deep in the

heart of Texas, where the Dallas Stars strutted their stirring triumph.

By 2000, the NHL will be a 30-team outfit. Most of the new entries dot the Sun Belt from coast to coast, some at the expense of Canadian markets. New arenas in the new cities forced the construction of new arenas in the old cities; with the Maple Leafs leaving the Gardens in 1999, none of the Original Six buildings is still in use.

More teams meant more players, and Europeans in the NHL are now commonplace. Several of the biggest stars are Europeans. The last three Hart Trophy winners have been players whose homeland is the Czech Republic. NHL players competed in the Olympics for the first time in 1998, in front of a worldwide audience.

Overseeing all of this has been the NHL's first commissioner, Gary B. Bettman, elected in December 1992 and in office by February 1993. Team owners saw their world expanding exponentially when they made the move to Bettman, less than a year after experiencing professional sports' preeminent growing pain: labor trouble.

Players' salaries had been on the rise – while Gretzky said he wanted to be traded to Los Angeles to be with his wife, actress Janet Jones, Oilers owner Peter Pocklington was said to be enduring financial trouble after having to pay the price of having a dynasty. Then, when Gretzky got to LA, his annual base salary was raised to nearly $2 million, easily setting a new standard in hockey.

Even though players' salaries were increasing – the average was about $230,000 in 1992 – they still paled in comparison to those in baseball, football and basketball. After the WHA had escalated salaries in the late 1970s, NHL president John Ziegler, NHL Players Association executive director Alan Eagleson and Bill Wirtz, the NHL's chairman of the Board of Governors and owner of the Chicago Blackhawks, stabilized franchises and their costs. Eventually, players became uneasy with the close relationship between their representative, Eagleson, and their bosses, the team owners. Players' agent Bob Goodenow joined the NHLPA as deputy executive director in September 1990, Eagleson stepped down in December 1991 and, on January 1, 1992, Goodenow was named as his replacement. (Eagleson was eventually convicted of stealing from the players' pension funds and lost his place in the Hall of Fame.)

In 1991-92, the NHL instituted video replay to help referees determine if goals were scored. The San Jose Sharks entered the league, becoming the first new team since the four WHA franchises were absorbed in 1979-80. By midway through the league's 75th anniversary season of 1991-92, the Tampa Bay Lightning and Ottawa Senators were given the approval to begin playing in 1992-93. Ottawa provided the NHL with what most observers felt was the last Canadian city with the resources to support a club; San Jose and Tampa Bay ignited the NHL's entry into the Sun Belt.

DAVE **McILWAIN**

HE SPENT 10 YEARS IN THE NHL, NONE MORE turbulent than 1991-92, when he played for four clubs, each in a different division. McIlwain started the season with the Winnipeg Jets (Smythe Division), was traded to the Buffalo Sabres (Adams) on October 11, then to the New York Islanders (Patrick) on October 25, and finally to the Toronto Maple Leafs (Norris) on March 10.

CRAIG MacTAVISH

AN ERA ENDED WHEN MacTAVISH RETIRED after 1996-97. He was the last player who didn't wear a helmet. MacTavish played before the league made headgear obligatory in 1979-80, having been a rookie that season. When the league mandated helmets, any player already in the league could sign a waiver to go bareheaded. MacTavish won four Stanley Cups, three with the Oilers and one with the New York Rangers.

issued his now-famous guarantee of a Game 6 victory. He even outdid his prediction by scoring a hat trick that ensured a Game 7. The series ended stunningly with Matteau scoring in double overtime. The Big Apple was delirious, and so was the NHL, which was reveling in its marquee team providing its all-time marquee season. So what's seven more games after 54 Cup-free seasons? The Canucks scarily pushed the Rangers the distance before New York forever put an end to the derisive chants of 'Nine-teen For-ty, Nine-teen For-ty'.

Phew!

What could be better?

Michael Jordan had retired from the NBA, leaving the NHL's main winter rival with an enormous void, and hockey interest was at its zenith, with Gretzky on one coast and the Rangers – the Stanley Cup-champion Rangers – on the other. *Sports Illustrated* proclaimed that the NHL was hotter than the NBA. The NHL was on a big-time roll.

Really, what could be better?

A New Deal

LESS THAN FOUR MONTHS AFTER THE EUPHORIA IN NEW York, the NHL went dark.

Without a collective bargaining agreement, Bettman and the owners, as promised, locked out Goodenow and the players, delaying the start of the season and, as the stalemate endured, jeopardizing the entire schedule. The season was slated to start on October 1, 1994. It began on January 20, 1995, and only after an 11th-hour deal was struck. The new pact, which eventually guaranteed labor peace into the next century, gave the players, expanded free agency, and gave the owners, a rein on players' salaries by putting a ceiling on what entry-level players may earn (although overall, the average player salary now easily exceeds $1 million). Among the casualties were the 1995 All-Star game, which was canceled.

After a brief "training camp", a 48-game schedule was set in motion. With the shortened season, a playoff mind-set was in place virtually from the start. It showed, as a defensive style of hockey permeated the league, greatly reducing scoring – a trend that continues to this day.

The Devils, who came so close to knocking off the Rangers the year before, played defense better than anyone

else. They got to the finals, but, employing a trapping, conservative style of play, they were roundly criticized as boring. For the Cup, New Jersey met high-octane Detroit, which, thanks to the Rangers, now owned the longest championship drought, last winning with Howe in 1955. Defense beat offense easily as the Devils swept the Red Wings.

The Quebec Nordiques had finished the shortened season at the top of the Eastern Conference, but were knocked off by the Rangers in the playoffs. It was their final act north of the border. Back in January, team owner Marcel Aubut voted for the collective bargaining agreement, but the Nordiques could not survive in Quebec City, by far the League's smallest (and probably most charming) city. The Nordiques were sold and became the Denver-based Colorado Avalanche.

The Nordiques, playing in a city dominated by government and devoid of the big businesses needed to support teams in today's sports climate, likely would not have survived no matter what. But they were dealt a humiliating blow a few years earlier when Eric Lindros, the brightest prospect since Lemieux, refused to play for them after being drafted first overall in 1991.

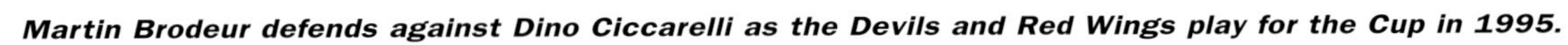

Martin Brodeur defends against Dino Ciccarelli as the Devils and Red Wings play for the Cup in 1995.

"WE'LL WIN"

Ever the rugged western Canadian pioneer, Eddie Shore epitomized the macho iceman of the early NHL and embodied the rough and tumble game of the late 1920s and 1930s.

The New York Jets of the upstart American Football League defeating the 18-point favorite Baltimore Colts of the NFL in Super Bowl III would have been a defining moment in the history of American sports even without Namath's promise. But his proclamation was so outlandish, so confidently delivered – and he played a major role in ensuring it became a reality – that it became lore.

Twenty-five years later, another larger-than-life New York athlete issued another startling guarantee. Like Namath, Mark Messier delivered. Like Namath, Messier played a large part in the delivery. His words, while not nearly as outrageous as Namath's – the Rangers, after all, were the NHL's top club during the 1993-94 regular season – constitute the defining moment of New York winning its first Stanley Cup in 54 years.

With the New Jersey Devils leading the Rangers three games to two in the Eastern Conference finals, Messier simply said, "We'll win." And then he went on to the ice and made sure.

Messier was traded to New York in 1991 with one charge from his new team's management: Win the Stanley Cup. From Rangers fans, it was more like Pleeeeease win the Stanley Cup.

Rangers fans, much like their counterparts who root for baseball's Chicago Cubs and Boston Red Sox, felt cursed. The Curse of 1940. They had seen their team – those who were old enough to – reach the finals only three times, in 1950, 1972 and 1979, since winning the Cup. So when Messier, who won five Cups with Edmonton, arrived, there was hope.

Still, when Messier led the Rangers to the league's best record in the 1991-92 regular season, the fans were only guardedly optimistic. Too much heartache over half a century will do that. Sure enough, after being extended to seven games by the Devils in the first round, the Rangers lost to the Pittsburgh Penguins in six – and that after Mario Lemieux broke his hand in Game 2 and missed the rest of the series. The curse lived!

The next season, the Rangers crashed, completely missing the postseason.

But, lo and behold, come 1993-94, the Rangers rebounded to win the Presidents' Trophy again. Let's not get ahead of ourselves, Rangers fans knew. The Rangers swept the hated Islanders in the first round, pelting them 22-3 in goals. A blowout, for sure, but let's not get ahead of ourselves, the fans knew. Then the Rangers beat the Washington Capitals in five. But let's not get ahead of ourselves, the fans knew.

Now it was on to the Devils, who had lost all six games with the Rangers during the regular season.

And they certainly knew it after Game 1, which the Devils won in double overtime after rallying to tie three times, lastly with 43 seconds left in regulation. What proceeded was one of the most dramatic series in Stanley Cup history, with the opening game just the first of three double-overtime thrillers in the seven-game epic.

Enter Messier. On the first shift of Game 2, Messier blasted the Devils' rugged defenseman Scott Stevens behind the net, stole a pass and stuffed the puck into the goal. The Rangers won 4-0. "Everything that happened in the game after that happened because of Mark," New York defenseman Brian Leetch said.

Game 3 went to double overtime, with the Rangers winning. New Jersey won Game 4 to even things at 2, with the series returning to Madison Square Garden. The Devils won Game 5 4-1 to put the Rangers on the brink. To that point, Messier had just that one goal in the entire series. Here we go again, Rangers fans knew.

At practice on May 24, the day before Game 6, Messier sensed that his teammates were apprehensive. When he spoke to reporters later, he said: "We're going to go in and win Game 6. I know we're going to go in and win Game 6 and bring it back here for Game 7."

The next night, the Devils raced to a 2-0 lead after one period. Near the end of the second period it was still 2-0. So much for guarantees.

But then Messier awoke. He found Alexei Kovalev to make it 2-1 after two. Less than three minutes into the third period, Kovalev found Messier, and the Rangers captain delivered for a 2-2 score. Midway through the period, Devils goaltender Martin Brodeur kicked out a Kovalev shot only to see the puck land on Messier's stick. Bang! It was 3-2, to the Rangers, at 12 minutes 12 seconds. New York erupted, New Jersey deflated.

The game went to the final minutes, when Brodeur was pulled for a sixth skater. Messier intercepted a pass in

Mark Messier's guarantee was made of desparation, but the result was plain to see: three goals and a win.

the Rangers' zone, fired the puck down ice. It went in. A hat trick for Messier, plus an assist.

The guarantee was delivered. "I played against Mark for nine years and nothing scared me more than when he got that real serious look of determination in his eye," said teammate Jay Wells. "In the third period, he had that. He was determined to back up his words and take the game into his own hands."

"That," said Rangers Coach Mike Keenan, "has to be the most impressive performance by any hockey player in the history of this league."

"This was a big game," Messier said. "But Game 7 is even bigger."

Oh, yeah. Game 7.

Back at the Garden two nights later, before 18,200 rabid fans, the Rangers took a 1-0 lead through Leetch's goal in the first period. The score stayed that way into the final minute of regulation, when Brodeur was pulled. Let's not get ahead – oh, heck, this was it, Rangers fans knew.

With the clock winding down, and a berth in the finals at stake, and every Rangers fan knowing that their team would have no trouble taking the Cup against the Vancouver Canucks – the Canucks? – the Devils' Valeri Zelepukin scored with 7.7 seconds left in regulation.

"*I knew it*," one rinkside Rangers fan screamed.

The curse continued.

"Hey, we'll play all night if we have to," Messier said in the locker room before overtime. "We'll win this game."

Play all night they almost did. There was still a third double-overtime game left in these two teams.

Four minutes 24 seconds into the second overtime, Rangers fans finally knew. Stephane Matteau, a name that will live on in Rangers history – and the Devils', too, for that matter – scored to end a remarkable game and a remarkable series.

Messier was handed the Prince of Wales Trophy, but the fans started chanting: "We want the Cup. We want the Cup."

The finals, expected to be a mere formality, turned out to be anything but. The Canucks took the opener in overtime at the Garden. Even after the Rangers won the next three, Rangers fans knew: Let's not get ahead of ourselves. Yep, Vancouver won the next two to force a deciding game in New York.

The Rangers won 3-2, with Messier's second-period goal the difference.

A Rangers fan holding a sign said it all: "Now I Can Die in Peace."

Waiting for Next One

HIS DEMAND LED TO ONE OF THE BLOCKBUSTER TRADES IN NHL history, as well as a bizarre and embarrassing moment for the league.

Marcel Aubut had agreed to trade Lindros to two clubs, the Rangers and Philadelphia Flyers. An arbitrator deemed that Lindros belonged to the Flyers. Lindros – a 6-ft 4-in, 235-lb rock of a center who combined speed, skill and power – was traded on June 30, 1992, for Peter Forsberg, Steve Duchesne, Kerry Huffman, Mike Ricci, Ron Hextall, Chris Simon and first-round draft picks in 1993 and 1994, plus $15 million.

Lindros began play with the Flyers in 1992-93. Forsberg, who was taken five places after Lindros in the 1991 draft and had scored the gold-medal-winning goal for Sweden in the 1994 Olympics, won the Calder Trophy for the Nordiques in 1995. He then became an integral part of the Avalanche's inaugural season in Colorado.

Eric Lindros's size and skill has been the stuff of dreams.

To the dismay of fans in Quebec City, the Avalanche thrived in 1995-96, especially after another trade that sent shock waves through the province. Patrick Roy, the three-time Vezina Trophy winner, demanded to leave Montreal after he surrendered nine goals in an 11-1 loss to Detroit on December 2. The goaltender felt coach Mario Tremblay embarrassed him by leaving him in the game for so long; he vowed never to play for the Canadiens again, and he and Mike Keane were dealt to Colorado for three players just four days later.

The Lindros deal proved to be a boon for Quebec/Colorado, even if it was not enough to keep the franchise in Canada. One of the players for whom Roy was traded, goaltender Jocelyn Thibault, was Quebec's choice with the 1993 draft pick secured from Philadelphia. Roy put the Avalanche over the top and, even though the Red Wings set an all-time record with 62 regular season wins, Colorado ousted Detroit in a bitter six-game Western Conference championship round. The Avalanche swept the third-year Florida Panthers in the Cup finals, but needed Roy to make 63 saves in a stirring, 1-0 triple-overtime clincher in Game 4.

It was a brilliant finish to a season that was marked with continued franchise upheaval, an emotional departure from Montreal even bigger than that of Roy, and another trade perhaps even bigger than the Roy deal – Wayne Gretzky.

Unhappy with the direction of the Kings after reaching the Cup finals in 1993, Gretzky wanted to go to a contender. He went, but not to a contender. He wound up with the St. Louis Blues on February 27. The Blues pushed the Red Wings to a double-overtime Game 7 in the second round of the playoffs, but that marked the end of Gretzky's brief stay in the Midwest. He signed with the Rangers as a free agent in the offseason, and was reunited with his Oilers' running mate, Messier.

Just three months after Roy left Montreal, the fabled Montreal Forum closed in favor of the sparkling Molson Centre. It was the third Original Six building to shut down in two years. Chicago Stadium had given way to the United Center in January 1995 and Boston Garden had been replaced by the FleetCenter the following September. In 1999, the last remaining old building, Maple Leaf Gardens, hosted its last NHL game, as

Lindros and John LeClair (10) have been two of the most effective teammates of the 1990s.

Expansion changed the look of the games.

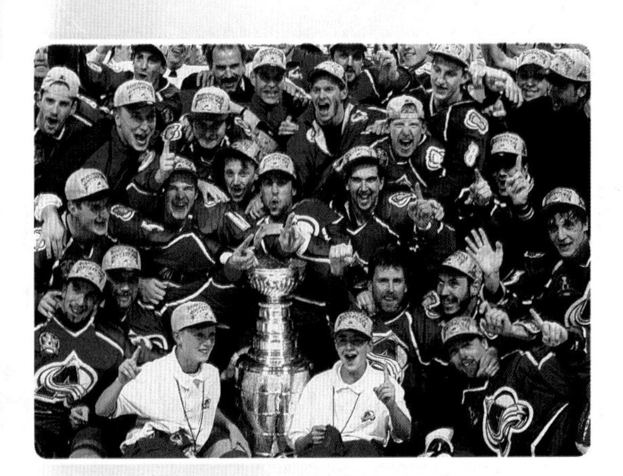

The Avalanche win the Cup in '96.

Toronto moved into Air Canada Centre. That left Pittsburgh's Civic Arena as the NHL's oldest facility, having opened in 1961.

During the 1990s, the NHL also moved into new venues in Anaheim, Buffalo, Carolina, Colorado, Florida, Los Angeles, Ottawa, Philadelphia, St. Louis, San Jose, Tampa Bay, Vancouver and Washington. And that list doesn't count the new buildings for each of the four latest expansion clubs which were awarded in 1997: the Nashville Predators (first season 1998-99), the Atlanta Thrashers (1999-2000), the Columbus (Ohio) Blue Jackets (2000-01) and the Minnesota Wild (2000-01).

What's that you say? Where did that Carolina team come from? That was one of the two franchise relocations later in the decade. After the 1996-97 season, the Hartford Whalers moved to North Carolina to become the Hurricanes. The year before, Canada had lost yet another club to the United States, with the Winnipeg Jets becoming the Phoenix Coyotes. With the shift of Quebec, Winnipeg and Hartford, the only team remaining of the four brought in from the WHA back in 1979 was Edmonton. And the Oilers have struggled to stave off the movers.

Predators Tom Fitzgerald and Panthers Rob Niedermayer at Nashville debut. In the 1990s, hockey became a Sun Belt sport.

Triumph and Disaster

THE 1996-97 SEASON WAS ONE OF TRIUMPH AND TRAGEDY for the NHL – but that could also be said of just one team, the Red Wings.

Gretzky, unthinkably, was now with his fourth club, the Rangers. Lemieux, who some observers felt could have challenged a number of Gretzky's now seemingly unattainable milestones, was in his final season. He didn't announce his retirement until after the season, but he had dropped enough hints that a career full of hardship was coming to a close.

Lemieux had his first surgery to repair a herniated disk back in the summer of 1990, an operation which caused him to miss 50 games in 1990-91 before coming back to direct the Penguins to their two consecutive Stanley Cups. Then, in January 1993, came the stunning news that Lemieux had Hodgkin's disease. He recovered from that and won the Art Ross and Hart Trophies. But he had to endure another back surgery in July 1993, limiting him to 22 games in 1993-94 and, in combination with his recuperation from the cancer, he was forced to sit out the 1994-95 season. Remarkably, he returned to win the Art Ross Trophy and the Hart Trophy in 1995-96. And, in 1996-97, in what turned out to be his final season, he won his sixth and final Ross Trophy.

For all the sadness in Pittsburgh, there was joy in Hockeytown. The Red Wings, who had flopped in the post-season each of the past two seasons, tried once again to end the NHL's longest championship drought. Finally adding enough defense and grit to their sleek skating club, highlighted by the Russian Five of Sergei Fedorov, Viacheslav Fetisov, Vladimir Konstantinov, Vyacheslav Kozlov and Igor Larionov, the Red Wings returned to the finals, much to the delight of their octopus-waving faithful.

Fans brought live octopi to the games and flung them onto the ice. The tradition was born in the 1950s, when the Red Wings were in their glory years and it took eight wins to secure the Stanley Cup. The fans threw the mollusks early and often in 1997, at least until Detroit dismissed Philadelphia in a four-game sweep. Lindros, for all his hype, finally had led the Flyers to the finals, after eliminating Lemieux's Penguins in the first round and Gretzky and Messier's Rangers in the Eastern Conference finals.

But the thrill of Detroit's first Cup celebration since 1955 was short-lived. Six days following the victory, a limousine carrying several Red Wings crashed, leaving Konstantinov and team masseur Sergei Mnatsakanov with life-threatening injuries. Neither man would be able to

MIKE **GARTNER**

GARTNER IS AMONG ONLY FIVE PLAYERS IN league history with 700 goals. He totaled at least 30 in 17 of his 19 seasons, including a record 15 consecutively, a streak that was ended in the shortened 1994-95 schedule. He also had more than 600 assists. He has played in seven All-Star games, representing four clubs. Gartner was one of the faster skaters in the league right up until his retirement after 1997-98.

return to his job.

The following season, 1997-98, the Red Wings won again, polishing off the Washington Capitals with the finals' fourth successive sweep and giving Scotty Bowman his eighth championship as a coach, which equalled Toe Blake. Afterward, captain Steve Yzerman placed the Stanley Cup in the lap of Konstantinov, who was wearing a Red Wings sweater and was pushed around the ice in his wheelchair.

The Russian Five constituted the most prominent example of how the NHL had become a worldwide entity in the 1990s. NHL players competed in the Olympics for the first time in 1998, with the league taking a two-week-plus break in February to participate.

The Red Wings' bid to join the Canadiens, Maple Leafs and Islanders as the only clubs to win at least three successive Cups failed, as they were ousted by their archrivals the Avalanche in 1998-99. After Detroit took a 2-0 lead in games in the Western Conference semifinals, the team – and the city – were silenced as Colorado won the next four. "This is Hockeytown," said the Wings' Darren McCarty, "and now there is no hockey."

Detroit's elimination ended a dominating spree for the NHL's northern clubs. In fact, throughout the decade, the southernmost team to win a Stanley Cup was the transplanted Avalanche – until a Sun-Belt club finally broke through at the very end. The Dallas Stars – themselves converts from Minnesota after the 1993-94 season – defeated Colorado in the Western Conference finals before beating the Sabres to win the Cup in the most thrilling championship series in years.

Konstantinov takes the Cup on an emotional ride.

THE MAGNIFICENT ONE

Apparently, Mario Lemieux was the last to know. Everyone else knew how great he would be long before he did.

MOST PEOPLE KNEW BY 1983-84, when Lemieux broke Quebec Major Junior Hockey League scoring records by totaling 133 goals and 282 points for Laval in winning the Canadian major junior player of the year. The Pittsburgh Penguins surely knew. They resisted all offers for the top pick in the 1984 draft. The Minnesota North Stars knew. They reportedly offered all their 1984 picks to Pittsburgh for the right to draft Lemieux.

If people didn't know by then, they certainly did after 1984-85, when 19-year-old Lemieux became only the third NHL player to score 100 points as a rookie. Still, Lemieux wasn't convinced.

"I am not admitting I ever doubted myself, but there was a time when I wasn't sure I could be a great hockey player," he recalled a few years later. "I thought I was a good hockey player, but a good hockey player is not a great one."

No, for Lemieux, it wasn't until he played alongside Wayne Gretzky and all the worldwide superstars in the 1987 Canada Cup that he understood.

"Just being with all those terrific players was an inspiration. I'm sure that was when I really reached the peak of my game. The fact that I was able to help win the Canada Cup gave me tremendous confidence."

OK, with that little self-doubt thing out of the way, Lemieux was able to go forward, despite enormous physical hardships, to become one of the NHL's all-time best. He is on everyone's very short list, along with Gretzky, Gordie Howe and Bobby Orr.

Mario Lemieux never knew how good he would be or how good he was.

The numbers Lemieux put up in his career – 613 goals, 1,494 points, six Art Ross Trophies, three Hart Trophies and two Conn Smythe Trophies won for the Penguins' two Stanley Cups in 1991 and 1992 – are as monumental as the ailments he overcame.

There was back surgery in July 1990 and there was another back surgery in July 1993. And then there was the cancer.

On January 6, 1993, Lemieux learned he had Hodgkin's disease. "I could hardly drive home because of the tears," he said. "I was crying all day." Two days later, he had a lymph node removed from his neck.

On February 1, Lemieux began radiation treatments. On February 12, he began intermittent skating with the Penguins. On March 2, the day of his last radiation session, he returned to the lineup. In mid-April, Lemieux said of the cancer: "That's all over now. That's really over."

Remarkably, he returned as if he had never left. In Lemieux's first 20 games back, he scored 56 points, including the second five-goal game of his career, to wrest back the scoring title that appeared lost. Lemieux won the Ross Trophy with 160 points, in only 60 games.

The per-game point total (2.67) is even better than when he notched his career-best 199 points in 76 games (2.62) in 1988-89. That was the last season that Lemieux, aged 23 at the time, was ever truly healthy.

He had the first surgery on his herniated disk before the 1990-91 season. He played in only 26 games, but came back to play in 23 of the Penguins' 24 playoff games, totaling 44 points as the long-hapless franchise won its first Stanley Cup. Pittsburgh won the Cup again the next season, with Lemieux winning another Ross Trophy, despite again missing substantial time because of his sore back.

Lemieux fought injuries, cancer and interference to score 613 goals and save a franchise.

The cancer struck in 1992-93, and then came the second back surgery in the summer. Lemieux played in only 22 games in 1993-94 and sat out all of the next season, in part because of his back and in part because of the aftereffects from the cancer.

All along, Lemieux had been growing disenchanted with the changing game on the ice, with the rules seemingly being relaxed to allow for a clogging of play in the neutral zone. As far back as 1991-92, he had been fined for what the NHL called comments detrimental to the league. After a February loss to Washington, Lemieux said: "It's a skating and passing game. That's what the fans want to see, but the advantage is to the marginal players now. That's the way this garage league is run."

That remark cost him $1,000, but he hoped it would help bring light to what he perceived to be a major problem. Despite being 6 ft 4 in and 225 lbs, Lemieux was even more graceful than he was powerful.

"He is definitely the most talented player ever to play the game," Flyers goaltender Ron Hextall said in 1997. "There is no way a guy can be more talented than this guy. It's humanly impossible."

But all the clutching and grabbing didn't allow Lemieux to play the way he thought hockey should be played. Still, he won the Ross Trophy again in 1995-96. The next season, most observers believed, would be Lemieux's last. He had made no announcement. But, at 31, his body was worn down from all the ailments, and he had lost his enjoyment, feeling not enough had been done to stem the interference taking place on the ice.

In 1996-97, Lemieux played 76 games and won the Ross Trophy with 122 points. The Penguins lost in the first round of the playoffs to the Philadelphia Flyers. And just like that, Lemieux was done. And just like that, the three-year waiting period to enter the Hall of Fame was waived for him.

Lemieux's 199 points in 1989-90 are surpassed only by Gretzky, who broke 200 four times, peaking at 215. "With the players I was with in the early 1990s, I thought I had a shot at it if my back would have stayed strong," Lemieux said of the 215.

For all that Lemieux did, his greatest accomplishment may have been saving hockey in Pittsburgh. When he arrived, the Penguins were at the bottom of the league – in the standings and at the gate – and Pittsburgh was a desultory hockey town. "He probably doesn't get enough credit," Gretzky said. "Pittsburgh was getting 6,000 people a game when he got there, so he basically saved that franchise and then won two Cups."

Said Lemieux: "I've played 12 seasons, I've won two Cups, some Conn Smythe Trophies, and in my prime I was able to challenge anyone one-on-one. I'm happy with what I accomplished."

Even with his playing career over, Lemieux continued to save hockey in Pittsburgh. In August 1999, an ownership group that he headed was preparing to take over the franchise. A bankruptcy judge ruled what everyone else already knew – no one was better suited to save the Pittsburgh Penguins than their once modest savior.

FROM THE SIDE TRACK

There was Scotty Bowman, taking a skate with his players, as he had done countless times throughout his long coaching career.

ONLY THIS ONE WAS A TAD different. During this skate, this one, glorious skate, Bowman was holding the Stanley Cup. The Detroit Red Wings had just won the 1996-97 NHL title. Bowman had just put the "Hockey" back in "Hockeytown" for the first time in 42 years. Joe Louis Arena was bedlam. Captain Steve Yzerman paraded with the Cup, reveling in the celebration, and so did Slava Fetisov and Igor Larionov and others. And then Bowman did.

"I decided to put on the skates because I always wanted to be an NHL player," said Bowman, 63 at the time. "My dreams got sidetracked, but I wanted to skate around with the Cup. So I said, 'Go for it.'"

"Sidetracked" doesn't quite explain how Bowman was lying on the ice in the Montreal Forum in 1952, bleeding and unconscious, after being whacked on the head from behind in the last minute of a Junior A playoff game. They put a metal plate in his head and he spent three weeks in the hospital, followed by a summer filled with headaches. An attempted comeback didn't take.

"There were only 30 seconds left in the game," he said. "I think about that sometimes. What if the game had been 30 seconds shorter?"

Perhaps Bowman would've gone on to become an NHL player, as he had dreamed. Perhaps he wouldn't have gone on to win a record-tying eight Stanley Cups as a coach and one more as Player Personnel Director of the 1991 Penguins. No. 7 came on the night he decided to take the Cup for a little spin.

"It's heavy, but it's light, too," he explained at the time.

There wasn't any underlying meaning in that remark, more Yogi Berra than anything else, but it's typical Bowman. His players and others always found him to be a cryptic, dichotomous person. An enigma.

"Trying to explain Scotty is like trying to explain an abstract painting," said Shawn Burr, who played for the Red Wings under Bowman and disliked him, then liked him.

Canadiens Hall of Famer Steve Shutt said that players "hated him for 364 days – and then on the other day you got your Stanley Cup ring".

That's the man most people know. That's not the man his family knows. Bowman is married and has five children, one of whom is handicapped. David, who is in his mid-twenties, was born with hydrocephalus (water on the brain). When doctors operated to

MANON **RHEAUME**

SHE IS THE ONLY WOMAN TO PLAY IN THE NHL. IN a preseason game on September 23, 1992, Rheaume started and played one period in goal for the Tampa Bay Lightning. She returned a year later to play in another preseason game, before 23,301 fans in the Lightning's first game in the ThunderDome. Rheaume also played for a number of men's minor league clubs and represented the Canadian women in the 1998 Olympics.

relieve the pressure on David's brain, he was left blind.

David had attended a special school for the blind in New York, where the family lived when Bowman coached the Buffalo Sabres. After Buffalo, Bowman worked as a TV analyst for *Hockey Night in Canada* and also with the Pittsburgh Penguins. Because of David, Bowman did not want to relocate his family. He commuted to Toronto, he commuted to Pittsburgh. In Detroit, he rented a house. The family remained in Buffalo.

Bowman has endured other hardships. Six days after the Red Wings won that Cup, player Vladimir Konstantinov and team masseur Sergei Mnatsakonov were critically injured in a limousine accident. Six days after the Red Wings retained the championship, this one celebrated with a brain-damaged Konstantinov on the ice with the Cup in his wheelchair, Bowman's younger brother, Jack, died of complications from heart surgery. Jack had been the Sabres' director of scouting and had joined the organization in 1980, hired by his brother.

Furthermore, Bowman was to have knee-replacement surgery in the offseason but, because of Jack, decided to have cardiac tests as well. Doctors found a blocked coronary artery, and he had an angioplasty. They said that if the blockage hadn't been detected, there could have been life-threatening complications during the knee operation.

When Bowman's playing days ended two years after his on-ice accident, he went to work in the Canadiens' organization as a junior coach and a scout. He made his NHL coaching debut with the expansion St Louis Blues in 1967-68 and spent four seasons with them, reaching the Cup finals the first three seasons. He joined Montreal in 1971-72 and won five Cups with the Canadiens, including a four-in-a-row dynasty at the end of the decade. Then it was off to Buffalo for seven seasons. After his stint on TV, Bowman returned to the NHL as the Pittsburgh Penguins' director of player development, helping build the club that won the Cup in 1991. The Penguins' coach, Bob Johnson, died of cancer after the season, and Bowman took over to guide Pittsburgh to another Cup.

With the Red Wings, Bowman became the first coach to win titles with three clubs, and he equalled the record of his idol, former Canadiens coach Toe Blake, with eight Cups overall. He entered the Hall of Fame in 1991, as a builder.

So what's left for Bowman? After the Red Wings' first Cup in 1997, Bowman was undecided about returning. He noted how Blake won his final game as coach. "Most times you aren't able to win your last game," Bowman said. But he returned and won another Cup, returned again and didn't win. When the Red Wings were eliminated by the Colorado Avalanche in the Western Conference semifinals in 1999, Bowman contemplated retirement, but the lure of coaching for a fifth decade, of trying for that ninth Cup, will keep him behind the Red Wings' bench.

No matter what happens, his place in history is set.

Ken Dryden, the Hall of Fame goaltender from that Canadiens dynasty, wrote in his book *The Game* that Bowman "is complex, confusing, misunderstood, unclear in every way but one. He is a brilliant coach, the best of his time".

LUC **ROBITAILLE**

THE CALDER TROPHY WINNER IN 1986-87 WITH the Los Angeles Kings, he has the NHL record for left wingers by scoring 40 goals in at least eight straight seasons. Robitaille surpassed 500 goals in his 13th season in 1998-99, finishing the year with 517.

Crying Foul

After the NHL endured final-round sweeps for four successive seasons, Dallas and Buffalo went to a Game 6, and then some. They played nearly two games' worth in one, coming within seconds of the longest match in finals history before Brett Hull scored at 14 minutes 51 seconds of the third overtime for a 2-1 Stars victory.

But while Hull was mobbed by jubilant teammates, the Sabres and their fans at Marine Midland Arena cried foul, saying Hull had scored a tainted goal. The always controversial, in-the-crease rule came into play. In short, the rule states that if an offensive player enters the crease before the puck does, and then a goal is scored, the goal shall not count. In this instance, the puck was in the crease before Hull was. But then he kicked the puck out of the crease – while he stayed in it – before shooting it in. It was ruled that Hull had maintained possession, which made the goal legal but did little to assuage a bunch of angered Sabres and their fans.

The rule had been in place for eight years. But in late March the NHL had reminded teams and officials that a player can stay in the crease after the puck exits the painted area as long as he maintains control of the puck. Still, the rule was due for a change and less than 48 hours after the goal, it was. Determinations of crease violations are now exclusively with the on-ice officials, removing such decisions from the replay judge.

For the jubilant Stars, Hull had joined his legendary father, Bobby, in winning a Cup. "It is unbelievable starting out as a kid growing up in that shadow and finally making a niche for myself," Hull said. "This finally completes the cycle. I hope someday my son or grandkids can do it."

As the decade, and the century, drew to a close, another cycle was completed: Gretzky retired following the 1998-99 season. The NHL thus lost its preeminent ambassador. The Hockey Hall of Fame waived its standard three-year waiting period for a player to become eligible for induction and Gretzky will become the 10th player so honored.

BRETT **HULL**

Among the most prolific goal scorers in history, Hull's 86 in 1990-91 rank behind only Wayne Gretzky's 92 in 1981-82 and 87 in 1983-84. But the biggest goal of his career came in the early morning of June 20, 1999, when he put the puck past Dominik Hasek late in the third overtime, giving the Dallas Stars their first Stanley Cup. He and his father, Hall of Famer Bobby Hull, are the only father-son duo with 500 goals each. He spent most of his career with the St. Louis Blues before signing with the Dallas Stars as a free agent in 1998-99. Hull was born in Belleville, Ontario, but has dual citizenship and played for the United States in the 1996 World Cup and the 1998 Olympics.

RAYMOND **BOURQUE**

THE DEFENSEMAN PLAYED HIS 20TH SEASON with the Boston Bruins in 1998-99. That is the most for any current player in any sport to have spent his entire career with one team. Bourque has won the Norris Trophy five times, behind only former Bruin Bobby Orr (eight) and Doug Harvey (seven). He has played in the All-Star game 18 times, behind only Gordie Howe (23). Bourque is the Bruins' all-time leader in assists and points, but surely would trade all his individual honors for a Stanley Cup. The Bruins have made the finals twice since Bourque won the Calder Trophy in 1980, losing to the Edmonton Oilers in 1988 and 1990.

TEEMU **SELANNE**

THE FINNISH FLASH – BURST UPON THE SCENE with Winnipeg in 1992-93, scoring 76 goals to obliterate Mike Bossy's rookie record of 53, and 132 points to easily outdistance Peter Stastny's rookie mark of 109. He was traded to the Mighty Ducks of Anaheim during 1995-96. In the 1998 Olympics he was the leading scorer (four goals, six assists), as Finland surprisingly won a bronze medal. He won the first Maurice "Rocket" Richard Trophy in 1999 with 47 goals.

THE DOMINATOR AND THE DREAM

To every boy who grows up playing hockey in North America, the dream is to win the Stanley Cup. The rest of the world, however, sees things differently.

"WHEN I GREW UP IT WAS always the Olympics. We knew nothing of the NHL," said Buffalo Sabres goaltender Dominik Hasek, from the Czech Republic. "My heroes were always from my country and when they went to the Olympics it was a big thing. Now, I know that to get the Stanley Cup is great and I would like to win one, but when I left to go to North America for another season [in 1997], nobody talked about the Stanley Cup with me. They talked about the Olympics."

In the Czech Republic, they were talking about hockey before the Olympics, during the Olympics and, most of all, after the Olympics.

With NHL players competing in the Games for the first time in Nagano in 1998, Canada and the United States were the favorites. But it was the Czech Republic, behind Hasek, that came out on top, touching off a celebration in Prague not seen since the fall of communism nearly a decade earlier.

The World Cup of Hockey had generated excitement in the summer of 1996, as the United States stunned Canada in a thrilling finale to the eight-nation event. Now, the NHL was hoping that having its players compete on the largest of sports stages would result in even more interest in the United States and beyond, even at the expense of shutting down its season for nearly three weeks in February. Despite Wayne Gretzky, Eric Lindros, Patrick Roy and Ray Bourque on Team Canada and Brett Hull, Brian Leetch, Mike Richter and John LeClair on Team USA, all did not go smoothly.

The time difference between Japan and the United States meant the matches were on at odd hours. Teams USA and Canada flopped and, worst of all, some of the American players trashed their rooms in the Olympic Village after being eliminated from medal contention. The actual damage was minimal; the image damage was extensive. Despite vows from Olympic and NHL officials to severely punish the guilty, the culprits were never identified.

Conversely, the women's tournament was a complete success, with the favorites,

DALE **HUNTER**

HUNTER IS THE ONLY PLAYER IN NHL HISTORY with at least 1,000 points and 3,000 penalty minutes (and also at least 300 goals). He totaled 323 goals and 1,020 points in a 19-year career with the Quebec Nordiques, Washington Capitals and Colorado Avalanche. Hunter's 3,565 penalty minutes are second all time to Dave 'Tiger' Williams's 3,966. Hunter also has the dubious distinction of having played in more playoff games without winning a Stanley Cup than anyone else. But he has had individual postseason success: his four overtime playoff goals give him joint second place in the all-time ratings, behind only Maurice Richard's six.

Canada and the United States, living up to the hype. Team USA won the gold-medal game with a 3-1 victory over the Canadians. And, perhaps in a message to the US men, forward Cammi Granato was chosen to be the US flag bearer in the closing ceremonies.

In the men's event, eight nations advanced to the championship round for round-robin play.

In Group A, a Russian squad led by Sergei Fedorov and Pavel Bure finished 3-0, ahead of the 2-1 Czech Republic, featuring Hasek and Jaromir Jagr. Finland, despite Teemu Selanne's tournament-high 10 points, was 1-2, followed by Kazakhstan at 0-3.

Team Canada cruised through Group B at 3-0, and in the most anticipated match of the tournament dropped the Americans 4-1. Sweden, with Peter Forsberg and Ulf Samuelsson, was 2-1. Team USA was 1-2, beating only lowly Belarus (0-3).

The Americans qualified for the quarterfinals, but were dismissed by the Czechs. They fired 39 shots at Hasek, who let in only one in a 4-1 decision. "We came here with expectations of gold," US coach Ron Wilson said. "It's something that will always be in the back of your mind: What if. We feel we let a lot of people down, but more than anyone we let ourselves down."

Not only were the Americans viewed as underachievers, but also, because of the Olympic Village incident, spoiled brats. Canada, Russia and Finland reached the semifinals, too, with Russia beating Finland 7-4 to gain the gold-medal game.

The Canada-Czech Republic game featured perhaps the world's two best goaltenders, Hasek and Roy. The teams played to a 1-1 tie through overtime, leading to a five-man shootout. Robert Reichel of the New York Islanders beat Roy on the first try for the Czechs, but Hasek stopped all five Canadian tries for the victory.

"Nobody can beat the Dominator. He's the man," teammate Martin Rucinsky said. "In big games like this, he's outstanding."

"It's devastating," said Gretzky, who, curiously, was not among the five Canadians chosen for the shootout. "They beat us fair and square. There are no excuses. But when you don't win, it's the worst feeling in the world."

The Canadians, without Olympic gold since 1952, offered little in the bronze-medal game, falling to Finland 3-2.

The finale between the Czechs and Russians went into the third period scoreless and stayed that way until Peter Svoboda connected at 11:52. That was all Hasek needed. He wasn't tested as often as he was in previous games, but his 20 saves were enough to give the Czechs a 1-0 victory and their first Olympic gold medal.

"I've never seen a better goalie," Czech captain Vladimir Ruzicka said. "Some of the saves he made [in the tournament] were unbelievable. His legs were going over here; his hands were going over there. He's the best goaltender in the world. We know we only have to score one or two goals."

About 70,000 people had jammed Prague's Old Town Square to watch the game, and afterwards a celebration took flight. The players flew to Prague for a national ceremony, after which Hasek and the other Czechs playing in the NHL returned to North America to resume their quest for that other honor, the Stanley Cup.

Dominik Hasek was the biggest star on the biggest stage when the Czech Republic won the Gold Medal in 1998.

THE FINAL DAYS

"Sometimes you go to funerals. Fortunately, sometimes you get to go to weddings and fun parties. And to me, this is a party. This is a celebration. I hope everyone understands that. I look upon these next few days as something to really enjoy" – Wayne Gretzky at his retirement news conference.

THERE WAS WAYNE Gretzky, two days before he played his final NHL game, telling everyone to view this as a celebration and not a funeral. There was Gretzky, behind a podium at Madison Square Garden, wearing a black suit, a white shirt and a black tie.

Truth be told, Gretzky's exit from the NHL after 20 seasons was both funereal and celebratory. There were friends and family. There were hugs and kisses. There were gifts and honors. There was music. There was even art – "99" was painted behind each goal in tribute to what was commonly called "Gretzky's office".

A pregame ceremony began with a five-minute ovation from the 18,000-plus wedged into the Garden (even the referee and linesmen were applauding). Then the likes of Glen Sather and Mario Lemieux and Mark Messier were introduced. Commissioner Gary Bettman announced that no NHL player would ever wear No. 99 again. The Rangers drove out a Mercedes-Benz for Gretzky.

Even though the match was played between two US clubs (the Pittsburgh Penguins were the opponents), the national anthems of the United States and Canada were sung, with a twist. Canadian rocker Bryan Adams, a longtime Gretzky friend, substituted the line "We Stand on Guard for Thee" from "O Canada" with "We're Going to Miss You, Wayne Gretz-keeeee". Not to be outdone, John Amirante sang the "The Star-Spangled Banner", and "O'er the Land of the Free" was turned into "O'er the Land of Wayne Gretz-keeeee".

The game itself, the 1,487th of Gretzky's career, was mostly uneventful – no one even considered fighting and there were only three minor penalties all day. Highlights of Gretzky were shown in between play. So was a message taped by Michael Jordan. The fans edged up in their seats every time Gretzky came onto the ice. For the record, he logged 22 minutes 30 seconds on 22 shifts. He had two shots. His passes looked as crisp as ever.

"Sitting there in the first period," said longtime Oilers teammate Paul Coffey, "I watched him make a pass over four sticks that nobody could make but him." What was different about these passes was that his teammates couldn't convert them into goals.

That had been a problem for the Rangers during Gretzky's last two seasons in New York, each of which ended without a playoff appearance. It was not

For his finale, Gretzky was surrounded by fans and family.

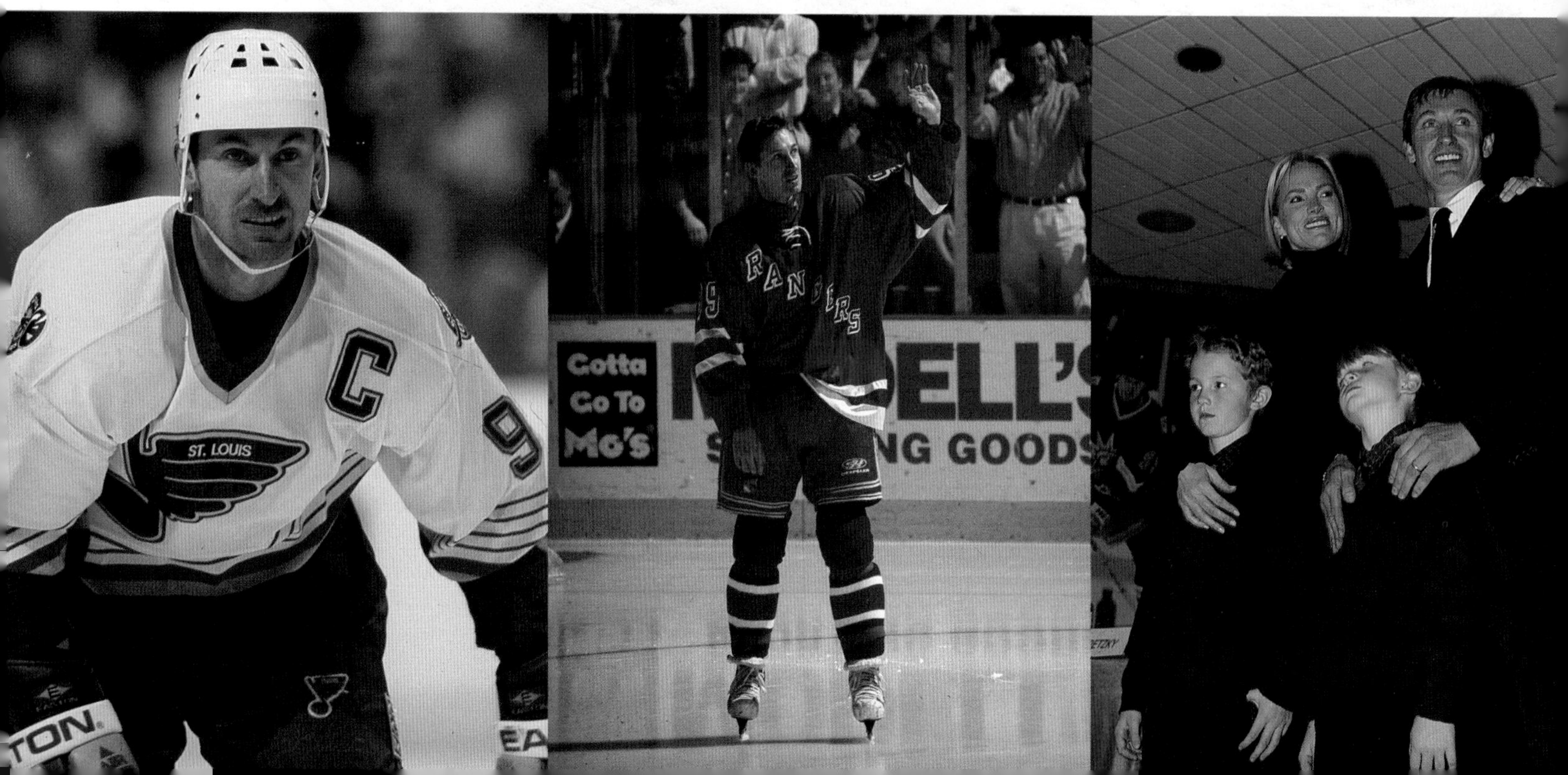

PAUL **COFFEY**

ONE OF THE SLEEKEST SKATERS THE NHL HAS ever seen, Coffey is the greatest scoring defenseman in league history and one of its top scorers at any position. He is second all-time in assists, behind only Wayne Gretzky. Coffey won three Stanley Cups with the Oilers, then one more with the Pittsburgh Penguins. He won three Norris Trophies, two with the Oilers and one with the Detroit Red Wings. He has played with eight clubs in his 19-year career, five of them in the past four seasons.

the way Gretzky, aged 38, wanted to go out. He had another year on his contract. But it was apparent that the Rangers were not close to contending for a Stanley Cup. Gretzky would have to settle for four titles, all with the Oilers under Sather, all in the 1980s.

The Penguins had already qualified for the postseason, but a win might have helped their playoff seeding. So, while everybody wanted Gretzky to go out a winner, the Penguins admitted to being conflicted. But they had won only one of their previous 11 games, and right winger Rob Brown said they weren't relishing "going into the playoffs with a loss".

With that in mind, Pittsburgh struck first, midway through the second period, on a goal by former Ranger Alexei Kovalev. Then, with Jaromir Jagr off for tripping, the fans got what they came for. On a wonderful tic-tac-toe play, Gretzky from the right circle passed into the slot to Mathieu Schneider, who found captain Brian Leetch to the left of the crease for a tap-in goal 30 seconds before the second intermission.

It was Gretzky's 1,963rd assist, his 2,857th point. They represent just two of his 61 solo or shared NHL records.

The third period wound down with no further scoring. Rangers coach John Muckler called a time out with 40 seconds left to announce he had become a grandfather and to tell Gretzky that "you've got to get the winner".

"Maybe when I was younger," Gretzky said later, adding that during the time-out it finally dawned on him that there was less than a minute left in his career.

Not quite. The game went into overtime. Then, stunningly, Jagr scored at one minute 22 seconds.

The building went silent. So did Jagr. "It was an accident," he said. "I didn't know what to do. Should I celebrate? I looked and [the Rangers] were all holding their heads and I just didn't know what to do."

After the stunned silence, the fans rose from their seats and cheered. Gretzky shook hands with all the Penguins. All the players left the ice. Only Gretzky was left. He skated around the rink, waving to the crowd. Then, suddenly, he was gone. But, like at a rock concert, the fans kept roaring, wanting more. Gretzky came back, took some laps, waving all the while, with a spotlight on him in the darkened Garden. He left again. But he had to come back a third and final time.

It was a full half-hour after the game when Gretzky went to his postgame news conference. He was still wearing his red, white and blue sweater.

"Probably, subconsciously, I didn't want to take it off," he said. "I'm not going to put it on ever again, so it's hard."

Gretzky, and everybody else, said it was fitting that Jagr, who had just won his second Ross Trophy, scored the winning goal.

Jagr was asked if he saw himself "replacing" Gretzky. With an incredulous look on his face, Jagr responded, "Replace Gretzky?"

"People talk about passing the torch," said Gretzky. "Well, it's been passed. He said: 'I didn't mean to do that.' I told him: 'That's what I used to say.'"

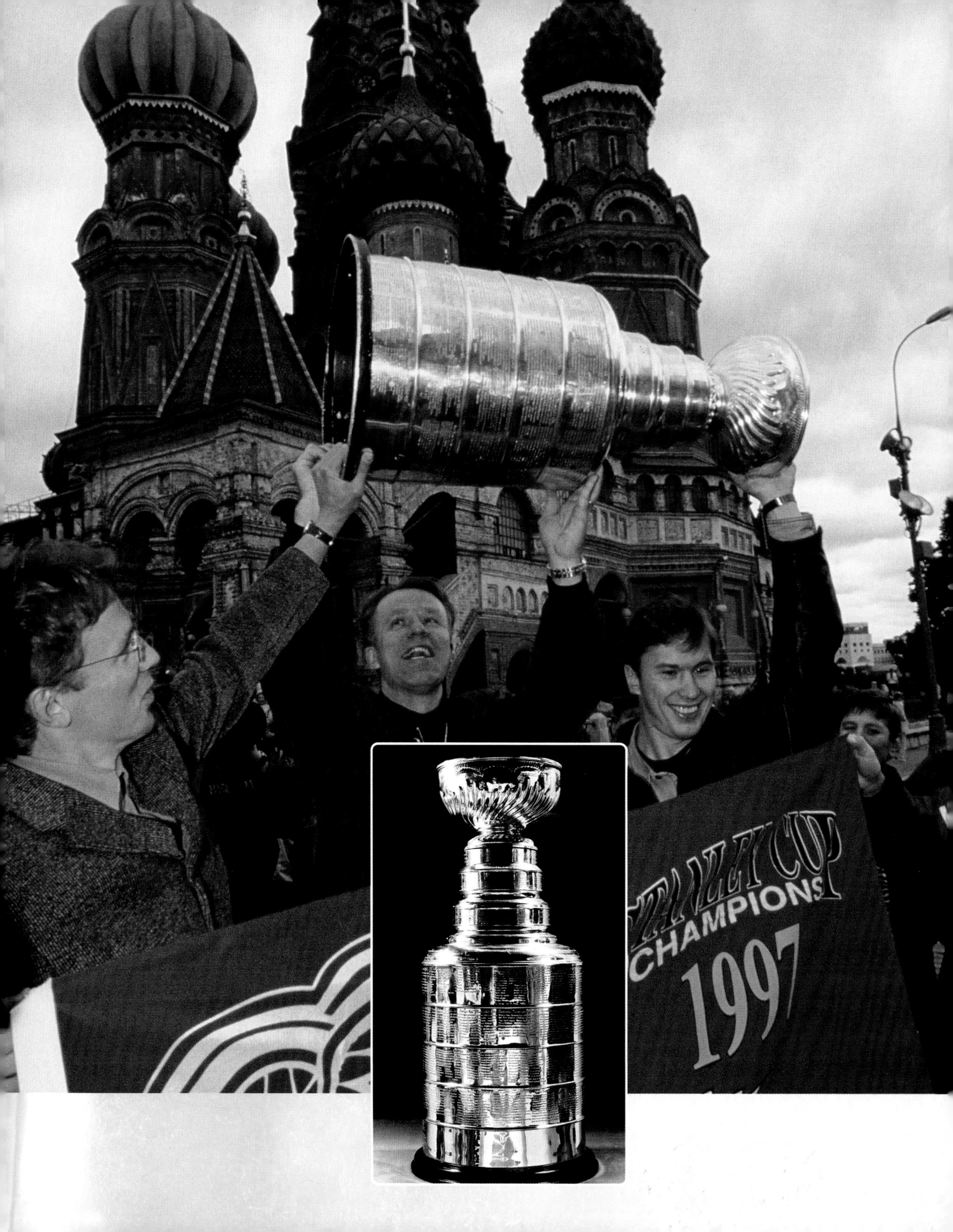
CUP
CHAMPIONS
1997

It has led quite a life. In fact, many people would be envious. It has traveled to some of the world's far-off places. Everywhere it has gone, people have waited in long lines just to get so much as a glimpse. It has been treated with reverence. It has bodyguards and round-the-clock security. It is famous. It has made little boys dream. It has made grown men cry ... It is the Stanley Cup.

Opposite page: Larionov, Fetisov and Kozlov take the Cup to Red Square in 1997.

Ever since it quietly came into existence late in the nineteenth century, the Stanley Cup has grown in size, stature, tradition and lore. It has triggered emotions and reactions from the reckless to the ridiculous.

The Cup has been paraded through Moscow's Red Square, it has been kicked into Ottawa's Rideau Canal, it has been left on the side of a road, it has been to bars and to swimming pools. Men have taken extreme measures to vie for the Cup, none more so than the Dawson City Klondikers, a bunch of gold miners who challenged for the Cup in 1905 (when challenges were the way you competed for it) and began their cross-continent journey in search of the Cup on dogsleds.

Back in 1892, Frederick Arthur Stanley, the Governor General of Canada who is more commonly remembered today as Lord Stanley (Lord Stanley of Preston, to be precise), decided that if hockey were to grow, it should have a yearly champion. There would be a challenge cup contested annually to determine the best club in Canada. And so, Lord Stanley purchased a silver, punch-bowl-shaped cup for $48.67 and named it the Dominion Hockey Challenge Cup.

The Cup given by Lord Stanley.

Quickly and forever, the trophy began being referred to as Lord Stanley's Cup. By the time it was first the object of a competition, Lord Stanley had returned to England and never saw a single Cup match played.

The first winner: Montreal AAA of 1893 (top); the toughest challenger, Dawson City, 1905.

The game of hockey has changed greatly since the Gay Nineties, but the feelings engendered by the Stanley Cup today were in place from the start. Back then, the course of determining a champion was not nearly as clear as it is today. The Montreal Amateur Athletic Association was deemed the best team in the Dominion in 1893, having survived a round-robin series of games against four other clubs. The Montreal AAA is the first team to have its name inscribed on the Cup.

Six Montreal clubs have won the Cup, and the city dominated the early years the way the Canadiens have controlled much of the modern era. Montreal teams won 11 times in the first 11 years of Cup play (1893-1903), although at that time the trophy often was contested more than once a year.

The Ottawa Silver Seven then took charge, winning in 1903 and 1904 before being challenged by Dawson City in 1905. A collection of Canadians lured to the Yukon in search of gold, they left Dawson City on December 19, 1904, beginning a 4,400-mile trek to Ottawa on dogsleds

Sugar Jim Henry congratulates Richard in 1952.

in temperatures of -20 degrees. Forty-six miles on the first day, forty-one on the second, thirty-six on the third, the ***Ottawa Journal*** reported. They were trying to get to Skagway to catch a boat to Seattle on their way to Vancouver to board a train.

They arrived in Skagway two hours late and had to wait five days for another boat. Arriving in Ottawa on January 12, 1905, the exhausted Klondikers asked for a one-week delay. The Silver Seven refused and the best-of-three series began the next day. Ottawa won 9-2. Three days later, Ottawa won 23-2, behind Frank McGee's 14 goals.

For the valiant if overmatched Klondikers, it was a case of "Thanks for coming, drive home safely".

The Silver Seven have a place in Stanley Cup history, and not just because they were perhaps hockey's first dynasty. They took part in what was one of many wacky incidents involving the Cup. Once, some of the players were returning from a victory banquet when it was suggested that they could kick the trophy into Rideau Canal. (It was just the bowl then, making the act, if not acceptable, possible.) One problem: They left it there. The next day, realizing what they had done, they returned to the canal and, luckily for them, found it frozen over, with the Cup where they had left it.

From 1893 to 1910, the Cup's recipient was determined via challenge matches contested by amateur and professional teams. By 1910, pro leagues began to dominate the Cup and, since 1912, the Cup has been contested only once per year. Beginning in 1913, the champions of the NHA and PCHA met for the Cup. That continued when the NHA morphed into the NHL in 1917 until the NHL took exclusive control of the Cup, commencing with the 1926-27 season.

Through it all, the ceremonial handshake has been part of Cup tradition. It is rare in sports that combatants end their battle with a show of sportsmanship – tennis players shake hands after matches – especially in such a fiercely brutal game as hockey. The hockey handshake dates to the early years of Cup play, but it didn't become a formal part of the game until the 1950s. At the end of a hard-fought series, the last thing many players – winners included, losers especially – want to do is shake hands with opponents they have learned to hate, at least temporarily. Rarely is anything more said than "Good series" or "Good luck", even among friends.

After the 1954 finals, when the Detroit Red Wings beat Montreal in overtime in Game 7, the Canadiens refused to shake hands. Led by their coach, Dick Irvin, the Canadiens simply left the ice following a goal by Tony Leswick.

"Did you see how they shook hands," Leswick said. "Not one of them came over."

Apparently, they were prevented from doing so by their coach. "If I had shaken hands, I wouldn't have meant it," Irvin said. "And I refuse to be a hypocrite."

The whole process may seem a bit hypocritical – trying figuratively to kill each other for a series and then being pleasant – but that is part of the Stanley Cup. And the 1954 Canadiens, in this instance, were an anomaly.

"The team on the losing end of the handshakes hates like heck to do it," said NHL veteran Dave Lowry, who was on the losing end when the Colorado Avalanche swept the Florida Panthers in 1996. "But it's a case of showing respect to your opponent."

Through the years, there also has been respect for the Cup itself. It's just that some players have a funny way of showing it. Take the 1924 Canadiens. After winning the trophy, some players loaded it into a car to drive to owner Leo Dandurand's home for a party. They got a flat tire along the way and everybody – Cup included – got out of the car. After the flat was fixed, everybody – Cup not included – got back into the car and proceeded to the

party. It wasn't until the players got to Dandurand's that they realized what they had done. Just like the Rideau Canal incident years earlier, the players scurried back and found the charmed Cup right where they had left it.

Despite surviving both Rideau Canal and a Montreal street unscathed, the Stanley Cup has undergone numerous planned alterations. At first, winning players scratched their own names into the bowl. Then silver bands were added to the bottom of the trophy to accommodate the names of the members of the winning clubs. The Cup underwent various changes through the years until the current one-piece Cup was introduced in 1958, with five silver bands. The original bowl was retired to the Hall of Fame in 1969, too brittle to continue, and a new Cup was created, sitting atop a barrel-shaped base. The 1991 Pittsburgh Penguins completed the bottom band of the original five-band trophy. At that point, the top band, denoting winners from 1928 to 1940, was removed and sent to the Hall.

Your name on the Cup, the dream of millions.

Three teams which didn't win the Cup nonetheless have their names engraved: The 1915 Ottawa Senators, the 1916 Portland (Oregon) Rosebuds and the 1917 Vancouver Millionaires each defeated the defending Cup holder in their league playoffs but then lost in the NHA-PCHA championship round.

A pair of enterprising kids almost got their names on the Cup. In 1925, with the trophy sitting in a cardboard box in their basement, Lynn and Muzz Patrick took a nail and attempted to scratch in their names. They were the sons of the legendary Lester Patrick, who had just coached the PCHA's Victoria Cougars to the title. Little did they know that 15 years later, both would get their names engraved onto the Cup in traditional fashion, as players on the New York Rangers.

Lester Patrick, having ended a 13-year run as Rangers coach just a season earlier, was part of the 1940 victory as the team's general manager. He also won two Cups in New York in 1928 and 1933. It was during the 1928 Cup finals that he was involved in one of the best-known moments in Stanley Cup history.

Having already lost the opener of the best-of-five series against the Montreal Maroons, the Rangers lost their one and only goaltender, Lorne Chabot, to an injury in the second period of a scoreless Game 2. Patrick asked the Maroons if he could use Alex Connell, the Ottawa Senators goaltender who happened to be in the Montreal Forum that night. The Maroons refused, suggesting that Patrick himself play goal.

"I will, by God, I will," growled the 44-year-old coach, who was a defenseman in his playing days.

Patrick kept the game scoreless until the Rangers tallied early in the third period. But the Maroons in turn connected to force overtime. That set the stage for the Rangers' Frank Boucher to score the winning goal. Patrick's players lifted him off the ice and carried him around the rink in celebration.

The Rangers endured an NHL-record 54-year drought before winning again in 1994. The Detroit Red Wings also had a decades-long barren stretch, though not quite as long. They dominated the early 1950s, winning four times in six seasons, ending in 1955. Then they went Cup-less until 1997.

Detroit also had suffered through a rugged 1940s. The Red Wings lost five finals in the decade (winning once in 1943), including the infamous 1942 series in which they became the only team to lose a finals after taking a 3-0 lead in games (against the Toronto Maple Leafs). Finally, Detroit broke through in 1950 and was presented with the Cup by NHL President Clarence Campbell. Until that day, the Cup was placed on a table in the center of the ice. And it stayed there during the celebration.

But when Ted Lindsay, having been on the last three of those runners-up clubs, saw the gleaming trophy that had been so elusive, he was practically salivating.

"Here it is face-to-face with you – what you've aspired to, what you've worked for, what you've finally achieved," Lindsay recalled years later. "You don't leave it just sitting there on a table in the middle of the ice. You reach for it."

And so Lindsay did. He picked it up and began skating. He skated over to the boards so fans could get a closer look. His teammates, perhaps stunned (along with Campbell), didn't join him to form the conga line that is the signature of today's celebrations.

Ted Lindsay, a 1966 Hall of Famer, is credited with

The 1999 Stanley Cup champions, the Dallas Stars: "What it's all about."

being the first player to hoist the Stanley Cup. The hoist and skate is one of the rituals that connects players across the years and the players to the fans who cheer them.

When the Red Wings ended their long drought in a whole different NHL – and a whole different world – they did something with Lord Stanley's Cup that had never been done in all its 104 years. With the fall of communism still fresh, three Red Wings – Viacheslav Fetisov, Igor Larionov and Vyacheslav Kozlov – took the vaunted trophy on a four-day tour of Russia in 1997. The Cup went to Lenin's Mausoleum in Red Square; it went to a soccer match in Moscow before 62,000 fans, including Russian President Boris Yeltsin; it went to the Russian White House, where Prime Minister Viktor Chernomyrdin sipped champagne from the Cup; it went to Russia's Hockeytown, Voskresensk, a small industrial village where Larionov and Kozlov played the game as boys.

The players and the Cup arrived via motorcade and were greeted by an exuberant, wide-eyed throng of 3,500. There was a jubilant celebration with dancers and musicians at the Khimik hockey school where Larionov first played at the age of seven. The townspeople eventually left the stands to go onto the ice to greet the players and to touch the Cup, 5,000 miles from Hockeytown, USA.

"I always dreamt about seeing them, but I never thought I would see them live, with the Stanley Cup," Dmitri Vorovjev, a 12-year-old defenseman at the time, said through an interpreter. "I was so nervous, I was going crazy. I will go over there some day and win the Cup myself."

"Even playing far from the Motherland, we could feel your support," Larionov told the crowd. "Now you can see what it's all about."

NHL Trophies

Every North American professional sports league honors its top personnel with end-of-season awards. But the NHL, more steeped in tradition than all the others, takes great strides in remembering its past while recognizing its present.

Only the NHL puts names – and faces – on all of its trophies. Also, only the NHL presents its awards as part of a televised extravaganza with thousands in attendance and hundreds of thousands watching at home. Six awards – Hart, Lady Byng, Masterton, Norris, Selke and Calder – are voted by the Professional Hockey Writers' Association. The other two that are awarded by vote are the Vezina, which is selected by NHL General Managers, and the Adams, which comes from a vote of NHL Broadcasters. And there are some that are purely achievement based – Art Ross, Jennings, Richard and Clancy.

HART MEMORIAL TROPHY

GIVEN TO THE PLAYER DEEMED "MOST VALUABLE TO HIS TEAM". THE Edmonton Oilers' Wayne Gretzky won the most Harts – nine, including eight in a row (1979-80 to 1988-89). In 1996-97, the Buffalo Sabres' Dominik Hasek became only the fifth goaltender in history to win both the Hart and the Vezina Trophy, which goes to the league's top goaltender, in the same season. Then he became the first player to do it twice, winning both honors the following season. The Hart Trophy was donated to the NHL in 1923 by David A. Hart, whose son, Cecil, became coach of the Montreal Canadiens in 1926-27 and later became their general manager. The trophy was retired to the Hall of Fame in 1960 and was replaced by the Hart Memorial Trophy. When Jaromir Jagr won the 1999 Trophy, he became the third straight winner from the Czech Republic.

ART ROSS TROPHY

THIS GOES TO THE SCORING CHAMPION AND IS ONE OF THE FEW MAJOR awards based on statistics – the Richard Trophy and the Jennings are the others. Wayne Gretzky has won it more than any other player – 10 times, seven consecutively with the Edmonton Oilers and three times with the Los Angeles Kings. Art Howie Ross, the former manager-coach of the Boston Bruins, presented this award to the NHL in 1947.

VEZINA TROPHY

AWARDED TO THE TOP GOALTENDER, THIS IS NAMED IN HONOR OF THE Canadiens' Georges Vezina, one of the NHL's first great goaltenders who collapsed during a game in 1925 and died of tuberculosis a few months later. Montreal's team owners gave the trophy to the NHL in 1926-27. Before 1981-82, it was given to the goaltender(s) of the team conceding the fewest goals. Jacques Plante won seven times under the old standard, six with the Montreal Canadiens and once sharing with Glenn Hall on the St. Louis Blues; the Buffalo Sabres' Domink Hasek won it five times (in six seasons) under the newer format. The only interruption to Hasek's run of prosperity came in 1995-96, when the Washington Capitals' Jim Carey was the victor. Carey proved to be a one-shot wonder, however, as he was traded to the Boston Bruins the following season before being demoted to the minors the year after that.

JAMES NORRIS MEMORIAL TROPHY

THE TOP DEFENSEMAN WINS THIS AWARD. IT HAS BEEN DOMINATED BY A select group since its inception in 1953, more than any other major NHL honor. The Boston Bruins' Bobby Orr won it a record eight times, and did so consecutively (1967-68 to 1974-75). Doug Harvey won it seven times in an eight-year span (1954-55 to 1961-62, excluding 1958-59, when fellow Montreal Canadien Tom Johnson was the recipient). In a recent 13-year stretch, from 1985 to 1997, four defensemen took turns winning the trophy. Boston's Raymond Bourque won it five times; the Chicago Blackhawks' Chris Chelios won it three times; Paul Coffey also won it three times, twice with the Edmonton Oilers and once with the Detroit Red Wings; and the Rangers' Brian Leetch won it twice. The Los Angeles Kings' Rob Blake ended the quartet's hold on the award by winning in 1997-98. Al MacInnis followed Blake with his near-unanimous selection in 1999. The trophy was presented in 1953 by Norris's four children in memory of their father, who owned the Red Wings.

LADY BYNG MEMORIAL TROPHY

PRESENTED TO THE PLAYER WHO EXHIBITS "THE BEST TYPE OF SPORTSMANSHIP and gentlemanly conduct combined with a high standard of play". The Chicago Blackhawks' Stan Mikita, always a great scorer, toned down his penalty-filled ways to win the trophy twice. Mikita had racked up a combined 300 penalty minutes in 1963-64 and 1964-65, but totaled only 26 in winning the Byng in 1966-67 and 1967-68. Interestingly, Mikita also won the Ross Trophy those same four seasons and the Hart Trophy in the latter two. In 1925, Lady Byng, wife of Canada's governor-general, unveiled the Lady Byng Trophy. After the New York Rangers' Frank Boucher won the award a record seven times in the first eight seasons, he was given the trophy to keep. Lady Byng donated another trophy in 1936 and, after her death in 1949, it became the Lady Byng Memorial Trophy. It will also be marked as the last trophy won by Wayne Gretzky as he took the 1999 Trophy.

JACK ADAMS TROPHY

THE TOP COACH RECEIVES THIS honor, and it has been in existence only since 1974. Pat Burns is the only one to receive the award three times, once each with the Montreal Canadiens (1988-89), the Toronto Maple Leafs (1992-93) and the Boston Bruins (1997-98). The award is named after the longtime coach of the Detroit Red Wings (1927-1947).

MAURICE "ROCKET" RICHARD TROPHY

AWARDED FOR THE FIRST TIME IN 1999 to Teemu Selanne of the Mighty Ducks of Anaheim. This trophy, presented to the League by the Montreal Canadiens in January 1999, goes to the leading goal scorer in the NHL each season. Selanne won the first with 47 goals. It honors the spectacular Rocket Richard, whose 50 goals in 50 games in 1944-45 remains the goal standard for all to follow, even as his record has been surpassed.

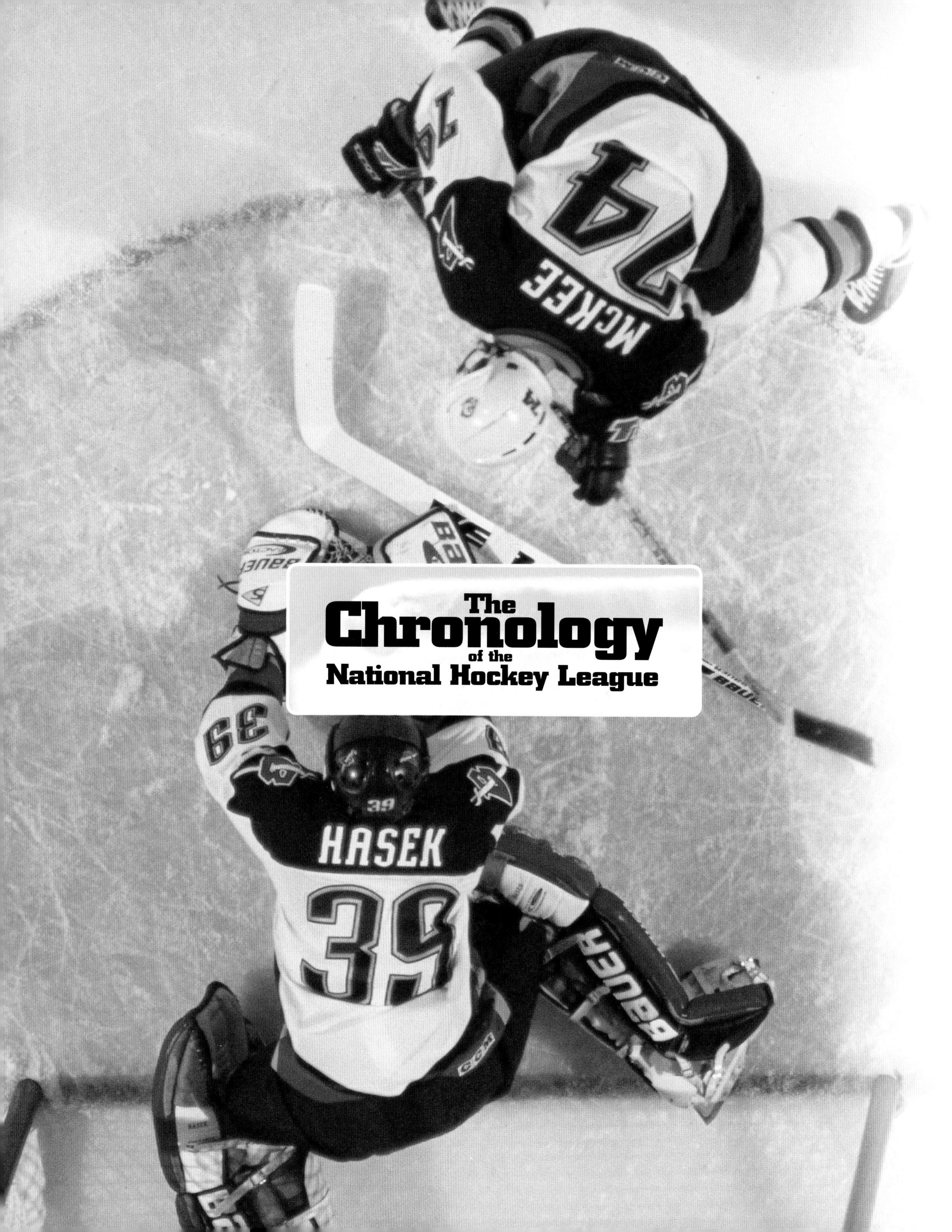

The Chronology of the National Hockey League

NOVEMBER 26, 1917: The NHL was formed with Frank Calder as its first president and the Montreal Canadiens, Montreal Wanderers, Ottawa Senators, and Quebec Bulldogs as founding members. The four teams from the defunct National Hockey Association of Canada Limited were soon joined by the Toronto Arenas.

DECEMBER 19, 1917: One minute into the first NHL game, Dave Ritchie of the Montreal Wanderers scored the first goal in NHL history. Seven hundred fans saw the Wanderers beat Toronto 10-9.

MARCH 30, 1918: Toronto was the first NHL team to play for the Stanley Cup as the Arenas played Vancouver of the PCHA. Toronto won the series, three games to two.

DECEMBER 28, 1918: Montreal Canadiens goalie Georges Vezina kicked a save to Newsy Lalonde, who then scored, giving Vezina the first assist for an NHL goalie.

APRIL 1, 1919: The final game of the Stanley Cup series between the Canadiens and the Seattle Metropolitans was cancelled due to the worldwide influenza epidemic. Joe Hall, star defenseman of the Canadiens, died of the flu on April 5. No Cup winner was determined.

JANUARY 31, 1920: Joe Malone became the first player to score seven goals in one game as Quebec beat Ottawa 10-4. The record still stands.

MARCH 2, 1922: The Toronto St. Patricks beat the Vancouver Millionaires 6-0 in the last game to feature seven players to a side in a professional game.

JANUARY 31, 1923: In the NHL's seventh season, the Canadiens defeated the Hamilton Tigers 5-4 in the first penalty-free game.

MARCH 22, 1923: Describing a game between two amateur minor-league teams over the telephone, Foster Hewitt delivered the first hockey broadcast.

MARCH 31, 1923: Ottawa's 18-year-old star King Clancy played all six positions in a 1-0 Stanley Cup-clinching victory over Edmonton.

FEBRUARY 9, 1924: The NHL's rich tradition of trophies began, as the Hart Trophy was created for the player deemed most valuable to his team. The first winner was Frank Nighbor of the Ottawa Senators, who had 13 points in 20 games.

DECEMBER 1, 1924: The Boston Bruins, the first United States-based team in the NHL, defeated the Montreal Maroons 2-1 at the Boston Arena, marking the first NHL game played in the United States.

APRIL 13, 1927: The Ottawa Senators defeated the Bruins for the Stanley Cup, the first time only NHL teams competed for the Cup. It was also the end of Ottawa's remarkable success in the league's early days, marking the franchise's fourth Cup in the league's first 10 seasons. By 1934, the franchise no longer existed.

SEPTEMBER 24, 1927: The league passed a rule allowing forward passes in the defensive end and neutral zone.

FEBRUARY 20, 1929: Clint Benedict was the first goaltender to wear a mask in the net when he donned temporary protection for a facial injury.

MARCH 28, 1929: In the first Stanley Cup Final featuring two American teams, the Boston Bruins swept the New York Rangers 2-0 and 2-1.

DECEMBER 16, 1929: The league adopted the offsides rule, which prevents players from entering the offensive zone ahead of the play. The change in the offside rule was necessitated by the legalization of forward passing in the offensive zone before the season.

MARCH 26, 1931: The first goaltender was pulled for an extra attacker when Boston's Art Ross yanked his goalie in a 1-0 loss to Montreal.

NOVEMBER 12, 1931: Maple Leaf Gardens opened in Toronto. The visiting Blackhawks won the game.

FEBRUARY 11, 1932: The first US-born player to score a hat trick was Boston's George Owen, who scored in a loss to the Montreal Maroons.

JANUARY 1, 1933: Foster Hewitt's radio broadcasts began going out over a national network of 20 stations, establishing Saturday as *Hockey Night in Canada*.

DECEMBER 28, 1933: Howie Morenz became the first player to score 250 career goals.

FEBRUARY 14, 1934: The league held its first All-Star game to raise money for injured player Ace Bailey. Toronto beat a team of stars from the other seven teams 7-4.

NOVEMBER 10, 1934: In the first season of the penalty shot rule, Toronto's George Hainsworth stopped the Canadiens' Armand Mondou on the first penalty shot ever. Three days later, Ralph Bowman scored the league's first penalty-shot goal.

MARCH 25, 1936: The longest game in NHL history, which began on March 24, ended on Mud Bruneteau's goal in the fifth overtime and with Detroit beating the Montreal Maroons, 1-0. Detroit went on to capture its first Stanley Cup.

JANUARY 30, 1937: Nels Stewart broke Howie Morenz's career goal-scoring record with his 270th.

MARCH 8, 1937: Howie Morenz died of an embolism.

APRIL 16, 1939: In the first Stanley Cup finals since the league expanded the series from best-of-five to best-of-seven, Boston beat Toronto in five games.

FEBRUARY 25, 1940: The New York Rangers beat the Canadiens 6-2 in the first game ever broadcast on TV in the US. Only 300 receivers in the New York area were set up to capture the broadcast.

SEPTEMBER 28, 1942: The Brooklyn (formerly New York) Americans ceased operations and "The Original Six" era began.

NOVEMBER 21, 1942: Due to a wartime restriction on train schedules, the league ended the 10-minute overtime rule for regular season games. The extra period was not reinstated until 1983.

JANUARY 23, 1944: Detroit scored a record 15 straight goals and crushed the Rangers 15-0.

MARCH 18, 1945: Maurice "Rocket" Richard scored his record 50th goal in the Montreal Canadiens' 50th and final game of the 1944-45 season.

SEPTEMBER 4, 1946: Clarence Campbell was elected as the third president of the NHL. He served until 1977.

OCTOBER 16, 1946: Gordie Howe of the Detroit Red Wings scored his first NHL goal as an 18-year-old rookie.

OCTOBER 13, 1947: First annual All-Star game matching the previous season's Stanley Cup champions against a squad of NHL All-Stars was played with the All-Stars defeated by the Maple Leafs 4-3.

OCTOBER 8, 1950: The first televised All-Star game was played in Detroit.

DECEMBER 20, 1950: Toronto goaltender Turk Broda was the first to reach 300 career victories.

APRIL 21, 1951: Bill Barilko of the Maple Leafs wrapped up the all-overtime final with a goal. That summer Barilko was killed in an airplane crash.

MARCH 23, 1952: In scoring three goals within a span of 21 seconds, Chicago's Bill Mosienko set the record for the fastest hat trick by one player.

NOVEMBER 1, 1952: First *Hockey Night in Canada* TV program beamed from Maple Leaf Gardens. On October 9, 1952, the first regular-season national TV coverage had come from the Montreal Forum in French. The first nationally televised game in the United States took place on January 5, 1957.

Chronology

MARCH 10, 1955: The Zamboni ice cleaning machine debuted in Montreal.

MARCH 17, 1955: At the first game following the suspension of the Canadiens' Maurice Richard for punching an official during a fight in a 4-2 loss to Boston, a riot broke out in Montreal. The Canadiens forfeited the game that night to the Red Wings.

APRIL 14, 1955: The Detroit Red Wings defeated the Canadiens four games to three in the Stanley Cup. The Red Wings dominated the first half of the decade with four Stanley Cups.

JUNE 6, 1955: The league modified the minor penalty rule to allow a player to return to the ice when the other team scored on the power play. Previously, penalties were served for the full two minutes.

NOVEMBER 1, 1959: Jacques Plante of Montreal donned a goalie's mask in a game for the first time.

APRIL 14, 1960: The Montreal Canadiens completed a four-game sweep of the Maple Leafs for their record fifth consecutive Stanley Cup. It was also Maurice "Rocket" Richard's last NHL game.

NOVEMBER 27, 1960: In his 938th game, Gordie Howe became the first NHL player to score 1,000 points.

AUGUST 26, 1961: The original Hockey Hall of Fame opened in Toronto.

JUNE 5, 1963: Twenty-one players were chosen in the league's first Amateur Draft.

NOVEMBER 10, 1963: Gordie Howe scored his 545th career goal, breaking the record held by Maurice Richard.

MARCH 12, 1966: Chicago's Bobby Hull became the first to score more than 50 goals in one season as he hit No. 51 in a 4-2 win over New York.

FEBRUARY 9, 1966: The league announced that six new franchises would be added for the 1967-68 season: Los Angeles, San Francisco, Philadelphia, Pittsburgh, Minneapolis, and St. Louis.

MAY 2, 1967: The Toronto Maple Leafs, the oldest team ever to win the Cup, defeated the Canadiens. They were the last champions of the Original Six era.

JANUARY 15, 1968: Minnesota's Bill Masterton died two days after being injured in a game, the first on-ice fatality in league history.

MARCH 2, 1969: Boston's Phil Esposito became the first player to score 100 points in a season. Bobby Hull and Gordie Howe also went on to crack 100.

MARCH 29, 1970: Chicago goaltender Tony Esposito set a modern NHL record with his 15th shutout in one season.

APRIL 15, 1970: Bobby Orr's assist gave him the scoring title with 33 goals and 120 points to make him the first defenseman ever to win the Art Ross Trophy.

NOVEMBER 9, 1971, AND DECEMBER 31, 1971: The NHL awarded franchises to the Atlanta Flames and New York Islanders, respectively.

SEPTEMBER 28, 1972: "Henderson has scored for Canada" was Foster Hewitt's call of the goal that gave the Summit Series to Canada over the Soviet Union.

MAY 19, 1974: Philadelphia became the first post-1967 expansion team to win the Stanley Cup.

JUNE 11, 1974: The NHL awarded franchises to the Kansas City Scouts and the Washington Capitals.

FEBRUARY 7, 1976: Toronto's Darryl Sittler got six goals and made four assists for a record 10 points in an 11-4 win against Boston.

JULY 14, 1976: The California Seals became the Cleveland Barons and the Kansas City Scouts became the Colorado Rockies.

SEPTEMBER 4, 1977: John A. Ziegler succeeded Clarence Campbell as President of the NHL.

JUNE 13, 1978: Cleveland folded and its players were added to Minnesota's roster.

MAY 21, 1979: The Montreal Canadiens won their fourth straight Stanley Cup, the second-longest streak ever. It was the last game for Hall of Famers Jacques Lemaire, Yvan Cournoyer and Ken Dryden. The next season, a new dynasty began when the New York Islanders won the first of their four straight Cups.

JUNE 22, 1979: Four World Hockey Association teams joined the NHL: the Edmonton Oilers, the Hartford Whalers, the Quebec Nordiques, and the Winnipeg Jets.

NOVEMBER 28, 1979: The Islanders' Billy Smith recorded the first goal for a goalie, as he was the last New York player to touch the puck before Colorado's Rob Ramage put it into his own net.

FEBRUARY 24, 1980: Wayne Gretzky, 19, scored 100 points in 61 games, making him the youngest 100-point scorer in history.

JUNE 24, 1980: The Flames moved from Atlanta to Calgary.

FEBRUARY 26, 1981: In a game between Boston and Minnesota, the teams combined for a record 406 penalty minutes.

MARCH 25, 1982: Wayne Gretzky got two goals and two assists to make him the first 200-point scorer in league history. He finished with a record 92 goals and 212 points.

MAY 27, 1982: The Colorado Rockies became the New Jersey Devils.

JANUARY 27, 1984: Wayne Gretzky of Edmonton scored in his 51st straight game. His streak ended in the Oilers' next game.

MARCH 31, 1984: The Islanders' Mike Bossy became the first player to score 50 goals in seven straight seasons.

MAY 19, 1984: The Edmonton Oilers started hockey's next dynasty by defeating the Islanders for the Stanley Cup. Edmonton won the title five times in the next seven seasons.

MARCH 26, 1986: Minnesota's Neal Broten became the first US-born player to score 100 points in one season.

DECEMBER 31, 1988: Mario Lemieux scored five goals in an 8-6 victory over the New Jersey Devils. The goals came at even strength, short-handed, on a power play, on a penalty shot and into an empty net. He also had three assists.

JUNE 6, 1989: Wayne Gretzky became the first player to win the same award nine times as he collected his ninth Hart Trophy as the league's MVP.

MAY 9, 1990: In a transaction involving the Minnesota North Stars, the NHL added the San Jose Sharks for the 1991-92 season.

JUNE 5, 1991: St. Louis' Brett Hull, son of Bobby Hull, won the Hart Trophy, making him part of the first father-son combination to win league MVP.

DECEMBER 16, 1991: The NHL awarded franchises to the Tampa Bay Lightning and the Ottawa Senators.

APRIL 1, 1992: The NHL Players' Association went on strike for 11 days.

DECEMBER 10, 1992: The NHL announced new teams in South Florida (Florida Panthers) and Anaheim (Mighty Ducks).

DECEMBER 11, 1992: Gary B. Bettman is elected as

the NHL's first commissioner.

MARCH 2, 1993: Mario Lemieux returned following his final cancer treatment to the Pittsburgh Penguins lineup. Despite his missing 24 games, Lemieux won the Art Ross Trophy with 160 points

MARCH 10, 1993: The Minnesota North Stars became the Dallas Stars.

JUNE 9, 1993: The Centennial Stanley Cup was won by the Montreal Canadiens after winning 10 overtime games in the playoffs.

JUNE 18, 1993: The Hockey Hall of Fame moved to its new site on Front Street, Toronto.

MARCH 23, 1994: Wayne Gretzky scored career goal No. 802 to pass Gordie Howe as the all-time leading goal scorer.

JUNE 14, 1994: After a 54-year drought, the New York Rangers won the Stanley Cup, defeating the Vancouver Canucks four games to three.

OCTOBER 1, 1994-JANUARY 19, 1995: An owner's lockout forced the cancellation of 468 games and the creation of an abbreviated 48-game schedule.

MAY 3, 1995: Pittsburgh's Jaromir Jagr scored 32 goals and 70 points in the lockout-shortened season to become the first European player to lead the NHL in scoring.

MAY 25, 1995: The Quebec Nordiques became the Colorado Avalanche and moved to Denver. In their first season in Colorado, the Avalanche defeated the Florida Panthers for the Stanley Cup.

JANUARY 19, 1996: The Winnipeg Jets sale was approved as was their move to Phoenix for the 1996-97 season, where they became the Phoenix Coyotes.

MARCH 25, 1997: The Hartford Whalers announced they would move to North Carolina and become the Carolina Hurricanes.

JUNE 7, 1997: The Detroit Red Wings won their first Stanley Cup in 42 seasons, sweeping the Philadelphia Flyers.

JUNE 25, 1997: The NHL announced it would expand to 30 teams with the addition of franchises in Columbus, Atlanta, Minnesota, and Nashville by 2000.

OCTOBER 3-4, 1997: The NHL played its first regular-season games off the North American continent as the Mighty Ducks of Anaheim and the Vancouver Canucks opened the season with two games in Tokyo.

DECEMBER 1, 1997: Montreal became the first NHL team to play 5,000 games. Their overall record stands at 2,625 wins, 1,603 losses and 772 ties since 1917.

FEBRUARY 22, 1998: The Czech Republic, led by goalie Dominik Hasek, defeated Russia 1–0 for the Olympic Gold Medal.

JUNE 16, 1998: Coach Scott Bowman's Detroit Red Wings won their second straight Stanley Cup. It was Bowman's eighth Cup as a coach, equalling Toe Blake's coaching record.

APRIL 18, 1999: The career of the NHL's greatest player, Wayne Gretzky ends as the Rangers lose in overtime to the Pittsburgh Penguins. The final numbers are 894 goals, 1,963 assists and 2,857 points and 61 NHL records.

JUNE 19-20, 1999: In triple overtime, the Dallas Stars won the franchise's first Cup by ousting the Buffalo Sabres, four games to two. It was the first Cup won by a team from the Sun Belt.

Glossary

ALL THE WAY: A face-off in the defensive zone after an off-side call brings the puck back all the way.

ALTERNATE CAPTAIN: A player who wears an "A" on the jersey and acts as a team leader with the team captain. There can be no more than two per team.

AMATEUR: A player who does not get paid to play.

ASSIST: Credit given to a player who passes to a teammate, who then scores a goal. A maximum of two players are credited on any goal and each assist counts as one point on a player's point total.

ASSISTANT COACH: A coach who helps the head coach either from the bench or above in the press box. Most specialize and work with specific units, such as defensemen, and many oversee practices and drills.

ATTACKING ZONE: The ice inside the opponent's blue line.

BACKCHECKERING: A forward skating deep into his own zone to check an opponent off the puck.

BACKHAND: A shot or pass using the back of the stick blade.

BACKLINER/BLUE-LINER: A defensemen.

BACKUP: A team's No 2 goaltender.

BANDY: A European game like hockey that is still played today.

BENCH BOSS: A coach.

BENCH MINOR: A two-minute penalty given to any player, coach, or team staff member on the bench. This is usually given for too many men on the ice or for unsportsmanlike conduct. These are served by one of the players on the ice.

BETWEEN THE PIPES: The goaltender's spot in the net.

BISCUIT: The puck.

BLOCKED SHOT: A shot kept away from the goal by a defensive player other than the goaltender.

BLOCKER: The large rectangular pad used by the goaltender on his stick-holding hand.

BLUE LINE: One of two lines which divide the ice into three zones.

BOARDING: Checking a player into the boards violently and punishable by a two-minute or a major penalty.

BODYCHECKING: Using one's body to block an opponent.

BOX: Formation used by a team in its own zone to kill a penalty. Four men each play a corner of the box in front of their goalie.

BREAKAWAY: A play where the player with the puck breaks away from the defense and enters the opponent's zone all alone.

BREAKOUT: When a team brings the puck out of its own defensive zone.

BROUHAHA: A fight.

BUSH LEAGUE: Pejorative for low level of play.

BUTT END: The taped knob of a player's stick.

BUTTERFLY: An increasingly popular style of goaltending where the player keeps his knees together and fans out his feet to block off the lower portion of the net.

CAGE: The goal net.

CALL-UP: When a player is transferred from a minor-league team to the NHL.

CAMP BY THE NET: When a player settles near the goal by the crease and waits for a pass.

CAPTAIN: The team leader who wears the "C" on his jersey and is allowed to have formal discussions with the on-ice officials.

CATCHING GLOVE: The large webbed trapper used only by goaltenders to catch the puck.

CENTER: One of three forward positions and usually the main person to take face-offs.

CENTER LINE: Red line that cuts the rink in half.

CHANGE ON THE FLY: When players substitute for tired teammates without a stoppage in play.

CHARGING: Taking two or more strides before hitting a player, usually bringing a penalty.

CHECKER: A player who is best at keeping the opposition's scorer from getting a goal.

CHEST PAD: Protective equipment worn by goalies under their sweaters.

CHIPPY: Used to describe dirty play.

CLEAR THE PUCK: Shooting the puck out of the defensive zone.

CLUTCH-AND-GRAB: A style used by slower teams or less talented teams to slow down opponents.

COINCIDENTAL PENALTIES: Given simultaneously against players on opposite teams. Neither team goes shorthanded.

CORNERS: The rounded-off parts of the rink between the goal line and end boards.

CROSSBAR: Pipe on top of the net.

CROSS-CHECK: An illegal check where players hit an opponent with the stick while holding it with both hands.

CUTTING DOWN THE ANGLE: Goaltenders' style where they move out to limit the shooter's view of the net.

CYCLING: Movement of the puck along the boards to a teammate.

DEFENSEMEN: The players on the ice who primarily guard the defensive zone.

DEFENSIVE ZONE: Area inside a team's blue line.

DEFLECTION: Redirecting the puck.

DEKE: A quick fake meant to trick the defense.

DELAY OF GAME: Minor penalty called when a player does something to stop the game intentionally and illegally.

DELAYED PENALTY: A penalty that is not called until the offending team takes control of the puck.

DIVE: A player falling intentionally in attempt to draw an official's penalty call.

DOWN A MAN: Being shorthanded.

DROP PASS: A backwards pass from an advancing player.

DROP THE GLOVES: Starting a fight.

EMPTY-NET GOAL: A goal scored in a goal left empty when the other team has pulled its goalie for an extra attacker.

ENFORCER: A frequent fighter.

FACE-OFF: Dropping the puck to start play.

FIVE HOLE: Open area between a goaltender's leg pads.

FORECHECKING: Aggressively checking the opponent deep in his own zone to try and steal the puck.

FORWARD: One of three players on the ice assigned to attack and score.

FREEZE THE PUCK: Pinning the puck to force the play to stop.

GAME MISCONDUCT: A penalty that includes the ejection and a fine.

GIVE AND GO: A nifty play where one player passes to another who then passes it right back to fool the defense.

GOAL CREASE: Blue area of the ice in front of the net. Only the goaltender can stand here unless the puck enters before an opposing player.

GOAL LINE: Red line connecting the goal posts. The puck must cross this line completely for a goal.

GOALTENDER: Player who defends the net with a wider stick and thicker padding. The goaltender is also the only player who can use his hands to handle the puck.

GOON: A player known as a constant fighter.

GRINDER: A hard-working overachieving player who checks well.

HACKER: A player who plays dirty with his stick.

HAND PASS: A pass from one player to another (not the goalie) using the glove.

HAT TRICK: Three goals by one player in one game. Three goals in a row by one player is a natural hat trick.

HIGH STICKING: Raising the stick above shoulder level. If a player hits the puck with a high stick, officials call this and play is stopped. If the stick hits another player, it's a penalty.

HIP CHECK: Using the hip to bounce an opponent.

HOLDING: Penalty for using the hands or arms to slow an opponent.

HOOKING: Penalty for using the stick to slow down an opposing player.

ICE TIME: Number of playing minutes per player.

ICING: Shooting the puck from behind the center red line and across the team's goal line, mainly used as a last-gasp defense. Play is stopped and a face-off is set in the offending team's defensive zone.

INSURANCE GOAL: A goal which widens a team's lead late in the game.

INTERFERENCE: Penalty for checking a player without the puck.

KICK SAVE: A save by the goaltender's leg.

KILLING A PENALTY: Surviving an opponent's man-advantage power play.

LINE CHANGE: Substitution of players.

LOWERING THE BOOM: Dropping a shoulder to cleanly check another player.

MAJOR PENALTY: Five-minute penalty often resulting from one player injuring another.

MASK: Protection for the face and head which each goalie wears.

MÊLÉE: Big brawl.

MINOR PENALTY: Two-minute penalty.

MISCONDUCT: Ten-minute penalty; does not result in a team playing a man short.

NEUTRAL ZONE: Area between the blue lines.

OFFICE: Area behind the net where an offensive player takes the puck to try to set up scoring chances. Wayne Gretzky made this area home for much of his career.

OFFSIDE: When a player illegally enters the attacking zone before the puck. Play is stopped and a face-off is held.

ONE-TIMER: A shot taken cleanly off a pass.

OVERTIME: Sudden-death play if a game is tied. In the regular season, teams play for five minutes, and if no one scores, it's a tie. In the playoffs, teams play additional 20-minute periods until someone wins.

PENALTY BOX: Area where penalized players sit opposite their team bench.

PENALTY SHOT: A free shot awarded for an infraction which clearly was intended to stop the other team from scoring.

PETER PUCK: A renowned animated character invented to explain the game to television viewers during the 1970s.

PLUS-MINUS: A statistic expressing defensive value. A player gets a plus each time he's on the ice when his team scores and a minus when the other team scores – all at even strength. The plus-minus is the result of subtracting the minuses from the pluses.

PULL THE GOALIE: Removing the goaltender from the game and replacing him with an extra attacker.

REBOUND: A puck which bounces off the goalie and back into play.

ROUGHING: Minor shoving or brief fighting.

RUT: An imperfection in the ice.

SCRATCH: A player who is on the roster but not in uniform, either for an injury or other reasons.

SCREENING: Legally blocking a goaltender's view of the puck on a shot.

SHINNY: An informal, wide-open version of hockey normally played on ponds.

SHUTOUT: A game in which a goaltender allows no goals.

SLAP SHOT: A full windup shot and the hardest in hockey.

SLASHING: Whacking an opponent with the stick.

SLOT: Area in front of the net.

SNAP SHOT: A quick wrist shot.

SPEARING: Jamming a stick blade into an opponent's stomach.

TWO-LINE PASS: An offside pass across two lines. This stops play for a face-off.

WRAPAROUND: A difficult but popular shot whereby the skater starts behind the net and swings in front of it to jam the puck past the recovering goaltender.

WRIST SHOT: Usually a slower, more accurate shot fired by snapping from the wrists without a clean windup.

ZAMBONI: Brand name for the machine which cleans the ice between periods. Developed by Frank Zamboni, it is used in so many places that the brand name now describes any ice-cleaning machine.

ZEBRA: Slang for the referee.

The Honored Members of the Hockey Hall of Fame

— P L A Y E R S —

NAMES	YEAR ELECTED	NAMES	YEAR ELECTED	NAMES	YEAR ELECTED
Sid Abel	1969	Butch Bouchard	1966	Roy Conacher	1998
Jack Adams	1959	Frank Boucher	1958	Alex Connell	1958
Syl Apps	1961	George Boucher	1960	Bill Cook	1952
George Armstrong	1975	Johnny Bower	1976	Bun Cook	1995
Ace Bailey	1975	Dubbie Bowie	1945	Art Coulter	1974
Dan Bain	1975	Frank Brimsek	1966	Yvon Cournoyer	1982
Hobey Baker	1945	Punch Broadbent	1962	Bill Cowley	1968
Bill Barber	1990	Turk Broda	1967	Rusty Crawford	1962
Marty Barry	1965	John Bucyk	1981	Jack Darragh	1962
Andy Bathgate	1978	Billy Burch	1974	Scotty Davidson	1950
Bobby Bauer	1996	Harry Cameron	1962	Hap Day	1961
Jean Beliveau	1972	Gerry Cheevers	1985	Alex Delvecchio	1977
Clint Benedict	1965	King Clancy	1958	Cy Denneny	1959
Doug Bentley	1964	Dit Clapper	1947	Marcel Dionne	1992
Max Bentley	1966	Bobby Clarke	1987	Gordie Drillon	1975
Toe Blake	1966	Sprague Cleghorn	1958	Graham Drinkwater	1950
Leo Boivin	1986	Neil Colville	1967	Ken Dryden	1983
Dickie Boon	1952	Charlie Conacher	1961	Woody Dumart	1992
Mike Bossy	1991	Lionel Conacher	1994	Tommy Dunderdale	1974

NAMES	YEAR ELECTED	NAMES	YEAR ELECTED	NAMES	YEAR ELECTED
Bill Durnan	1964	Red Horner	1965	Frank Mahovlich	1981
Red Dutton	1958	Tim Horton	1977	Joe Malone	1950
Babe Dye	1970	Gordie Howe	1972	Sylvio Mantha	1960
Phil Esposito	1984	Syd Howe	1965	Jack Marshall	1965
Tony Esposito	1988	Harry Howell	1979	Fred Maxwell	1962
Arthur Farrell	1965	Bobby Hull	1983	Lanny McDonald	1992
Fernie Flaman	1990	Bouse Hutton	1962	Frank McGee	1945
Frank Foyston	1958	Harry Hyland	1962	Billy McGimsie	1962
Frank Fredrickson	1958	Dick Irvin	1958	George McNamara	1958
Bill Gadsby	1970	Busher Jackson	1971	Stan Mikita	1983
Bob Gainey	1992	Ching Johnson	1958	Dickie Moore	1974
Chuck Gardiner	1945	Ernie Johnson	1952	Paddy Moran	1958
Herb Gardiner	1958	Tom Johnson	1970	Howie Morenz	1945
Jimmy Gardner	1962	Aurel Joliat	1947	Bill Mosienko	1965
Eddie Giacomin	1987	Duke Keats	1958	Frank Nighbor	1947
Rod Gilbert	1982	Red Kelly	1969	Reg Noble	1962
Billy Gilmour	1962	Ted Kennedy	1966	Buddy O'Connor	1988
Moose Goheen	1952	Dave Keon	1986	Harry Oliver	1967
Ebbie Goodfellow	1963	Elmer Lach	1966	Bert Olmstead	1985
Michel Goulet	1998	Guy Lafleur	1988	Bobby Orr	1979
Mike Grant	1950	Newsy Lalonde	1950	Bernie Parent	1984
Shorty Green	1962	Jacques Laperriere	1987	Brad Park	1988
Wayne Gretzky	1999	Guy Lapointe	1993	Lester Patrick	1947
Si Griffis	1950	Edgar Laprade	1993	Lynn Patrick	1980
George Hainsworth	1961	Jack Laviolette	1962	Gilbert Perrault	1990
Glenn Hall	1975	Percy LeSeur	1961	Tom Phillips	1945
Joe Hall	1961	Hughie Lehman	1958	Pierre Pilote	1975
Doug Harvey	1973	Jacques Lemaire	1984	Didier Pitre	1962
George Hay	1958	Mario Lemieux	1997	Jacques Plante	1978
Riley Hern	1962	Herbie Lewis	1989	Denis Potvin	1991
Bryan Hextall	1969	Ted Lindsay	1966	Babe Pratt	1966
Hap Holmes	1972	Harry Lumley	1980	Joe Primeau	1963
Tom Hooper	1962	Mickey MacKay	1952	Marcel Pronovost	1978

— PLAYERS —
(CONTINUED)

NAMES	YEAR ELECTED	NAMES	YEAR ELECTED	NAMES	YEAR ELECTED
Bob Pulford	1991	Earl Seibert	1963	Cyclone Taylor	1947
Harvey Pulford	1945	Oliver Seibert	1961	Tiny Thompson	1959
Bill Quackenbush	1976	Eddie Shore	1947	Vladislav Tretiak	1989
Frank Rankin	1961	Steve Shutt	1993	Harry Trihey	1950
Jean Ratelle	1985	Babe Siebert	1964	Bryan Trottier	1997
Chuck Rayner	1973	Joe Simpson	1962	Norm Ullman	1982
Kenny Reardon	1966	Darryl Sittler	1989	Georges Vezina	1945
Henri Richard	1979	Alf Smith	1962	Jack Walker	1960
Maurice Richard	1961	Billy Smith	1993	Marty Walsh	1962
George Richardson	1950	Clint Smith	1991	Harry 'Moose' Watson	1962
Gordie Roberts	1971	Hooley Smith	1972	Harry Percival Watson	1994
Larry Robinson	1995	Tommy Smith	1973	Cooney Weiland	1971
Art Ross	1945	Allan Stanley	1981	Harry Westwick	1962
Borje Salming	1996	Barney Stanley	1962	Fred Whitcroft	1962
Serge Savard	1986	Peter Stastny	1998	Phat Wilson	1962
Terry Sawchuk	1971	Jack Stewart	1964	Gump Worsley	1980
Fred Scanlan	1965	Nels Stewart	1962	Roy Worters	1969
Milt Schmidt	1961	Bruce Stuart	1961		
Sweeney Schriner	1962	Hod Stuart	1945		

— BUILDERS —

NAMES	YEAR ELECTED	NAMES	YEAR ELECTED	NAMES	YEAR ELECTED
Charles Adams	1960	Al Arbour	1996	Walter Brown	1962
Weston Adams	1972	Harold Ballard	1977	Frank Buckland	1975
Frank Ahearn	1962	Father David Bauer	1989	Jack Butterfield	1980
Bunny Ahearne	1977	J. P. Bickell	1978	Frank Calder	1947
Sir Montagu Allan	1945	Scott Bowman	1991	Angus Campbell	1964
Keith Allen	1992	George Brown	1961	Clarence Campbell	1966

NAMES	YEAR ELECTED	NAMES	YEAR ELECTED	NAMES	YEAR ELECTED
Joseph Cattarinich	1977	Al Leader	1969	Sen. Donat Raymond	1958
Leo Dandurand	1963	Thomas Lockhart	1965	John Ross Robinson	1947
Frank Dilio	1964	Paul Loicq	1961	Claude Robinson	1947
George Dudley	1958	John Mariucci	1985	Phillip Ross	1976
James Dunn	1968	Frank Mathers	1992	Gunther Sabetzki	1995
Emile Francis	1982	Frederic McLaughlin	1963	Glen Sather	1997
Jack Gibson	1976	Jake Milford	1984	Frank Selke	1960
Tommy Gorman	1963	Sen. Hartland Molson	1973	Harry Sinden	1983
Frank Griffiths	1993	Ian 'Scotty' Morrison	1999	Frank Smith	1962
Bill Hanley	1986	Monsignor A. Murray	1998	Conn Smythe	1958
Charles Hay	1974	Francis Nelson	1947	Ed Snider	1988
Jim Hendy	1968	Bruce Norris	1969	Lord Stanley of Preston	1945
Foster Hewitt	1965	James Norris	1962	Capt James Sutherland	1947
W. A. Hewitt	1947	James Norris Sr	1958	Anatoli Tarasov	1974
Fred Hume	1962	William Northey	1947	Bill Torry	1995
Punch Imlach	1984	J. Ambrose O'Brien	1962	Lloyd Turner	1958
Tommy Ivan	1974	Brian Francis O'Neill	1994	William Tutt	1978
William Jennings	1975	Frederick Page	1993	Carl Voss	1974
Bob Johnson	1992	Frank Patrick	1958	Fred Waghorne	1961
Gordon Juckes	1979	Allen Pickard	1958	Arthur Wirtz	1971
John Kilpatrick	1960	Rudy Pilous	1985	Bill Wirtz	1976
Seymour Knox	1993	Norman 'Bud' Polie	1990	John A. Ziegler Jr	1987
Robert LeBel	1970	Sam Pollock	1978		

– REFEREES & LINESMEN –

NAMES	YEAR ELECTED	NAMES	YEAR ELECTED	NAMES	YEAR ELECTED
Neil Armstrong	1991	George Hayes	1988	Cooper Smeaton	1961
John Ashley	1981	Bobby Hewitson	1963	Red Storey	1967
Bill Chadwick	1964	Mickey Ion	1961	Frank Udvari	1973
John D'Amico	1993	Matt Pavelich	1987	Andy van Hellemond	1999
Chaucer Elliott	1961	Mike Rodden	1962		

Records

INDIVIDUAL RECORDS

MOST GOALS

GOALS	PLAYER	TEAM	SEASON (G)
92	Wayne Gretzky	Edmonton Oilers	1981-82 (80)
87	Wayne Gretzky	Edmonton Oilers	1983-84 (80)
86	Brett Hull	St. Louis Blues	1990-91 (80)
85	Mario Lemieux	Pittsburgh Penguins	1988-89 (80)
76	Phil Esposito	Boston Bruins	1970-71 (78)
76	Alex Mogilny	Buffalo Sabres	1992-93 (84)
76	Teemu Selanne	Winnipeg Jets	1992-93 (84)

MOST ASSISTS

ASSISTS	PLAYER	TEAM	SEASON (G)
163	Wayne Gretzky	Edmonton Oilers	1985-86 (80)
135	Wayne Gretzky	Edmonton Oilers	1984-85 (80)
125	Wayne Gretzky	Edmonton Oilers	1982-83 (80)
122	Wayne Gretzky	Los Angeles Kings	1990-91 (80)
121	Wayne Gretzky	Edmonton Oilers	1986-87 (80)

MOST POINTS

POINTS (G/A)	PLAYER	TEAM	SEASON (G)
215 (52/163)	Wayne Gretzky	Edmonton Oilers	1985-86 (80)
212 (92/120)	Wayne Gretzky	Edmonton Oilers	1981-82 (80)
208 (73/135)	Wayne Gretzky	Edmonton Oilers	1984-85 (80)
205 (87/118)	Wayne Gretzky	Edmonton Oilers	1983-84 (80)
199 (85/114)	Mario Lemieux	Pittsburgh Penguins	1988-89 (80)

PENALTIES

PEN MIN.	PLAYER	TEAM	SEASON
472	Dave Schultz	Philadelphia Flyers	1974-75
409	Paul Baxter	Pittsburgh Penguins	1981-82
408	Mike Peluso	Chicago Blackhawks	1991-92
405	Dave Schultz	Philadelphia Flyers	1977-78

GOALTENDER VICTORIES

VICTORIES	GOALIE	TEAM	SEASON
47	Bernie Parent	Philadelphia Flyers	1973-74
44	Bernie Parent	Philadelphia Flyers	1974-75
44	Terry Sawchuk	Detroit Red Wings	1950-51
44	Terry Sawchuk	Detroit Red Wings	1951-52

SHUTOUTS	GOALIE	TEAM	SEASON
22	George Hainsworth	Montreal Canadiens	1928-29
15	Alex Connell	Ottawa Senators	1925-26
15	Alex Connell	Ottawa Senators	1927-28
15	Hal Winkler	Boston Bruins	1927-28
15	Tony Esposito	Chicago Blackhawks	1969-70

INDIVIDUAL RECORDS

MOST SEASONS: Gordie Howe, 1946-47 through 1970-71 (Detroit) and 1979-80 (Hartford), 26 seasons.

MOST GAMES: Gordie Howe, 1,767

MOST GOALS ONE GAME: 7, Joe Malone, Quebec Bulldogs, 1920

MOST GOALS BY A DEFENSEMAN: 385, Paul Coffey and Raymond Bourque

MOST GOALS BY A DEFENSEMAN, SEASON: 48, Paul Coffey, Edmonton Oilers, 1985-86

MOST GOALS BY ROOKIE: 76, Teemu Selanne, Winnipeg Jets, 1992-93

MOST ASSISTS BY A ROOKIE: 70, Peter Stastny, Quebec Nordiques, 1980-81, and Joe Juneau, Boston Bruins, 1992-93

MOST POINTS BY A ROOKIE: 132, Teemu Selanne, Winnipeg Jets, 1992-93

MOST 50 GOAL SEASONS: 9, Mike Bossy and Wayne Gretzky

MOST 100 POINT SEASONS: 13, Wayne Gretzky

MOST THREE OR MORE GOAL GAMES, CAREER: 50, Wayne Gretzky

CAREER LEADERS

GOALS

894	Wayne Gretzky, 20 seasons
801	Gordie Howe, 26 seasons
731	Marcel Dionne, 18 seasons
717	Phil Esposito, 18 seasons
708	Mike Gartner, 19 seasons
613	Mario Lemieux, 12 seasons
610	Bobby Hull, 16 seasons
610	Mark Messier, 20 seasons
608	Dino Ciccarelli, 19 seasons
601	Jari Kurri, 17 seasons

ASSISTS

1,963	Wayne Gretzky, 20 seasons
1,102	Paul Coffey, 19 seasons
1,083	Ray Bourque, 20 seasons
1,050	Mark Messier, 20 seasons
1,049	Gordie Howe, 26 seasons
1,040	Marcel Dionne, 18 seasons
1,037	Ron Francis, 18 seasons
926	Stan Mikita, 22 seasons
901	Bryan Trottier, 18 seasons
891	Dale Hawerchuk, 16 seasons

POINTS

2,852	Wayne Gretzky, 20 seasons
1,850	Gordie Howe, 26 seasons
1,771	Marcel Dionne, 18 seasons
1,656	Mark Messier, 20 seasons
1,590	Phil Esposito, 18 seasons
1,494	Mario Lemieux, 12 seasons
1,482	Paul Coffey, 19 seasons
1,476	Ron Francis, 18 seasons
1,473	Steve Yzerman, 16 seasons
1,467	Stan Mikita, 22 seasons

SHUTOUTS

103	Terry Sawchuk
94	George Hainsworth
84	Glenn Hall
82	Jacques Plante
81	Tiny Thompson
81	Alex Connell
76	Tony Esposito
73	Lorne Chabot
71	Harry Lumley
66	Roy Worters

GOALTENDER VICTORIES

447	Terry Sawchuk, 21 seasons
434	Jacques Plante, 18 seasons
423	Tony Esposito, 16 seasons
407	Glenn Hall, 18 seasons
405	Patrick Roy, 14 seasons
392	Grant Fuhr, 17 seasons

372	Andy Moog, 18 seasons
355	Rogie Vachon, 16 seasons
347	Mike Vernon, 15 seasons
343	Tom Barrasso, 15 seasons

PENALTY MINUTES

3,966	Dave Williams, 14 seasons
3,548	Dale Hunter, 19 seasons
3,300	Marty McSorley, 16 seasons
3,146	Tim Hunter, 16 seasons
3,043	Chris Nilan, 13 seasons

ASSISTS LEADERS

1956-57	Ted Lindsay	55
1957-58	Henri Richard	52
1958-59	Dickie Moore	55
1959-60	Don McKenney	49
1960-61	Jean Beliveau	58
1961-62	Andy Bathgate	56
1962-63	Henri Richard	50
1963-64	Andy Bathgate	58
1964-65	Stan Mikita	59
1965-66	Jean Beliveau	48
	Stan Mikita	48
	Bobby Rousseau	48
1966-67	Stan Mikita	62
1967-68	Phil Esposito	49
1968-69	Phil Esposito	77
1969-70	Bobby Orr	87
1970-71	Bobby Orr	102
1971-72	Bobby Orr	80
1972-73	Phil Esposito	75
1973-74	Bobby Orr	90
1974-75	Bobby Clarke	89
	Bobby Orr	89
1975-76	Bobby Clarke	89
1976-77	Guy Lafleu	80
1977-78	Bryan Trottier	77
1978-79	Bryan Trottier	87
1979-80	Wayne Gretzky	86
1980-81	Wayne Gretzky	109
1981-82	Wayne Gretzky	120
1982-83	Wayne Gretzky	125
1983-84	Wayne Gretzky	118
1984-85	Wayne Gretzky	135
1985-86	Wayne Gretzky	163
1986-87	Wayne Gretzky	121
1987-88	Wayne Gretzky	109
1988-89	Wayne Gretzky	114
	Mario Lemieux	114
1989-90	Wayne Gretzky	102
1990-91	Wayne Gretzky	122
1991-92	Wayne Gretzky	90
1992-93	Adam Oates	97
1993-94	Wayne Gretzky	92
1994-95	Ron Francis	48
1995-96	Ron Francis	92
	Mario Lemieux	92
1996-97	Wayne Gretzky	72
	Mario Lemieux	72
1997-98	Wayne Gretzky	67
	Jaromir Jagr	67
1998-99	Jaromir Jagr	83

GOALTENDER LEADERS

1933-34	Wilf Cude	1.47
1934–35	Lorne Chabot	1.80
1935-36	Tiny Thompson	1.68
1936-37	Norman Smith	2.05
1937-38	Tiny Thompson	1.80
1938-39	Frank Brimsek	1.56
1939-40	Dave Kerr	1.54
1940-41	Turk Broda	2.00
1941-42	Frank Brimsek	2.35
1942-43	Johnny Mowers	2.47
1943-44	Bill Durnan	2.18
1944-45	Bill Durnan	2.42
1945-46	Bill Durnan	2.60
1946-47	Bill Durnan	2.30
1947-48	Turk Broda	2.38
1948-49	Bill Durnan	2.10
1949-50	Bill Durnan	2.20
1950-51	Al Rollins	1.77
1951-52	Terry Sawchuk	1.90
1952-53	Terry Sawchuk	1.90
1953-54	Harry Lumley	1.86
1954-55	Terry Sawchuk	1.94
1955-56	Jacques Plante	1.86
1956-57	Jacques Plante	2.02
1957-58	Jacques Plante	2.11
1958-59	Jacques Plante	2.16
1959-60	Jacques Plante	2.54
1960-61	Johnny Bower	2.50
1961-62	Jacques Plante	2.37
1962-63	Jacques Plante	2.49
1963-64	Johnny Bower	2.11
1964-65	Johnny Bower	2.38
1965-66	Johnny Bower	2.25
1966-67	Glenn Hall	2.38
1967-68	Gump Worsley	1.98
1968-69	Jacques Plante	1.96
1969-70	Ernie Wakely	2.11
1970-71	Jacques Plante	1.88
1971-72	Tony Esposito	1.77
1972-73	Ken Dryden	2.26
1973-74	Bernie Parent	1.89
1974-75	Bernie Parent	2.03
1975-76	Ken Dryden	2.03
1976-77	Michel Larocque	2.09
1977-78	Ken Dryden	2.05
1978-79	Ken Dryden	2.30
1979-80	Bob Sauve	2.36
1980-81	Richard Sevigny	2.40
1981-82	Denis Herron	2.64
1982-83	Pete Peeters	2.36
1983-84	Pat Riggin	2.66
1984-85	Tom Barrasso	2.66
1985-86	Bob Froese	2.55
1986-87	Brian Hayward	2.81
1987-88	Pete Peeters	2.78
1988-89	Patrick Roy	2.47
1989-90	Mike Liut	2.53
1990-91	Ed Belfour	2.47
1991-92	Patrick Roy	2.36
1992-93	Felix Potvin	2.50
1993-94	Dominik Hasek	1.95
1994-95	Dominik Hasek	2.11
1995-96	Ron Hextall	2.17
1996-97	Martin Brodeur	1.88
1997-98	Ed Belfour	1.88
1998-99	Ron Tugnutt	1.79

GOAL LEADERS

1928-29	Ace Bailey	22
1929-30	Cooney Weiland	43
1930-31	Charlie Conacher	31
1931-32	C.Conacher/Bill Cook	34
1932-33	Bill Cook	28
1933-34	Charlie Conacher	32
1934-35	Charlie Conacher	36
1935-36	C.Conacher/Bill Thoms	23
1936-37	Larry Aurie/Nels Stewart	23
1937-38	Gordie Drillon	26
1938-39	Roy Conacher	26
1939-40	Bryan Hextall	24
1940-41	Bryan Hextall	26
1941-42	Lynn Patrick	32
1942-43	Doug Bentley	33
1943-44	Doug Bentley	38
1944-45	Maurice Richard	50
1945-46	Gaye Stewart	37
1946-47	Maurice Richard	45
1947-48	Ted Lindsay	33
1948-49	Sid Abel	28
1949-50	Maurice Richard	43
1950-51	Gordie Howe	43
1951-52	Gordie Howe	47
1952-53	Gordie Howe	49
1953-54	Maurice Richard	37
1954-55	M. Richard/B. Geoffrion	38
1955-56	Jean Beliveau	47
1956-57	Gordie Howe	44
1957-58	Dickie Moore	36
1958-59	Jean Beliveau	45
1959-60	Bobby Hull	39
1960-61	Bernie Geoffrion	50
1961-62	Bobby Hull	50
1962-63	Gordie Howe	38
1963-64	Bobby Hull	43
1964-65	Norm Ullman	42
1965-66	Bobby Hull	54
1966-67	Bobby Hull	52
1967-68	Bobby Hull	44
1968-69	Bobby Hull	58
1969-70	Phil Esposito	43
1970-71	Phil Esposito	76
1971-72	Phil Esposito	66
1972-73	Phil Esposito	55
1973-74	Phil Esposito	68
1974-75	Phil Esposito	61
1975-76	Reggie Leach	61
1976-77	Steve Shutt	60
1977-78	Guy Lafleur	60
1978-79	Mike Bossy	69
1979-80	C.Simmer/D. Gare	56
1980-81	Mike Bossy	68
1981-82	Wayne Gretzky	92
1982-83	Wayne Gretzky	71
1983-84	Wayne Gretzky	87
1984-85	Wayne Gretzky	73
1985-86	Jari Kurri	68
1986-87	Wayne Gretzky	62
1987-88	Mario Lemieux	70
1988-89	Mario Lemieux	85
1989-90	Brett Hull	72
1990-91	Brett Hull	86
1991-92	Brett Hull	70
1992-93	T. Selanne/A. Mogilny	76
1993-94	Pavel Bure	60
1994-95	Peter Bondra	34
1995-96	Mario Lemieux	69
1996-97	Keith Tkachuk	52
1997-98	P. Bondra/T. Selanne	52
1998-99	T. Selanne	47

NHL LEADING SCORERS

SEASON	NAME, TEAM	GOALS	ASS	P
1917-18	Joe Malone, Montreal	44	4	48
	Cy Denneny, Ottawa	36	10	46
1918-19	Newsy Lalonde, Montreal	23	10	33
	Odie Cleghorn, Montreal	21	6	27
1919-20	Joe Malone, Quebec	39	10	49
	Newsy Lalonde, Montreal	37	9	46
1920-21	Newsy Lalonde, Montreal	32	11	43
	Babe Dye, Ham./Tor.	35	5	40
1921-22	Punch Broadbent, Ottawa	32	14	46
	Cy Denneny, Ottawa	27	12	39
1922-23	Babe Dye, Toronto	26	11	37
	Cy Denneny, Ottawa	21	10	31
1923-24	Cy Denneny, Ottawa	22	1	23
	Billy Boucher, Montreal	16	6	22
1924-25	Babe Dye, Toronto	38	6	44
	Cy Denneny, Ottawa	27	15	42
1925-26	Nels Stewart, Montreal (M)	34	8	42
	Cy Denneny, Ottawa	24	12	36
1926-27	Bill Cook, NYR	33	4	37
	Dick Irvin, Chicago	18	18	36
1927-28	Howie Morenz, Montreal (C)	33	18	51
	Aurel Joliat, Montreal (C)	28	11	39
1928-29	Ace Bailey, Toronto	22	10	32
	Nels Stewart, Montreal (M)	21	8	29
1929-30	Cooney Weiland, Boston	43	30	73
	Frank Boucher, NYR	26	36	62
1930-31	Howie Morenz, Montreal (C)	28	23	51
	Ebbie Goodfellow, Detroit	25	23	48
1931-32	Busher Jackson, Toronto	28	25	53
	Joe Primeau, Toronto	13	37	50
1932-33	Bill Cook, NYR	28	22	50
	Busher Jackson, Toronto	27	17	44
1933-34	Charlie Conacher, Toronto	32	20	52
	Joe Primeau, Toronto	14	32	46
1934-35	Charlie Conacher, Toronto	36	21	57
	Syd Howe, St.L/Det	22	25	47
1935-36	Sweeney Schriner, NYA	19	26	45
	Marty Barry, Detroit	21	19	40
1936-37	Sweeney Schriner, NYA	21	25	46
	Syl Apps, Toronto	16	29	45
1937-38	Gordie Drillon, Toronto	26	26	52
	Syl Apps, Toronto	21	29	50
1938-39	Toe Blake, Montreal	24	23	47
	Sweeney Schriner, NYA	13	31	44
1939-40	Milt Schmidt, Boston	22	30	52
	Woody Dumart, Boston	22	21	43
1940-41	Bill Cowley, Boston	17	45	62
	Bryan Hextall, NYR	26	18	44
1941-42	Bryan Hextall, NYR	24	32	56
	Lynn Patrick, NYR	32	22	54
1942-43	Doug Bentley, Chicago	33	40	73
	Bill Cowley, Boston	27	45	72
1943-44	Herb Cain, Boston	36	46	82
	Doug Bentley, Chicago	38	39	77
1944-45	Elmer Lach, Montreal	26	54	80
	Maurice Richard, Montreal	50	23	73
1945-46	Max Bentley, Chicago	31	30	61
	Gaye Stewart, Toronto	37	15	52
1946-47	Max Bentley, Chicago	29	43	72
	Maurice Richard, Montreal	45	26	71
1947-48	Elmer Lach, Montreal	30	31	61
	Buddy O'Connor, NYR	24	36	60
1948-49	Roy Conacher, Chicago	26	42	68
	Doug Bentley, Chicago	23	43	66
1949-50	Ted Lindsay, Detroit	23	55	78
	Sid Abel, Detroit	34	35	69
1950-51	Gordie Howe, Detroit	43	43	86
	Maurice Richard, Montreal	42	24	66
1951-52	Gordie Howe, Detroit	47	39	86
	Ted Lindsay, Detroit	30	39	69
1952-53	Gordie Howe, Detroit	49	46	95
	Ted Lindsay, Detroit	32	39	71
1953-54	Gordie Howe, Detroit	33	48	81
	Maurice Richard, Montreal	37	30	67
1954-55	Bernie Geoffrion, Montreal	38	37	75
	Maurice Richard, Montreal	38	36	74
1955-56	Jean Beliveau, Montreal	47	41	88
	Gordie Howe, Detroit	38	41	79
1956-57	Gordie Howe, Detroit	44	45	89
	Ted Lindsay, Detroit	30	55	85
1957-58	Dickie Moore, Montreal	36	48	84
	Henri Richard, Montreal	28	52	80
1958-59	Dickie Moore, Montreal	41	55	96
	Jean Beliveau, Montreal	45	46	91
1959-60	Bobby Hull, Chicago	39	42	81
	Bronco Horvath, Boston	39	41	80
1960-61	Bernie Geoffrion, Montreal	50	45	95
	Jean Beliveau, Montreal	32	58	90
1961-62	Bobby Hull, Chicago	50	34	84
	Andy Bathgate, NYR	28	56	84
1962-63	Gordie Howe, Detroit	38	48	86
	Andy Bathgate, NYR	35	46	81
1963-64	Stan Mikita, Chicago	39	50	89
	Bobby Hull, Chicago	43	44	87
1964-65	Stan Mikita, Chicago	28	59	87
	Norm Ullman, Detroit	42	41	83
1965-66	Bobby Hull, Chicago	54	43	97
	Stan Mikita, Chicago	30	48	78
1966-67	Stan Mikita, Chicago	35	62	97
	Bobby Hull, Chicago	52	28	80
1967-68	Stan Mikita, Chicago	40	47	87
	Phil Esposito, Boston	35	49	84
1968-69	Phil Esposito, Boston	49	77	126
	Bobby Hull, Chicago	58	49	107
1969-70	Bobby Orr, Boston	33	87	120
	Phil Esposito, Boston	43	56	99
1970-71	Phil Esposito, Boston	76	76	152
	Bobby Orr, Boston	37	102	139
1971-72	Phil Esposito, Boston	66	67	133
	Bobby Orr, Boston	37	80	117
1972-73	Phil Esposito, Boston	55	75	130
	Bobby Clarke, Philadelphia	37	67	104
1973-74	Phil Esposito, Boston	68	77	145
	Bobby Orr, Boston	32	90	122
1974-75	Bobby Orr, Boston	46	89	133
	Phil Esposito, Boston	61	66	127
1975-76	Guy Lafleur, Montreal	56	69	125
	Bobby Clarke, Philadelphia	30	89	119
1976-77	Guy Lafleur, Montreal	56	80	136
	Marcel Dionne, LA	53	69	122
1977-78	Guy Lafleur, Montreal	60	72	132
	Bryan Trottier, NYI	46	77	123
1978-79	Bryan Trottier, NYI	47	87	134
	Marcel Dionne, LA	59	71	130
1979-80	Marcel Dionne, LA	53	84	137
	Wayne Gretzky, Edmonton	51	86	137
1980-81	Wayne Gretzky, Edmonton	55	109	164
	Marcel Dionne, LA	58	77	135
1981-82	Wayne Gretzky Edmonton	92	120	212
	Mike Bossy, NYI	64	83	147
1982-83	Wayne Gretzky, Edmonton	71	125	196
	Peter Stastny, Quebec	47	77	124
1983-84	Wayne Gretzky, Edmonton	87	118	205
	Paul Coffey, Edmonton	40	86	126
1984-85	Wayne Gretzky, Edmonton	73	135	208
	Jari Kurri, Edmonton	71	64	135
1985-86	Wayne Gretzky, Edmonton	52	163	215
	Mario Lemieux, Pittsburgh	48	93	141
1986-87	Wayne Gretzky, Edmonton	62	121	183
	Jari Kurri, Edmonton	54	54	108
1987-88	Mario Lemieux, Pittsburgh	70	98	168
	Wayne Gretzky, Edmonton	40	109	149
1988-89	Mario Lemieux, Pittsburgh	85	114	199

Season	Player	G	A	Pts
	Wayne Gretzky, LA	54	114	168
1989-90	Wayne Gretzky, LA	40	102	142
	Mark Messier, Edmonton	45	84	129
1990-91	Wayne Gretzky, LA	41	122	163
	Brett Hull, St Louis	86	45	131
1991-92	Mario Lemieux, Pittsburgh	44	87	131
	Kevin Stevens, Pittsburgh	54	69	123
1992-93	Mario Lemieux, Pittsburgh	69	91	160
	Pat LaFontaine, Buffalo	53	95	148
1993-94	Wayne Gretzky, LA	38	92	130
	Sergei Fedorov, Detroit	56	64	120
1994-95	Jaromir Jagr, Pittsburgh	32	38	70
	Eric Lindros, Philadelphia	29	41	70
1995-96	Mario Lemieux, Pittsburgh	69	92	161
	Jaromir Jagr, Pittsburgh	62	87	149
1996-97	Mario Lemieux, Pittsburgh	50	72	122
	Teemu Selanne, Anaheim	51	58	109
1997-98	Jaromir Jagr, Pittsburgh	35	67	102
	Peter Forsberg, Colorado	25	66	91
1998-99	Jaromir Jagr, Pittsburgh	44	83	127
	Teemu Selanne, Anaheim	47	60	107

CALDER TROPHY

Year	*Winner*	*Team*
1999	Chris Drury	Colorado Avalanche
1998	S. Samsonov	Boston Bruins
1997	Bryan Berard	New York Islanders
1996	Dan Alfredsson	Ottawa Senators
1995	Peter Forsberg	Quebec Nordiques
1994	Martin Brodeur	New Jersey Devils
1993	Teemu Selanne	Winnipeg Jets
1992	Pavel Bure	Vancouver Canucks
1991	Ed Belfour	Chicago Blackhawks
1990	Sergei Makarov	Calgary Flames
1989	Brian Leetch	New York Rangers
1988	Joe Nieuwendyk	Calgary Flames
1987	Luc Robitaille	Los Angeles Kings
1986	Gary Suter	Calgary Flames
1985	Mario Lemieux	Pittsburgh Penguins
1984	Tom Barrasso	Buffalo Sabres
1983	Steve Larmer	Chicago Blackhawks
1982	Dale Hawerchuk	Winnipeg Jets
1981	Peter Stastny	Quebec Nordiques
1980	Ray Bourque	Boston Bruins
1979	Bobby Smith	Minnesota N.Stars
1978	Mike Bossy	New York Islanders
1977	Willi Plett	Atlanta Flames
1976	Bryan Trottier	New York Islanders
1975	Eric Vail	Atlanta Flames
1974	Denis Potvin	New York Islanders
1973	Steve Vickers	New York Rangers
1972	Ken Dryden	Montreal Canadiens
1971	G. Perreault	Buffalo Sabres
1970	Tony Esposito	Chicago Blackhawks
1969	Danny Grant	Minnesota N.Stars
1968	D. Sanderson	Boston Bruins
1967	Bobby Orr	Boston Bruins
1966	Brit Selby	Toronto Maple Leafs
1965	Roger Crozier	Detroit Red Wings
1964	J. Laperriere	Montreal Canadiens
1963	Kent Douglas	Toronto Maple Leafs
1962	Bob Rousseau	Montreal Canadiens
1961	Dave Keon	Toronto Maple Leafs
1960	Bill Hay	Chicago Blackhawks
1959	R. Backstrom	Montreal Canadiens
1958	F. Mahovlich	Toronto Maple Leafs
1957	Larry Regan	Boston Bruins
1956	Glenn Hall	Detroit Red Wings
1955	Ed Litzenberger	Chicago Blackhawks
1954	Camille Henry	New York Rangers
1953	Lorne Worsley	New York Rangers
1952	B. Geoffrion	Montreal Canadiens
1951	Terry Sawchuk	Detroit Red Wings
1950	Jack Gelineau	Boston Bruins
1949	Pentti Lund	New York Rangers
1948	Jim McFadden	Detroit Red Wings
1947	Howie Meeker	Toronto Maple Leafs
1946	Edgar Laprade	New York Rangers
1945	Frank McCool	Toronto Maple Leafs
1944	Gus Bodnar	Toronto Maple Leafs
1943	Gaye Stewart	Toronto Maple Leafs
1942	Grant Warwick	New York Rangers
1941	Johnny Quilty	Montreal Canadiens
1940	K. MacDonald	New York Rangers
1939	Frank Brimsek	Boston Bruins
1938	Cully Dahlstrom	Chicago Blackhawks
1937	Syl Apps	Toronto Maple Leafs
1936	Mike Karakas	Chicago Blackhawks
1935	Dave Schriner	New York Americans
1934	Russ Blinko	Montreal Maroons
1933	Carl Voss	Detroit Red Wings

FRANK J. SELKE TROPHY

Year	*Winner*	*Team*
1999	Jere Lehtinen	Dallas Stars
1998	Jere Lehtinen	Dallas Stars
1997	Michael Peca	Buffalo Sabres
1996	Sergei Fedorov	Detroit Red Wings
1995	Ron Francis	Pittsburgh Penguins
1994	Sergei Fedorov	Detroit Red Wings
1993	Doug Gilmour	Toronto Maple Leafs
1992	G. Carbonneau	Montreal Canadiens
1991	Dirk Graham	Chicago Blackhawks
1990	Rick Meagher	St Louis Blues
1989	G. Carbonneau	Montreal Canadiens
1988	G. Carbonneau	Montreal Canadiens
1987	Dave Poulin	Philadelphia Flyers
1986	Troy Murray	Chicago Blackhawks
1985	Craig Ramsay	Buffalo Sabres
1984	Doug Jarvis	Washington Capitals
1983	Bobby Clarke	Philadelphia Flyers
1982	Steve Kasper	Boston Bruins
1981	Bob Gainey	Montreal Canadiens
1980	Bob Gainey	Montreal Canadiens
1979	Bob Gainey	Montreal Canadiens
1978	Bob Gainey	Montreal Canadiens

JACK ADAMS AWARD

Year	*Winner*	*Team*
1999	Jacques Martin	Ottawa Senators
1998	Pat Burns	Boston Bruins
1997	Ted Nolan	Buffalo Sabres
1996	Scotty Bowman	Detroit Red Wings
1995	Marc Crawford	Quebec Nordiques
1994	J. Lemaire	New Jersey Devils
1993	Pat Burns	Toronto Maple Leafs
1992	Pat Quinn	Vancouver Canucks
1991	Brian Sutter	St Louis Blues
1990	Bob Murdoch	Winnipeg Jets
1989	Pat Burns	Montreal Canadiens
1988	J. Demers	Detroit Red Wings
1987	J. Demers	Detroit Red Wings
1986	Glen Sather	Edmonton Oilers
1985	Mike Keenan	Philadelphia Flyers
1984	Bryan Murray	Washington Capitals
1983	Orval Tessier	Chicago Blackhawks
1982	Tom Watt	Winnipeg Jets
1981	G. Berenson	St. Louis Blues
1980	Pat Quinn	Philadelphia Flyers
1979	Al Arbour	New York Islanders
1978	Bobby Kromm	Detroit Red Wings
1977	Scotty Bowman	Montreal Canadiens
1976	Don Cherry	Boston Bruins
1975	Bob Pulford	Los Angeles Kings
1974	Fred Shero	Philadelphia Flyers

LADY BYNG MEMORIAL TROPHY

Year	*Winner*	*Team*
1999	Wayne Gretzky	New York Rangers
1998	Ron Francis	Pittsburgh Penguins
1997	Paul Kariya	Anaheim Mighty Ducks
1996	Paul Kariya	Anaheim Mighty Ducks
1995	Ron Francis	Pittsburgh Penguins
1994	Wayne Gretzky	Los Angeles Kings
1993	Pierre Turgeon	New York Islanders
1992	Wayne Gretzky	Los Angeles Kings
1991	Wayne Gretzky	Los Angeles Kings

VEZINA TROPHY

Year	*Winner*	*Team*
1999	Dominik Hasek	Buffalo Sabres
1998	Dominik Hasek	Buffalo Sabres
1997	Dominik Hasek	Buffalo Sabres
1996	Jim Carey	Washington Capitals
1995	Dominik Hasek	Buffalo Sabres
1994	Dominik Hasek	Buffalo Sabres
1993	Ed Belfour	Chicago Blackhawks
1992	Patrick Roy	Montreal Canadiens
1991	Ed Belfour	Chicago Blackhawks
1990	Patrick Roy	Montreal Canadiens
1989	Patrick Roy	Montreal Canadiens
1988	Grant Fuhr	Edmonton Oilers
1987	Ron Hextall	Philadelphia Flyers
1986	J. Vanbiesbrouck	New York Rangers
1985	Pelle Lindbergh	Philadelphia Flyers
1984	Tom Barrasso	Buffalo Sabres
1983	Pete Peeters	Boston Bruins
1982	Billy Smith	New York Islanders
1981	Denis Herron	Montreal Canadiens
	Richard Sevigny	Montreal Canadiens
	M. Larocque	Montreal Canadiens
1980	Don Edwards	Buffalo Sabres
	Bob Sauve	Buffalo Sabres
1979	Ken Dryden	Montreal Canadiens
	Glenn Resch	Montreal Canadiens
	Michel Larocque	Montreal Canadiens
1978	Ken Dryden	Montreal Canadiens
	Michel Larocque	Montreal Canadiens
1977	Ken Dryden	Montreal Canadiens
	Michel Larocque	Montreal Canadiens
1976	Ken Dryden	Montreal Canadiens
1975	Bernie Parent	Philadelphia Flyers
1974	Bernie Parent	Philadelphia Flyers
	Tony Esposito	Chicago Blackhawks

1973	Ken Dryden	Montreal Canadiens
1972	Tony Esposito	Chicago Blackhawks
	Gary Smith	Chicago Blackhawks
1971	Ed Giacomin	New York Rangers
	Gilles Villemure	New York Rangers
1970	Tony Esposito	Chicago Blackhawks
1969	Glenn Hall	St. Louis Blues
	Jacques Plante	St. Louis Blues
1968	Lorne Worsley	Montreal Canadiens
	Rogatien Vachon	Montreal Canadiens
1967	Denis DeJordy	Chicago Blackhawks
	Glenn Hall	Chicago Blackhawks
1966	Charlie Hodge	Montreal Canadiens
	Lorne Worsley	Montreal Canadiens
1965	Johnny Bower	Toronto Maple Leafs
	Terry Sawchuk	Toronto Maple Leafs
1964	Charlie Hodge	Montreal Canadiens
1963	Glenn Hall	Chicago Blackhawks
	Don Simmons	Toronto Maple Leafs
1962	Jacques Plante	Montreal Canadiens
1961	Johnny Bower	Toronto Maple Leafs
1960	Jacques Plante	Montreal Canadiens
1959	Jacques Plante	Montreal Canadiens
1958	Jacques Plante	Montreal Canadiens
	Lorne Worsley	New York Rangers
1957	Jacques Plante	Montreal Canadiens
1956	Jacques Plante	Montreal Canadiens
1955	Terry Sawchuk	Detroit Red Wings
1954	Harry Lumley	Toronto Maple Leafs
1953	Terry Sawchuk	Detroit Red Wings
1952	Terry Sawchuk	Detroit Red Wings
1951	Al Rollins	Toronto Maple Leafs
1950	Bill Durnan	Montreal Canadiens
1949	Bill Durnan	Montreal Canadiens
1948	Turk Broda	Toronto Maple Leafs
1947	Bill Durnan	Montreal Canadiens
1946	Bill Durnan	Montreal Canadiens
1945	Bill Durnan	Montreal Canadiens
	Frank McCool	Toronto Maple Leafs
1944	Bill Durnan	Montreal Canadiens
1943	Johnny Mowers	Detroit Red Wings
1942	Frank Brimsek	Boston Bruins
1941	Turk Broda	Toronto Maple Leafs
	Johnny Mowers	Detroit Red Wings
1940	Dave Kerr	New York Rangers
1939	Frank Brimsek	Boston Bruins
1938	Tiny Thompson	Boston Bruins
1937	Normie Smith	Detroit Red Wings
1936	Tiny Thompson	Boston Bruins
1935	Lorne Chabot	Chicago Blackhawks
1934	Charlie Gardiner	Chicago Blackhawks
1933	Tiny Thompson	Boston Bruins
1932	Charlie Gardiner	Chicago Black Hawks
1931	Roy Worters	New York Americans
1930	Tiny Thompson	Boston Bruins
1929	G. Hainsworth	Montreal Canadiens
1928	G. Hainsworth	Montreal Canadiens
1927	G. Hainsworth	Montreal Canadiens

**Note: awarded to goalie who played a minimum of 25 games for the team that concieved the fewest amount of goals.*

MASTERTON TROPHY

Year	*Winner*	*Team*
1999	John Cullen	Tampa Bay Lightning
1998	Jamie McLennan	St. Louis Blues
1997	Tony Granato	San Jose Sharks
1996	Gary Roberts	Calgary Flames
1995	Pat LaFontaine	Buffalo Sabres
1994	Cam Neely	Boston Bruins
1993	Mario Lemieux	Pittsburgh Penguins
1992	Mark Fitzpatrick	NY Islanders
1991	Dave Taylor	Los Angeles Kings
1990	Gord Kluzak	Boston Bruins
1989	Tim Kerr	Philadelphia Flyers
1988	Bob Bourne	Los Angeles Kings
1987	Doug Jarvis	Hartford Whalers
1986	Charlie Simmer	Boston Bruins
1985	Anders Hedberg	NY Rangers
1984	Brad Park	Detroit Red Wings
1983	Lanny McDonald	Calgary Flames
1982	Glenn Resch	Colorado Avalanche
1981	Blake Dunlop	St. Louis Blues
1980	Al MacAdam	Minnesota
1979	Serge Savard	Montreal Canadiens
1978	Butch Goring	Los Angeles Kings
1977	Ed Westfall	NY Islanders
1976	Rod Gilbert	NY Rangers
1975	Don Luce	Buffalo Sabres
1974	Henri Richard	Montreal Canadiens
1973	L. MacDonald	Pittsburgh Penguins
1972	Bobby Clarke	Philadelphia Flyers
1971	Jean Ratelle	NY Rangers
1970	Pit Martin	Chicago Blackhawks
1969	Ted Hampson	Oakland
1968	Claude Provost	Montreal Canadiens

KING CLANCY TROPHY

Year	*Winner*	*Team*
1999	Rob Ray	Buffalo Sabres
1998	Kelly Chase	St. Louis Blues
1997	Trevor Linden	Vancouver Canucks
1996	Kris King	Winnipeg Jets
1995	Joe Nieuwendyk	Calgary Flames
1994	Adam Graves	NY Rangers
1993	Dave Poulin	Boston Bruins
1992	Ray Bourque	Boston Bruins
1991	Dave Taylor	Los Angeles Kings
1990	Kevin Lowe	Edmonton Oilers
1989	Bryan Trottier	NY Islanders
1988	Lanny McDonald	Calgary Flames

JAMES NORRIS MEMORIAL TROPHY

Year	*Winner*	*Team*
1999	Al MacInnis	St. Louis Blues
1998	Rob Blake	Los Angeles Kings
1997	Brian Leetch	New York Rangers
1996	Chris Chelios	Chicago Blackhawks
1995	Paul Coffey	Detroit Red Wings
1994	Ray Bourque	Boston Bruins
1993	Chris Chelios	Chicago Blackhawks
1992	Brian Leetch	New York Rangers
1991	Ray Bourque	Boston Bruins
1990	Ray Bourque	Boston Bruins
1989	Chris Chelios	Montreal Canadiens
1988	Ray Bourque	Boston Bruins
1987	Ray Bourque	Boston Bruins
1986	Paul Coffey	Edmonton Oilers
1985	Paul Coffey	Edmonton Oilers
1984	Rod Langway	Washington Capitals
1983	Rod Langway	Washington Capitals
1982	Doug Wilson	Chicago Blackhawks
1981	Randy Carlyle	Pittsburgh Penguins
1980	Larry Robinson	Montreal Canadiens
1979	Denis Potvin	New York Islanders
1978	Denis Potvin	New York Islanders
1977	Larry Robinson	Montreal Canadiens
1976	Denis Potvin	New York Islanders
1975	Bobby Orr	Boston Bruins
1974	Bobby Orr	Boston Bruins
1973	Bobby Orr	Boston Bruins
1972	Bobby Orr	Boston Bruins
1971	Bobby Orr	Boston Bruins
1970	Bobby Orr	Boston Bruins
1969	Bobby Orr	Boston Bruins
1968	Bobby Orr	Boston Bruins
1967	Harry Howell	New York Rangers
1966	J. Laperriere	Montreal Canadiens
1965	Pierre Pilote	Chicago Blackhawks
1964	Pierre Pilote	Chicago Blackhawks
1963	Pierre Pilote	Chicago Blackhawks
1962	Doug Harvey	New York Rangers
1961	Doug Harvey	Montreal Canadiens
1960	Doug Harvey	Montreal Canadiens
1959	Tom Johnson	Montreal Canadiens
1958	Doug Harvey	Montreal Canadiens
1957	Doug Harvey	Montreal Canadiens
1956	Doug Harvey	Montreal Canadiens
1955	Doug Harvey	Montreal Canadiens
1954	Red Kelly	Detroit Red Wings

HART MEMORIAL TROPHY WINNERS

Year	*Winner*	*Team*
1999	Jaromir Jagr	Pittsburgh Penguins
1998	Dominik Hasek	Buffalo Sabres
1997	Dominik Hasek	Buffalo Sabres
1996	Mario Lemieux	Pittsburgh Penguins
1995	Eric Lindros	Philadelphia Flyers
1994	Sergei Fedorov	Detroit Red Wings
1993	Mario Lemieux	Pittsburgh Penguins
1992	Mark Messier	New York Rangers
1991	Brett Hull	St. Louis Blues
1990	Mark Messier	Edmonton Oilers
1989	Wayne Gretzky	Edmonton Oilers
1988	Mario Lemieux	Pittsburgh Penguins
1987	Wayne Gretzky	Edmonton Oilers
1986	Wayne Gretzky	Edmonton Oilers
1985	Wayne Gretzky	Edmonton Oilers
1984	Wayne Gretzky	Edmonton Oilers
1983	Wayne Gretzky	Edmonton Oilers
1982	Wayne Gretzky	Edmonton Oilers
1981	Wayne Gretzky	Edmonton Oilers
1980	Wayne Gretzky	Edmonton Oilers
1979	Bryan Trottier	New York Islanders
1978	Guy Lafleur	Montreal Canadiens
1977	Guy Lafleur	Montreal Canadiens
1976	Bobby Clarke	Philadelphia Flyers
1975	Bobby Clarke	Philadelphia Flyers
1974	Phil Esposito I	Boston Bruins
1973	Bobby Clarke	Philadelphia Flyers
1972	Bobby Orr	Boston Bruins
1971	Bobby Orr	Boston Bruins
1970	Bobby Orr	Boston Bruins
1969	Phil Esposito	Boston Bruins
1968	Stan Mikita	Chicago Blackhawks
1967	Stan Mikita	Chicago Blackhawks
1966	Bobby Hull	Chicago Blackhawks
1965	Bobby Hull	Chicago Blackhawks
1964	Jean Beliveaul	Montreal Canadiens
1963	Gordie Howe	Detroit Red Wings
1962	Jacques Plante	Montreal Canadiens
1961	Bernie Geoffrion	Montreal Canadiens
1960	Gordie Howe	Detroit Red Wings
1959	Andy Bathgate	New York Rangers
1958	Gordie Howe	Detroit Red Wings
1957	Gordie Howe	Detroit Red Wings
1956	Jean Beliveaul	Montreal Canadiens
1955	Ted Kennedy	Toronto Maple Leafs

1954	Al Rollins	Chicago Blackhawks
1953	Gordie Howe	Detroit Red Wings
1952	Gordie Howe	Detroit Red Wings
1951	Milt Schmidt	Boston Bruins
1950	Chuck Rayner	New York Rangers
1949	Sid Abel	Detroit Red Wings
1948	Buddy O'Connor	New York Rangers
1947	Maurice Richard	Montreal Canadiens
1946	Max Bentley	Chicago Blackhawks
1945	Elmer Lach	Montreal Canadiens
1944	Babe Pratt	Toronto Maple Leafs
1943	Bill Cowley	Boston Bruins
1942	Tom Anderson	New York Americans
1941	Bill Cowleyl	Boston Bruins
1940	Ebbie Goodfellow	Detroit Red Wings
1939	Toe Blake	Montreal Canadiens
1938	Eddie Shore	Boston Bruins
1937	Babe Siebert	Montreal Canadiens
1936	Eddie Shore	Boston Bruins
1935	Eddie Shore	Boston Bruins
1934	Aurel Joliat	Montreal Canadiens
1933	Eddie Shore	Boston Bruins
1932	Howie Morenz	Montreal Canadiens
1931	Howie Morenz	Montreal Canadiens
1930	Nels Stewart	Montreal Maroons
1929	Roy Worters	New York Americans
1928	Howie Morenz	Montreal Canadiens
1927	Herb Gardiner	Montreal Canadiens
1926	Nels Stewart	Montreal Maroons
1925	Billy Burch	Hamilton Tigers
1924	Frank Nighbor	Ottawa Senators

CONN SMYTHE TROPHY WINNERS

Year	*Winner*	*Team*
1999	Joe Nieuwendyk	Dallas Stars
1998	Steve Yzerman	Detroit Red Wings
1997	Mike Vernon	Detroit Red Wings
1996	Joe Sakic	Colorado Avalanche
1995	Claude Lemieux	New Jersey Devils
1994	Brian Leetch	New York Rangers
1993	Patrick Roy	Montreal Canadiens
1992	Mario Lemieux	Pittsburgh Penguins
1991	Mario Lemieux	Pittsburgh Penguins
1990	Bill Ranford	Edmonton Oilers
1989	Al MacInnis	Calgary Flames
1988	Wayne Gretzky	Edmonton Oilers
1987	Ron Hextall	Philadelphia Flyers
1986	Patrick Roy	Montreal Canadiens
1985	Wayne Gretzky	Edmonton Oilers
1984	Mark Messier	Edmonton Oilers
1983	Bill Smith	New York Islanders
1982	Mike Bossy	New York Islanders
1981	Butch Goring	New York Islanders
1980	Bryan Trottier	New York Islanders
1979	Bob Gainey	Montreal Canadiens
1978	Larry Robinson	Montreal Canadiens
1977	Guy Lafleur	Montreal Canadiens
1976	Reggie Leach	Philadelphia Flyers
1975	Bernie Parent	Philadelphia Flyers
1974	Bernie Parent	Philadelphia Flyers
1973	Yvan Cournoyer	Montreal Canadiens
1972	Bobby Orr	Boston Bruins
1971	Ken Dryden	Montreal Canadiens
1970	Bobby Orr	Boston Bruins
1969	Serge Savard	Montreal Canadiens
1968	Glenn Hall	St. Louis Blues
1967	Dave Keon	Toronto Maple Leafs
1966	Roger Crozier	Detroit Red Wings
1965	Jean Beliveau	Montreal Canadiens

PLAYOFF RECORD HOLDERS

GOALS

Career: Wayne Gretzky, 122; Mark Messier, 109; Jari Kurri, 106
Season: Reggie Leach, Philadelphia, 1976, 19; Jari Kurri, Edmonton, 1985, 19; Joe Sakic, Colorado, 1996, 18
Series other than final: Jari Kurri Edmonton, 1985 Conference Final, 12
Final series: Babe Dye, Toronto, 1922, 9 in 5 games.
Game: Newsy Lalonde, Montreal, 1919, 5; Maurice Richard, Montreal, 1944, 5; Darryl Sittler, Toronto, 1976, 5, Reggie Leach, Philadelphia, 1976, 5; Mario Lemieux, Pittsburgh, 1989, 5.

ASSISTS

Career: Wayne Gretzky, 260; Mark Messier 186
Season: Wayne Grezky 31, 1988; Wayne Gretzky, 30, 1985
Series other than final: Rick Middleton, Boston, Division Final 1983, 14
Final series: Wayne Gretzky, Edmonton, 1988, 10
Game: Mikko Leinonen, NY Rangers, 1982, 6; Wayne Gretzky, Edmonton, 1987, 6

POINTS

Career: Wayne Gretzky, 382
Season: Wayne Gretzky, Edmonton, 1985, 47
Series other than final: Rick Middleton, Boston, 1983, 19
Final Series: Wayne Gretzky, Edmonton, 1988, 13
Game: Patrik Sundstrom, New Jersey, 1988, 8; Mario Lemieux, Pittsburgh, 1989, 8

GOALTENDING

Career Victories: Patrick Roy, 110
Career Shutouts: Clint Benedict, 15
Season Shutouts: Clint Benedict, Mtl. Maroons, 1926, 4; Clint Benedict, Mtl. Maroons, 1928, 4; Dave Kerr, NY Rangers, 1937, 4; Frank McCool, Toronto, 1945, 4; Terry Sawchuk, Detroit, 1952, 4; Bernie Parent, Philadelphia, 1975, 4; Ken Dryden, Monteal, 1977, 4; Mike Richter, NY Rangers, 1994, 4; Kirk McLean, Vancouver, 1994, 4; Olaf Kolzig, 1998, 4

STANLEY CUP FINALS

From 1918 to 1926, the Cup winner was determined in a series between the NHL and PCHA champion. Since 1927, the NHL champion has won the Cup.

Year	*Champion*	*Runner-up*	*Games*
1999	Dallas	Buffalo	4-2
1998	Detroit	Washington	4-0
1997	Detroit	Philadelphia	4-0
1996	Colorado	Florida	4-0
1995	New Jersey	Detroit	4-0
1994	NY Rangers	Vancouver	4-3
1993	Montreal	Los Angeles	4-1
1992	Pittsburgh	Chicago	4-0
1991	Pittsburgh	Minnesota	4-2
1990	Edmonton	Boston	4-1
1989	Calgary	Montreal	4-2
1988	Edmonton	Boston	4-0
1987	Edmonton	Philadelphia	4-3
1986	Montreal	Calgary	4-1
1985	Edmonton	Philadelphia	4-1
1984	Edmonton	NY Islanders	4-1
1983	NY Islanders	Edmonton	4-0
1982	NY Islanders	Vancouver	4-0
1981	NY Islanders	Minnesota	4-1
1980	NY Islanders	Philadelphia	4-2
1979	Montreal	NY Rangers	4-1
1978	Montreal	Boston	4-2
1977	Montreal	Boston	4-0
1976	Montreal	Philadelphia	4-0
1975	Philadelphia	Buffalo	4-2
1974	Philadelphia	Boston	4-2
1973	Montreal	Chicago	4-2
1972	Boston	NY Rangers	4-2
1971	Montreal	Chicago	4-3
1970	Boston	St. Louis	4-0
1969	Montreal	St. Louis	4-0
1968	Montreal	St. Louis	4-0
1967	Toronto	Montreal	4-2
1966	Montreal	Detroit	4-2
1965	Montreal	Chicago	4-3
1964	Toronto	Detroit	4-3
1963	Toronto	Detroit	4-1
1962	Toronto	Chicago	4-2
1961	Chicago	Detroit	4-2
1960	Montreal	Toronto	4-0
1959	Montreal	Toronto	4-1
1958	Montreal	Boston	4-2
1957	Montreal	Boston	4-1
1956	Montreal	Detroit	4-1
1955	Detroit	Montreal	4-3
1954	Detroit	Montreal	4-3
1953	Montreal	Boston	4-1
1952	Detroit	Montreal	4-0
1951	Toronto	Montreal	4-1
1950	Detroit	NY Rangers	4-3
1949	Toronto	Detroit	4-0
1948	Toronto	Detroit	4-0
1947	Toronto	Montreal	4-2
1946	Montreal	Boston	4-1
1945	Toronto	Detroit	4-3
1944	Montreal	Chicago	4-0
1943	Detroit	Boston	4-0
1942	Toronto	Detroit	4-3
1941	Boston	Detroit	4-0
1940	NY Rangers	Toronto	4-2
1939	Boston	Toronto	4-1
1938	Chicago	Toronto	3-1
1937	Detroit	NY Rangers	3-2
1936	Detroit	Toronto	3-1
1935	Mtl. Maroons	Toronto	3-0
1934	Chicago	Detroit	3-1
1933	NY Rangers	Toronto	3-1
1932	Toronto	NY Rangers	3-0
1931	Montreal	Chicago	3-2
1930	Montreal	Boston	2-0
1929	Boston	NY Rangers	2-0
1928	NY Rangers	Mtl. Maroons	3-2
1927	Ottawa	Boston	2-0-2
1926	Mtl. Maroons	Victoria	3-1
1925	Victoria	Montreal	3-1
1924	Montreal	Van. Maroons	2-0
		Calgary Tigers	2-0
1923	Ottawa	Van. Maroons	3-1
		Edm. Eskimos	2-0
1922	Tor. St Patricks	Van. Millionaires	3-2
1921	Ottawa	Van. Millionaires	3-2
1920	Ottawa	Seattle	3-2
1919	*No champion; series between Montreal and Seattle halted because of flu epidemic.*		
1918	Tor. Arenas	Van. Millionaires	3-2

TEAM RECORDS

MOST GOALS:

Goals	*Team (games)*	*Season*
446	Edmonton Oilers	1983-84 (80)
426	Edmonton Oilers	1985-86 (80)
424	Edmonton Oilers	1982-83 (80)

417	Edmonton Oilers	1981-82 (80)
401	Edmonton Oilers	1984-85 (80)

MOST ASSISTS:

Ass.	***Team***	***Season***
737	Edmonton Oilers	1985-86
736	Edmonton Oilers	1983-84
706	Edmonton Oilers	1981-82

GOALS AGAINST AVERAGE (G.A.A.):
LOWEST:

G.A.A.	***Team***	***Season (games)***
0.98	Montreal Canadiens	1928-29 (44)
1.09	Montreal Canadiens	1927-28 (44)
1.17	Ottawa Senators	1925-26 (36)

**The record for fewest goals allowed in a season is 42 by the 1925-26 Ottawa Senators in 36 games. For a minimum 70-game season the record is 131 by the Toronto Maple Leafs in 1953-54 and the Montreal Canadiens in 1955-56.*

HIGHEST:

G.A.A.	***Team***	***Season (g)***
7.38	Quebec Bulldogs	1919-20 (24)
6.20	N.Y. Rangers	1943-44 (50)

MOST POINTS:

P	***Team***	***Season (W-L-T)***
132	Mon. Canadiens	1976-77 60-8-12
131	Detroit Red Wings	1995-96 62-13-7
129	Mon. Canadiens	1977-78 59-10-11

TEAM PENALTY MINUTES:

Pen Mins	***Team***	***Season(g)***
2,713	Buffalo Sabres	1991-92 (80)
2,670	Pitt. Penguins	1988-89 (80)
2,663	Chicago B'hawks	1991-92 (80)

OTHER TEAM RECORDS

Longest winning streak one season: Pittsburgh Penguins, March 9-April 10 1993, 17 games
Longest undefeated streak one season: Philadelphia Flyers, October 14, 1979-January 6, 1980, 35 games (25 wins, 10 ties)
Longest losing streak one season: Washington Capitals, February 18-March 26, 1975, 17 games / San Jose Sharks, January 4-February 12, 1993, 17 games
Longest winless streak one season: Winnipeg Jets, October 19-December 20, 1980, 30 games
Most Goals/game: 16, Montreal Canadiens, March 3, 1920.Defeated Quebec Bulldogs, 16-3
Most 50 goal scorers one season: 3, Edmonton Oilers, 1983-84 (Wayne Gretzky 87, Glenn Anderson 54, Jari Kurri 52) / 3, Edmonton Oilers 1985-86 (Jari Kurri 68, Glenn Anderson 54, Wayne Gretzky 52)

POSTSEASON ALL-STAR TEAMS

**First team only.*
Voting for the NHL All-Star Team is conducted among the represnetatives of the Professional Hockey Writers Association at the end of each season.

1930-31
G – Chuck Gardiner, Chi.
D – Eddie Shore, Bos.
D – King Clancy, Tor.
C – Howie Morenz, Mtl.
RW – Bill Cook, NYR
LW – Aurel Joliat, Mtl.
Coach – Lester Patrick, NYR

1931-32
G – Chuck Gardiner, Chi.
D – Eddie Shore, Bos.
D – Ivan Johnson, NYR
C – Howie Morenz, Mtl.
RW – Bill Cook, NYR
LW – Harvey Jackson, Tor.
Coach – Lester Patrick, NYR

1932-33
G – John Ross Roach, Det.
D –Eddie Shore, Bos.
D –Ivan Johnson, NYR
C –Frank Boucher, NYR
RW – Bill Cook NYR
LW – Baldy Northcott, Mtl Maroons
Coach – Lester Patrick, NYR

1933-34
G – Chuck Gardiner, Chi.
D – King Clancy, Tor.
D – Lionel Conacher, Chi.
C – Frank Boucher, NYR
RW – Charlie Conacher, Tor.
LW – Harvey Jackson, Tor.
Coach – Lester Patrick, NYR

1934-35
G – Lorne Chabot, Chi.
D – Eddie Shore, Bos.
D – Earl Seibert, NYR
C – Frank Boucher, NYR
RW – Charlie Conacher, Tor.
LW – Harvey Jackson, Tor.
Coach – Lester Patrick, NYR

1935-36
G – Tiny Thompson, Bos.
D – Eddie Shore, Bos.
D – Babe Siebert, Bos.
C – Hooley Smith, Mtl. Maroons
RW – Charlie Conacher, Tor.
LW – Sweeney Schriner, NYA
Coach – Lester Patrick, NYR

1936-37
G – Norman Smith, Det.
D – Babe Siebert, Mtl.
D – Ebbie Goodfellow, Det.
C – Marty Barry, Det.
RW – Larry Aurie, Det.
LW – Harvey Jackson, Tor.
Coach – Jack Adams, Det.

1937-38
G – Frank Brimsek, Bos.
D – Jack Stewart, Det.
D – Bill Quackenbush, Det.
C – Max Bentley, Chi.
RW – Bobby Bauer, Bos.
LW – Woody Dumart, Bos.
Coach – Lester Patrick, NYR

1938-39
G – Frank Brimsek, Det.
D – Eddie Shore, Bos.
D – Dit Clapper, Bos.
C – Syl Apps Sr., Tor.
RW – Gordie Drillon, Tor.
LW – Toe Blake, Mtl.
Coach – Art Ross, Bos.

1939-40
G – Dave Kerr, NYR
D – Dit Clapper, Bos.
D – Ebbie Goodfellow, Det.
C – Milt Schmidt, Bos.
RW – Bryan Hextall Sr., NYR
LW – Toe Blake, Mtl.
Coach – Paul Thompson, Chi.

1940-41
G – Turk Broda, Tor.
D – Dit Clapper, Bos.
D – Wally Stanowski, Tor.
C – Bill Cowley, Bos.
RW – Bryan Hextall Sr., NYR
LW – Sweeney Schriner, Tor.
Coach – Cooney Weiland, Bos.

1941-42
G – Frank Brimsek, Bos.
D – Earl Seibert, Chi.
D – Tom Anderson, Bro.
C – Syl Apps Sr, Tor.
RW – Bryan Hextall, NYR
LW – Lynn Patrick, NYR
Coach – Frank Boucher, NYR

1942-43
G – Johnny Mowers, Det.
D – Earl Seibert, Chi.
D – Jack Stewart, Det.
C – Bill Cowley, Bos.
RW – Lorne Carr, Tor.
LW – Doug Bentley, Chi.
Coach – Jack Adams, Det.

1943-44
G – Bill Durnan, Mtl.
D – Earl Seibert, Chi.
D – Babe Pratt, Tor.
C – Bill Cowley, Bos.
RW – Lorne Carr, Tor.
LW – Doug Bentley, Chi.
Coach – Dick Irvin, Mtl.

1944-45
G – Bill Durnan, Mtl.
D – Butch Bouchard, Mtl.
D – Flash Hollett, Det.
C – Elmer Lach, Mtl.
RW – Maurice Richard, Mtl.
LW – Toe Blake, Mtl.
Coach – Dick Irvin, Mtl.

1945-46
G – Bill Durnan, Mtl.
D – Jack Crawford, Bos.
D – Butch Bouchard, Mtl.
C – Max Bentley, Chi.
RW – Maurice Richard, Mtl.
LW – Gaye Stewart, Tor.
Coach – Dick Irvin, Mtl.

1946-47
G – Bill Durnan, Mtl.
D – Ken Reardon, Mtl.
D – Butch Bouchard, Mtl.
C – Milt Schmidt, Bos.
RW – Maurice Richard, Mtl.
LW – Doug Bentley, Chi

1947-48
G – Turk Broda, Tor.
D – Bill Quackenbush, Det.
D – Jack Stewart, Det.
C – Elmer Lach, Mtl.
RW – Maurice Richard, Mtl.
LW – Ted Lindsay, Det.

1948-49
G – Bill Durnan, Mtl.
D – Bill Quackenbush, Det.
D – Jack Stewart, Det.
C – Sid Abel, Det.
RW – Maurice Richard, Mtl.
LW – Roy Conacher, Chi.

1949-50
G – Bill Durnan, Mtl.
D – Gus Mortson, Tor.
D – Ken Reardon, Mtl.
C – Sid Abel, Det.
RW – Maurice Richard, Mtl.
LW – Ted Lindsay, Det.

1950-51
G – Terry Sawchuk, Det.
D – Red Kelly, Det.
D – Bill Quackenbush, Bos.
C – Milt Schmidt, Bos.
RW – Gordie Howe, Det.
LW – Ted Lindsay, Det.

1951-52
G – Terry Sawchuk, Det.
D – Red Kelly, Det.
D – Doug Harvey, Mtl.
C – Elmer Lach, Mtl.
RW – Gordie Howe, Det.
LW – Ted Lindsay, Det.

1952-53
G – Terry Sawchuk, Det.
D – Red Kelly, Det.
D – Doug Harvey, Mtl.
C – Fleming Mackell, Bos.
RW – Gordie Howe, Det.
LW – Ted Lindsay, Det.

1953-54
G – Harry Lumley, Tor.
D – Red Kelly, Det.
D – Doug Harvey, Mtl.
C – Kenny Mosdell, Mtl.
RW – Gordie Howe, Det.
LW – Ted Lindsay, Det.

1954-55
G – Harry Lumley, Tor.
D – Red Kelly, Det.
D – Doug Harvey, Mtl.
C – Jean Beliveau, Mtl.
RW – Maurice Richard, Mtl.
LW – Sid Smith, Tor

1955-56
G – Jacques Plante, Mtl.
D – Doug Harvey, Mtl.
D – Bill Gadsby, NYR
C – Jean Beliveau, Mtl.
RW – Maurice Richard, Mtl.
LW – Ted Lindsay, Det.

1956-57
G – Glenn Hall, Det.
D – Doug Harvey, Mtl.
D – Red Kelly, Det.
C – Jean Beliveau, Mtl.
RW – Gordie Howe, Det.
LW – Ted Lindsay, Det.

1957-58
G – Glenn Hall, Det.
D – Doug Harvey, Mtl.
D – Bill Gadsby, NYR
C – Henri Richard, Mtl.
RW – Gordie Howe, Det.
LW – Dickie Moore Mtl.

1958-59
G – Jacques Plante, Mtl.
D – Tom Johnson, Mtl.
D – Bill Gadsby, NYR
C – Jean Beliveau, Mtl.
RW – Andy Bathgate, NYR
LW – Dickie Moore, Mtl.
1959-60
G – Glenn Hall, Chi.
D – Doug Harvey, Mtl.
D – Marcel Pronovost, Det.
C – Jean Beliveau, Mtl.
RW – Gordie Howe, Det.
LW – Bobby Hull, Chi.
1960-61
G – Johnny Bower, Tor.
D – Doug Harvey, Mtl.
D – Marcel Pronovost, Det.
C – Jean Beliveau, Mtl.
RW – Bernie Geoffrion, Mtl.
LW – Frank Mahovlich, Tor.
1961-62
G – Jacques Plante, Mtl.
D – Doug Harvey, Mtl.
D – Jean-Guy Talbot, Mtl.
C – Stan Mikita, Chi.
RW – Andy Bathgate, NYR
LW – Bobby Hull, Chi.
1962-63
G – Glenn Hall, Chi.
D – Oierre Pilote, Chi.
D – Carl Brewer, Tor.
C – Stan Mikita, Chi.
RW – Gordie Howe, Det.
LW – Frank Mahovlich, Tor.
1963-64
G – Glenn Hall, Chi.
D – Pierre Pilote, Chi.
D – Tim Horton, Tor.
C – Stan Mikita, Chi
RW – Kenny Wharram, Chi.
LW – Bobby Hull, Chi.
1964-65
G – Roger Crozier, Det.
D – Pierre Pilote, Chi.
D – Jacques Laperriere
C – Norm Ullman, Det.
RW – Claude Provost, Mtl.
LW – Bobby Hull, Chi.
1965-66
G – Glenn Hall, Chi.
D – Jacques Laperriere
D – Pierre Pilote, Chi.
C – Stan Mikita, Chi.
RW – Gordie Howe, Det.
LW – Bobby Hull, Chi.
1966-67
G – Ed Giacomin, NYR
D – Pierre Pilote, Chi.
D – Harry Howell, NYR
C – Stan Mikita, Chi
RW – Kenny Wharram, Chi.
LW – Bobby Hull, Chi.
1967-68
G – Gump Worsley, Mtl.
D – Bobby Orr, Bos.
D – Tim Horton, Tor.
C – Stan Mikita, Chi.
RW – Gordie Howe, Det.
LW – Bobby Hull, Chi.
1968-69
G – Glenn Hall, St.L
D – Bobby Orr, Bos.
D – Tim Horton, Tor.
C – Phil Esposito, Bos.
RW – Gordie Howe, Det.
LW – Bobby Hull, Chi.
1969-70
G – Tony Esposito, Chi.
D – Bobby Orr, Bos.
D – Brad Park, NYR
C – Phil Esposito, Bos.
RW – Gordie Howe, Det.
LW – Bobby Hull, Chi.
1970-71
G – Ed Giacomin, NYR
D – Bobby Orr, Bos.
D – J.C. Tremblay, Mtl.
C – Phil Esposito, Bos.
RW – Ken Hodge, Bos.
LW – John Bucyk, Bos.
1971-72
G – Tony Esposito, Chi.
D – Bobby Orr, Bos.
D – Brad Park, NYR
C – Phil Esposito, Bos.
RW – Rod Gilbert, NYR
LW – Bobby Hull, Chi.
1972-73
G – Ken Dryden, Mtl.
D – Bobby Orr, Bos.
D – Guy Lapointe, Mtl.
C – Phil Esposito, Bos.
RW – Mickey Redmond, Det.
LW – Frank Mahovlich, Mtl.
1973-74
G – Bernie Parent, Phi.
D – Bobby Orr, Bos.
D – Brad Park, NYR
C – Phil Esposito, Bos.
RW – Ken Hodge, Bos.
LW – Rick Martin, Buf.
1974-75
G – Bernie Parent, Phi.
D – Bobby Orr, Bos.
D – Denis Potvin, NYI
C – Bobby Clarke, Phi.
RW – Guy Lafleur, Mtl.
LW – Rick Martin, Buf.
1975-76
G – Ken Dryden, Mtl.
D – Denis Potvin, NYI
D – Brad Park, Bos.
C – Bobby Clarke, Phi.
RW – Guy Lafleur, Mtl.
LW – Bill Barber, Phi.
1976-77
G – Ken Dryden, Mtl.
D – Larry Robinson, Mtl.
D – Borje Salming, Tor.
C – Marcel Dionne, LA
RW – Guy Lafleur, Mtl.
LW – Steve Shutt, Mtl.
1977-78
G – Ken Dryden, Mtl.
D – Denis Potvin, NYI
D – Brad Park, Bos.
C – Bryan Trottier, NYI
RW – Guy Lafleur, Mtl.
LW – Clark Gilles, NYI
1978-79
G – Ken Dryden, Mtl.
D – Denis Potvin, NYI
D – Larry Robinson, Mtl.
C – Bryan Trottier, NYI
RW – Guy Lafleur, Mtl.
LW – Clark Gilles, NYI
1979-80
G – Tony Esposito, Chi.
D – Larry Robinson, Mtl.
D – Ray Bourque, Bos.
C – Marcel Dionne, LA
RW – Guy Lafleur, Mtl.
LW – Charlie Simmer, LA
1980-81
G – Mike Liut, St.L
D – Denis Potvin, NYI
D – Randy Carlyle, Pitt.
C – Wayne Gretzky, Edm.
RW – Mike Bossy, NYI
LW – Charlie Simmer, LA
1981-82
G – Billy Smith, NYI
D – Doug Wilson, Chi.
D – Ray Bourque, Bos.
C – Wayne Gretzky, Edm.
RW – Mike Bossy, NYI
LW – Mark Messier, Edm.
1982-83
G – Pete Peeters, Bos.
D – Mark Howe, Phi.
D – Rod Langway, Wash.
C – Wayne Gretzky, Edm.
RW – Mike Bossy, NYI
LW – Mark Messier, Edm.
1983-84
G – Tom Barrasso, Pitt.
D – Rod Langway, Wash.
D – Ray Bourque, Bos.
C – Wayne Gretzky, Edm.
RW – Mike Bossy, NYI
LW – Michel Goulet, Que.
1984-85
G – Pelle Lindbergh, Phi.
D – Paul Coffey, Edm.
D – Ray Bourque, Bos.
C – Wayne Gretzky, Edm.
RW – Jari Kurri, Edm.
LW – John Ogrodnick, Det.
1985-86
G – John Vanbiesbrouck, NYR
D – Paul Coffey, Edm.
D – Mark Howe, Phi.
C – Wayne Gretzky, Edm.
RW – Mike Bossy, NYI
LW – Michel Goulet, Que.
1986-87
G – Ron Hextall, Phi.
D – Ray Bourque, Bos.
D – Mark Howe, Phi.
C – Wayne Gretzky, Edm.
RW – Jari Kurri, Edm.
LW – Michel Goulet, Que.
1987-88
G – Grant Fuhr, Edm.
D – Ray Bourque, Bos.
D – Scott Stevens, Wash.
C – Mario Lemieux, Pitt.
RW – Hakan Loob, Cgy.
LW – Luc Robitaille, LA
1988-89
G – Patrick Roy, Mtl.
D – Chris Chelios, Mtl.
D – Paul Coffey, Pitt.
C – Mario Lemieux, Pitt.
RW – Joe Mullen, Cgy.
LW – Luc Robitaille, LA
1989-90
G – Patrick Roy, Mtl.
D – Ray Bourque, Bos.
D – Al MacInnis, Cgy.
C – Mark Messier, Edm.
RW – Brett Hull, St.L
LW – Luc Robitaille, LA
1990-91
G – Ed Belfour, Chi.
D – Ray Bourque, Bos.
D – Al MacInnis, Cgy.
C – Wayne Gretzky, LA
RW – Brett Hull, St.L
LW – Luc Robitaille, LA
1991-92
G – Patrick Roy, Mtl.
D – Brian Leetch, NYR
D – Ray Bourque, Bos.
C – Mark Messier, NYR
RW – Brett Hull, St.L
LW – Kevin Stevens, Pitt.
1992-93
G – Ed Belfour, Chi.
D – Chris Chelios, Chi.
D – Ray Bourque, Bos.
C – Mario Lemieux, Pitt.
RW – Teemu Selanne, Winn.
LW – Luc Robitaille, LA
1993-94
G – Dominik Hasek, Buf.
D – Ray Bourque, Bos.
D – Scott Stevens, NJ
C – Sergei Fedorov, Det.
RW – Pavel Bure, Van.
LW – Brendan Shanhan, StL.
1994-95
G – Dominik Hasek, Buf.
D – Paul Coffey, Det.
D – Chris Chelios, Chi.
C – Eric Lindros, Phi.
RW – Jaromir Jagr, Pitt.
LW – John LeClair, Mtl/Phi.
1995-96
G – Jim Carey, Was.
D – Chris Chelios, Chi.
D – Ray Bourque, Bos.
C – Mario Lemieux, Pitt.
RW – Jaromir Jagr, Pitt.
LW – Paul Kariya, Ana.
1996-97
G – Dominik Hasek, Buf.
D – Brian Leetch, NYR
D – Sandis Ozolinsh, Colo.
C – Mario Lemieux, Pitt.
RW – Teemu Selanne, Ana.
LW – Paul Kariya, Ana.
1997-98
G – Dominik Hasek, Buf.
D – Nicklas Lidstrom, Det.
D – Rob Blake, LA
C – Peter Forsberg, Colo.
RW – Jaromir Jagr, Pitt.
LW – John LeClair, Phi.
1998-99
G – Dominik Hasek, Buf.
D – Nicklas Lidstrom, Det.
D – Al MacInnis, St. L.
C – Peter Forsberg, Colo.
RW – Jaromir Jagr, Pitt.
LW – Paul Kariya, Ana.

INDEX

Note: page numbers in italics refer to illustrations.

Index

PICTURE ACKNOWLEDGMENTS

The publishers would like to thank the following sources for their kind permission to reproduce the pictures in this book:

Allsport USA 150l, 165, 170, 182, /Al Bello 171, Steve Powell 152t, Jamie Squire 187
Corbis 130b, 135
Hockey Hall Of Fame 13r, 14c, 15t, 16, 17, 18, 20, 21l, 22, 23, 25, 26, 28, 29, 30, 33, 34, 35, 36, 40, 46, 49, 50, 51, 52, 53, 57, 64, 65l, 78, 80, 91, 92, 94, 95, 97, 108, 120, 134b, 138, 139, 151b, 155, 162, 164, 169, 172, 179t, 192b, 193, 196, 197/Wayne Arnold 161r, Graphic Artists 78, 101t, 102, 104, 105, 106t, 107, 112, 114, 115, 116, 118, 121, 127b, 128, 133, 137, 140, 141, 143, 150r, Imperial Oil-Turofsky 13l, 21r, 37, 38, 42, 43, 44, 45, 47r, 54, 58-9, 61, 62-3, 65r, 66, 67, 68, 69, 70, 73, 75, 76, 77, 81, 83b, 84, 89, 99, 100, 101b, Fred Kennan 126, James McCarthy 130t, Doug MacLellan 15b, 155bl, 159, 161l, 168, 173, Peter Mecca 134t,
NHL 109, 113, 190b, 192t, 194, Miles Nadal 145, O-Pee-Chee Collection 31, 123, Frank Prazak 82, 83t, 85, 96, 98, 117, 122, 129, 132, 156, James Rice 26, 48
NHL Images 2, 7, 10, 14r, 41, 47l, 72, 87, 106b, 127t, 131, 142, 146, 153, 181, 188l, 192c, /Allsport: Elsa Hasch 184, Craig Jones 9, Ezra Shaw 190t, Rick Stewart 177br /Paul Bereswell 177t, 188c, Andrew D Bernstein 189, Brantford Expositor 124, Tim DeFrisco 6, 204, Barry Gossage 210, 216, Mitchell Layton 149, 154, 175, 183, Craig Melvin 176, 195, 202, 206, 212, 218, Richard Pilling Inc. 148, 163, Matt Polk 179b, 180, Nevin Reid 186, Dave Sandford 4, 185t, 198, Kent Smith 185b, Diane Sobolewski 166, 188r, 200, 208, 214, Ron Vesely 177bl, 178,
Howard Shooter/©Carlton Books Ltd. 1, 3

Every effort has been made to acknowledge correctly and contact the source and/or copyright holder of each picture, and Carlton Books Limited apologises for any unintentional errors or omissions which will be corrected in future editions of this book.